OPEN AT THE CLOSE

OPEN

AT THE

CLOSE

Literary Essays on

HARRY POTTER

Edited by

CECILIA KONCHAR FARR

UNIVERSITY PRESS OF MISSISSIPPI / JACKSON

The University Press of Mississippi is the scholarly publishing agency of the Mississippi Institutions of Higher Learning: Alcorn State University, Delta State University, Jackson State University, Mississippi State University, Mississippi University for Women, Mississippi Valley State University, University of Mississippi, and University of Southern Mississippi.

www.upress.state.ms.us
The University Press of Mississippi is a member
of the Association of University Presses.

Note on the text: All references to the *Harry Potter* novels throughout are from the Scholastic paper editions and include abbreviations as noted:

Rowling, J. K. *Harry Potter and the Sorcerer's Stone*. New York: Scholastic, 1997. Print. (*SS*)
Rowling, J. K. *Harry Potter and the Chamber of Secrets*. New York: Scholastic, 1998. Print. (*CS*)
Rowling, J. K. *Harry Potter and the Prisoner of Azkaban*. New York: Scholastic, 1999. Print. (*PA*)
Rowling, J. K. *Harry Potter and the Goblet of Fire*. New York: Scholastic, 2000. Print. (*GF*)
Rowling, J. K. *Harry Potter and the Order of the Phoenix*. New York: Scholastic, 2003. Print. (*OP*)
Rowling, J. K. *Harry Potter and the Half-Blood Prince*. New York: Scholastic, 2005. Print. (*HBP*)
Rowling, J. K. *Harry Potter and the Deathly Hallows*. New York: Scholastic, 2007. Print. (*DH*)

First printing 2022
∞

Library of Congress Cataloging-in-Publication Data

Names: Farr, Cecilia Konchar, 1958– editor.
Title: Open at the close : literary essays on Harry Potter / edited by Cecilia Konchar Farr.
Description: Jackson : University Press of Mississippi, 2022. | Includes bibliographical references and index.
Identifiers: LCCN 2022003339 (print) | LCCN 2022003340 (ebook) | ISBN 978-1-4968-3931-2 (hardback) | ISBN 978-1-4968-3932-9 (trade paperback) | ISBN 978-1-4968-3934-3 (epub) | ISBN 978-1-4968-3933-6 (epub) | ISBN 978-1-4968-3936-7 (pdf) | ISBN 978-1-4968-3935-0 (pdf)
Subjects: LCSH: Rowling, J. K. Harry Potter series—Criticism and interpretation. | Children's literature—Criticism and interpretation.
Classification: LCC PR6068.O93 Z8 2022 (print) | LCC PR6068.O93 (ebook) | DDC 823/.914—dc23/eng/20220307
LC record available at https://lccn.loc.gov/2022003339
LC ebook record available at https://lccn.loc.gov/2022003340

British Library Cataloging-in-Publication Data available

This book is dedicated to the folks at
Chestnut Hill College who have been gathering
Harry Potter fans, scholars, and Quidditch players together in
mad, magical, democratic exchange since 2011.

Most of the essays gathered here were first developed for their annual conference.
Thanks especially to the conference's prescient and persistent organizers,
Patrick McCauley and Karen Wendling.

CONTENTS

Introduction... xi
Cecilia Konchar Farr

Section 1: Horcruxes

1   *Ascendio*: A Close and Distant Reading
    of Progressive Complexity in the *Harry Potter* Series............ 3
    Cecilia Konchar Farr and Amy Mars

2   Said Hermione Earnestly: *Harry Potter*'s Prose,
    and Why It Doesn't Matter 35
    Emily Strand

3   Say the Magic Word: Spellwork and the Legacy of Nonsense..... 48
    Christina Phillips-Mattson

4   Magical Medicine: Healers, Healing Spells,
    and Medical Humanities.................................. 65
    Jennifer M. Reeher

5   Rowling's Paratextual Gifts: Thresholds to
    Community in *Harry Potter and the Deathly Hallows* 77
    Marie Schilling Grogan

6   Communities of Interpretation in Jane Austen
     and *Harry Potter* 93
     Beatrice Groves

7   The Russian Formalist Heart of the *Harry Potter* Series. 106
     John Granger

Section 2: Hallows

8   Reading *Harry* with the Risk of Trust
     and a Hopeful Search for Meaning 121
     Patrick McCauley

9   "Always Dependably, Solidly Present":
     The Preeminence of Minerva McGonagall 135
     Kate Glassman

10   "Loony, Loopy Lupin": (Sexual) Nonnormativity,
     Transgression, and the Werewolf. 154
     Jonathan A. Rose

11   Sorry, Not Sorry: The Limits of Empathy
     for Nonhuman Creatures 166
     Keridiana Chez

12   "All Was Well"?: The Sociopolitical Struggles
     of House-Elves, Goblins, and Centaurs. 178
     Juliana Valadão Lopes

13   The Face of Evil: Physiognomy in Potter. 188
     Lauren R. Camacci

14   Slytherin Safety: The Rhetoric of Antiassimilation
     in the Wizarding World. 201
     Nusaiba Imady

15   *Harry Potter* and the Management of Trauma................ 212
     Tolonda Henderson

     A Coda: She-Who-Must-Not-Be-Named 223
     Tolonda Henderson

     Contributors... 227

     Index 233

INTRODUCTION

Cecilia Konchar Farr

This book took shape as readers in the United States marked twenty years since J. K. Rowling published her first *Harry Potter* novel here. In those twenty years, a generation of readers came of age with Harry, Ron, and Hermione as they tracked the publication of the series across their teenage years. Midnight book release parties, all day reading binges, cosplay with robes and wands, and long hours of constructing fan theories and fictional fill-ins are among the memories that Millennials take with them into adulthood. And it's not just Millennials who are having a nostalgic *Harry Potter* moment. There has never been a more successful book series (500 million copies sold and counting), nor a more culturally prominent literary phenomenon, with three expanding theme parks, ten movies and more in production, multiple follow-up e-books and short stories, new editions of the original novels (illustrated, translated, available in your House colors), a variety of podcasts, an Internet home in *Pottermore*, several Hogwarts-themed charitable organizations, and Rowling's joint envisioning of a grown-up Harry in *The Cursed Child*, a successful play on the London stage that opened on Broadway and claimed five Tony awards. Still today the series holds a venerable place on the *New York Times* Bestseller List—for more than 625 weeks as of this writing—and "Muggle" is officially in the Oxford dictionary.[1] All of this represents an expansive world of Potter-philia.

Yet, despite such phenomenal success, literary critical assessment of Rowling's novels has lagged behind the parade. While popular books, articles, and blogs for general readers proliferate, while philosophers, historians, theologians, sociologists, psychologists, even business professors have taken on book-length studies and edited essay collections about *Harry Potter*, literature scholars, outside of the children's literature community, have paid comparatively little attention to the wizarding world.[2] This is due, at least in part, to a longstanding reluctance to recognize popular novels, and particularly those with genre labels "children's literature" or "fantasy," as worthy subjects for academic study, even after years of vociferous protest from scholars in middlebrow and reception studies, new historicism, cultural studies and other disciplines. Despite deconstructing traditional literary categories, challenging the foundation of aesthetic assessments, opening up "text" to include every artifact of our diverse multimedia cultures, and calling out white male bias in reviewing and publishing, literature professors, graduate students, publishers, and critics still cordon off the "important" from the "trivial."

This book challenges that division, assembling and foregrounding some of the best literary critical work by scholars trying to move the needle on these novels to reflect their importance to literate twenty-first-century culture. We've taken to calling ourselves *Harry Potter* scholars, even as most of us toil away in other fields of literature, often fitting this work into the margins of our academic lives. Many of us gather with fans at *Harry Potter* conferences and festivals around the world and discuss the novels in classrooms and lecture halls, in blogs and on podcasts. In *Open at the Close*, we consciously address *Harry Potter* primarily as a literary phenomenon rather than a cultural one. And while we interrogate the novels on many levels, from multiple perspectives and with various conclusions, we come together here as literature scholars to address the overarching questions: *What is it about these books?* At their heart, what is it that makes these novels so exceptionally compelling, so irresistible to their readers, and so relevant in our time?

Mind the Gap

My attempt at an introductory answer to those questions begins with the three-year gap between the publication dates of *Goblet of Fire* and *Order of the Phoenix*, from the summer of 2000 all the way through to the summer of 2003. Those were long years of waiting for the news of Voldemort's return, like Harry hiding behind the hydrangea bushes underneath the Dursleys' window. "What happened, what happened?" we kept asking one another, as nearly every reader I know, young or wizened, emerging or practiced, was becoming a critic, formulating their own theories. [3]

During those same three years in the United States, our world was upended by the terror of 9-11, when the sense of safety and security that many privileged children (and adults) had enjoyed shifted dramatically. Like Harry, young readers in the United States searched for information and explanations and often got, instead, the equivalent of waterskiing budgerigars on the evening news. For this reason, at least in part, those three years were a *productive gap*, as we say in literary theory. And it was all the more productive for being massive, particularly to young readers. The first four books in the series appeared only a year apart in the United States, and the three that followed only two years apart, so the space between these two middle novels and the nature of the narrative stopping place, at the very moment of Voldemort's return, at the beginning of the pandemonium of an all-out wizarding war, left readers anxious.

From my multiple perspectives as a mother of readers, a professor of English teaching literature courses, and a reader myself, the sense of urgency of these *Harry Potter* fans—their desire for news, their need for comfort, even their yearning for escape—changed everything. It conjured a more active readership that multiplied quickly in online forums; MuggleNet started in 1999, and the Leaky Cauldron, in 2000 and then grew exponentially in the years that followed. These readers took matters into their own hands, sharing ideas, and creating their own *Harry Potter* stories. As they did this, they complicated the relationship between reader and text in ways literary critics had never seen before.

To understand these engaged readers, we need to first grant that the *Harry Potter* novels are record-setting bestsellers for a reason. They are exceptionally good, particularly the later ones, which meet nearly every criterion of technical excellence we introduce in literature classes (see Strand's essay in this collection). They have vivid, dynamic characters (see Glassman) and a complex structure around a compelling plot (see Grogan and Konchar Farr and Mars); they deploy innovative and imaginative language (Phillips-Mattson), address complex philosophical (McCauley), psychological (Henderson), and social ideas (Reeher and Camacci) and introduce thought-provoking moral dilemmas (Chez and Lopes). They pay attention to literary tradition in their themes and allusions (Groves and Granger) and draw attention to the issues of our time in their implications (Rose and Imady). And they also seem fresh and funny, even after multiple rereadings. Here, however, I will home in on two reader-centered qualities of literary excellence, what I've called elsewhere "absorption" and "relatability," because these two move us closer to understanding what happened to *Harry Potter* in that productive gap.[4]

I begin with absorption, the one that may be hardest to define. Other literary theorists have different terms for it; it's one of the reader responses that Janice A. Radway develops in *A Feeling for Books*, and Rita Felski, in *Uses of Literature*, theorizes something similar, calling it "enchantment." But no matter what we call it, all of us recognize it when we fall into it. It's that can't-put-it-down quality, that read-past-any-reasonable-bedtime compulsion that avid readers yearn for. Novels have long been a preferred form of entertainment, especially for women, at least in part because this opportunity for sustained indulgence is so satisfying.[5] It's what keeps us waiting for our Hogwarts letters. It's what inspired my college students when, after studying the *Harry Potter* novels intensively for three weeks on a study abroad course in London, Oxford, and Edinburgh, they walked into Universal Orlando's Wizarding World and said, "I'm home." The truth is (and don't tell them I told you) some of them even cried; it felt so overpoweringly familiar, as if they'd been there before.

Absorption has something to do with setting, certainly, and something to do with a plot that draws you in and won't let you go. If you want to get lost in a book, there has to be a there there, to misappropriate Gertrude Stein. If there is any single quality that can explain why these novels are exceptional, this one may be it. Once you're in, you're all in. Some Potterphiles will recall rereading every one of the previous novels before a new one came out and then waiting in line at a midnight release party and spending the rest of the early morning hours nonstop reading. If you were really hooked, you got up late the next day and immediately started rereading the one you just finished. (Not that I would know. Not that I, a grown woman, would ever sternly send my kids to bed so I could have the book to myself.)

Absorption is the gold standard for avid readers. We're always looking for books that claim us like this, books we can get lost in. And, truthfully, I have never encountered another novel that does this better than the *Harry Potter* novels do or another author more skilled at it than Rowling, no matter what I think of her personally (more on that in a moment). With this quality, she is masterful. A small indication of how deftly she achieves this is found in how chapters end and begin, how insistently the texts demand that you turn that page. Take this scene from the very beginning of *Sorcerer's Stone*, the end of chapter 3 to the beginning of chapter 4:

The lighted dial of Dudley's watch [. . .] told Harry he'd be eleven in ten minute's time.

He lay and watched his birthday tick nearer. [. . .]

Five minutes to go. Harry heard something creak outside. [. . .]

Three minutes to go. Was that the sea, slapping hard on the rock like that? And (two minutes to go) what was that funny crunching noise? Was the rock crumbling into the sea?

One minute to go and he'd be eleven. Thirty seconds . . . ten . . . nine—maybe he'd wake Dudley up, just to annoy him—three . . . two . . . one . . .

BOOM.

The whole shack shivered and Harry sat bolt upright, staring at the door. Someone was outside, knocking to come in.

I defy anyone, let alone a young impressionable reader, NOT to turn the page.

Turning the page, then:

Chapter Four

BOOM. They knocked again. (45–46)

Most of us know what happens next. It's like there's a monster at the end of this chapter, though we find out later it's just loveable furry old Hagrid. Threshold crossings, dreams ending, niggling questions left unanswered—Rowling consistently ends chapters in a way that makes a reader need to turn the page, even in the later novels aimed at more mature readers. Here are just a few chapter endings from *Deathly Hallows*, for example: "*The Ministry has fallen. Scrimgeour is dead. They are coming*" (159). And "Hermione's hand was suddenly vice-like on his and everything went dark again" (267). And this one: "The slope-shouldered figure of Alecto Carrow was standing before him, and even as Harry raised his wand, she pressed a stubby forefinger to the skull and snake branded on her forearm" (588).

The second reader-centered quality I highlight here is "relatability," because this is often the first quality readers identify when they like a book, using a word that Miriam Webster has not yet recognized.[6] "This book was really relatable," they will say, meaning they connected with it, often through the main character. If a book is relatable, you think: "This could have happened to me." With *Harry Potter* you might take that up a notch to: "This *should* have happened to me." Rowling manages to excel at this quality, a characteristic of craft, not inexplicable happenstance. In her drive to be a writer, in her years of reading and studying literature (in college and beyond), she certainly encountered lonely boys and smart girls, big, loving families and solitary outsiders, wise mentors and smarmy tormentors. And so, in the *Harry Potter* novels, she carefully constructs characters who are not only believable but also relatable, characters who readers can enter her books through—characters who aren't perfect and sometimes not even likable. Many readers have told me, for example, that they relate most deeply to Draco Malfoy or Severus Snape (witness the popularity of the "Always" tattoo).

Recall how she introduces Harry as just a normal kid, "small and skinny for his age" with "a thin face, knobbly knees, black hair and bright green eyes." He wore hand-me-down clothes and "round glasses held together with a lot of Scotch tape because of all the times Dudley had punched him on the nose" (20). Ron and Hermione, too, are set up as pretty unremarkable, certainly not charismatic as Cedric Diggory, Cho Chang, or Fleur Delacour. For some of the nerdier readers, there's Luna Lovegood to enter the texts through, with her strange beliefs and dirigible plum earrings. Carrie Matthews, one of the contributors to our collection of student essays, *A Wizard of Their Age*, found the unlikely Neville Longbottom an inspiration, exactly the character she needed to get through a tough time in her life. She writes:

> Throughout the series I watched this boy with low self-esteem slowly grow into the courageous young man he becomes in *Deathly Hallows*. This young man, fictional though he may be, has a lack of confidence and an awkwardness that is very relatable. . . . Neville never stops trying, even when he is completely terrified. (183–84)

The point I underline here, then, is that these novels are popular because they *deserve* to be. Rowling, the writer, pursued her craft relentlessly, and she mastered these two reader-centered qualities, absorption and relatability, which account for much of her novels' success. Let's examine, then, the alchemy of these two qualities and what reactions they produce in proximity. If a book is so absorbing that you can't put it down, if it's so relatable you feel like you could happily live inside it, well, maybe if you're young or hopeful, if the world around you is a mess, you decide to do just that. You move into Hogwarts.

As a former *Harry Potter* student, now a collections and metadata librarian, Kate McManus writes in her essay "Loading the Canon," Rowling "often receives credit for getting kids to read, but perhaps she should also be credited with getting kids to write" because the burst of fan fictional energy Kate studies was a result of this chemistry (35). Other scholars have written about the phenomenon of reader interaction on the Internet, first by way of Oprah's Book Club, then Goodreads, and now innumerable sites catering to readers of every sort.[7] This two-way interaction, super-charged by laptops, tablets, and smartphones, is not new, however. Readers, particularly women readers, have formed groups to discuss novels since there were novels, as in the Women's Improvement Societies of the late nineteenth century and the Consciousness Raising groups of the early feminist second wave in the United States.[8] Most of us know someone—a mother, aunt, or friend—who is in a book club, if we're not in one ourselves. Wherever you find them, readers talk to one another, and sometimes writers, too, join the conversation, historically exchanging letters, and now sharing re-Tweets or Facebook likes. When online groups entered the conversation, early fandom was mostly (and notoriously) active around TV shows. Fans of the *X-Files*, *Buffy the Vampire Slayer*, and *Star Trek* reimagined characters, and Mary-Sue-ed their way into fictional worlds, gayer worlds, worlds full of adventure and sex. Dominated by young women, these fan sites began to turn a two-way interaction into a multidimensional one.[9]

But what I watched happen with *Harry Potter* fandom was something quite different, what Anne Jamison in *Fic: Why Fanfiction Is Taking Over the World*, called a "megafandom." According to Percy Weasely—or, actually, Chris Rankin who played Percy in the *Harry Potter* films and went on to write a senior thesis on *Harry Potter* fan fiction—what distinguishes this fandom is that they aren't "fans of J. K. Rowling, Warner Bros., Daniel Radcliffe or of any other individual. They are fans of a book series . . . [I]n their hearts, what they connect with is the literature," Rankin writes (157).

And the fact of this literary connection is significant. I can't help but think that the immersive and relatable qualities I have cited are some of the things make the *Harry Potter* universe more than a "Fandom." Beyond letters, beyond book group discussions, even beyond fanfic, romantic "ships" and Alternate Universes (AUs) where Spock is sorted into Ravenclaw, the

Harry Potter novels yielded empowered participants, readers who connected deeply with the stories they were reading, felt a sense of ownership because of that connection, and had something to say about the wizarding world they now belonged to. And they also had a worldwide community to say it to. Again, readers entered this magical realm because the texts skillfully invited them in. And arriving there, they felt free to interact, to talk back, to rethink everything from minor plot details to the race and sexuality of characters.

Revolutionary Readers

These readers became a Dumbledore's Army, a veritable girl gang of radical literary critics who took the novels into their own hands.[10] They talked, some of them wrote, they reread, rethought, and talked some more. When they didn't like something, they imagined it differently. When the author fell short, they challenged her and filled in the gaps. And, completing this multidimensional sphere of interaction, there has never been a more active author conversing with readers. If you want to know if Dumbledore is gay or Hermione is Black, you ask her, and she'll tell you—on *Pottermore*, on a lecture tour, or in a Tweet.

Three brief examples of recent reader responses will illustrate how distinctive, how qualitatively different the *Harry Potter* literary community has been. The first famously took place at the 2013 National Poetry Slam in New York City, Rachel Rostad's three-and-half minute performance called, "To JK Rowling from Cho Chang."[11] This fierce, insistent critique of how the text's principle Asian character is portrayed was viewed over a million times on YouTube. In it, Rostad addresses Rowling directly, accusing her of taking blind shortcuts through popular culture to create another tragic Asian woman who "cries more than she talks," a "subordinate, submissive, subplot." Her accusations are relentless, one after the other, and by the end they're undeniable.

Rostad's insights cut deep, and the fury that drives her performance is clearly earned. She elaborates, more pointedly, in a follow-up video. The text, she argues, purposely sets up a weak Asian love interest for Harry to make Ginny, Harry's white love interest, look stronger. "And, of course, I doubt that J. K. Rowling was aware of the racist implications," she says, "but that doesn't mean they're not there, and that doesn't mean we shouldn't critique or question them."[12] Despite the intensity of her critique, Rostad insists that she sees herself as part of the devoted *Harry Potter* literary community. "I grew up on these books," she tells us. For her, *Harry Potter* "was all about equality and compassion." Calling attention to the novels' shortcomings is an act of loyalty, then. "Social justice," she insists, "is about holding each other accountable."

The next reader I want to highlight is hard to trace, because she is one of many young bloggers who created portraits of what fandom calls Racebent Hermione, or Black Hermione, mostly on Tumblr, and used textual evidence to support that choice. These images appeared years before Rowling finally allowed the possibility they presented, years before these portraits created such a powerful countercanon that a Black actor was cast as Hermione in *The Cursed Child* when it opened in London in the summer of 2016. The play went on to win a record-breaking nine awards for British theater in 2017, including Best New Play and Best Actress in a Supporting Role (for the actor who played Hermione), before opening on Broadway in 2018, with the same actor in the Hermione role. Blogger Alanna Bennet, cataloguing and defending Black Hermione on *Buzzfeed* in February 2015, quotes Junot Díaz:

> You guys know about vampires? . . . You know, vampires have no reflections in a mirror? . . . what I've always thought isn't that monsters don't have reflections in a mirror. It's that if you want to make a human being into a monster, deny them, at the cultural level, any reflection of themselves. And growing up, I felt like a monster in some ways. I didn't see myself reflected at all. I was like, "Yo, is something wrong with me? That the whole society seems to think that people like me don't exist?" And part of what inspired me, was this deep desire that before I died, I would make a couple of mirrors. That I would make some mirrors so that kids like me might see themselves reflected back and might not feel so monstrous for it.

Rostad's call for accountability met this reader-empowered spirit that brought us Black Hermione and thrust us into hyperengagement in the pandemic summer of 2020, the final example of reader engagement I want to explore. When Rowling used her sizeable Twitter pulpit to denounce transwomen as something other than women—a topic that had, on the surface, nothing to do with the *Harry Potter* novels—it tore a painful hole through the fandom. At that time I was moderating a summer reading group for about 100 alumnae at my women's college, all seven novels in three months, and we immediately lost our way. Putting our schedule aside, we began with a question: Can these novels be saved?

This also took place while our community—Minnesota's Twin Cities—rose up in protest of the murder of George Floyd, an unarmed Black man, at the hands of the Minneapolis police. Our school, founded by activist nuns, cherishes their legacy (our senior capstone core course is The Global Search for Justice), so Rowling's choice to publicly support an outspoken bigot and then follow up with her own (beautifully written) bigotry, presented us with a grim quandary, made even more urgent by the activist context we were living in. And Rostad's call for accountability won the day. My book clubbers called Rowling out and drew each another in, generously embracing one another's varied responses and choices while emphatically rejecting the transphobia—or trans-exclusionary radical feminism (TERF)—that Rowling defended. These two posts are typical of their online conversation. First, Lydia Fasteland, an alumna who works in the book industry:

> I definitely have been thinking back to your "the author is dead" teachings in the last few weeks . . . and I have made the decision that any continued interaction I have with the novels will be strictly through fan-based organizations, art, fanfic. . . . I respect people who reject her outright and reject everything she had worked on and I respect people who are choosing to interact with the content in ways not involving her directly. Transwomen are women and her continued stance on this is disappointing.

Another participant, Jessica Remme, an entrepreneur who identifies as queer, wrote:

> I have been matching a lot of weird parallels to my Catholic faith and JK's TERFness. I think in many ways you can quickly dismiss all the beautiful teachings and values of the books because of JK's views but I also think it's not just JK's views that [give us] reasons to dismiss the teachings. There are things in the books like the goblins' Jewish tropes that could lend to it as well. That being said, I think if we dismissed every work of art or literature because the author, work or artist has/had problems we'd be left with nothing. I think instead we should use them as teaching tools, don't sweep the elephant under the rug, embrace the good, teach and discuss the bad because the books were written to grow with us. I think it's a perfect tool to use for these

conversations. Also, I think it can be unfair to erase the pain of trans readers by completely writing JK out of the picture. I'm a believer that once your work is in the world it belongs to the reader but also by say we no longer know the author—or JK is dead—gives her a pass.[13]

Most of the fandom came to similar conclusions that summer, posting pro-trans memes and offering up ideas for protest. "Queer the fandom," one Tweeted, urging the creation of more LGBTQIA interventions on TikTok. The moderators of the popular podcast *Harry Potter and the Sacred Text* turned their show over to trans readers for a week. The Harry Potter Alliance, a social justice organization that sprang from Potter fandom, MuggleNet and the Leaky Cauldron all condemned Rowling's position, affirmed that trans women are women, and encouraged readers to continue to use the *Harry Potter* books "to explore their own identities while spreading love and acceptance" (from the MuggleNet and Leaky Caudron joint statement). The cast members of the films were among the first to respond, with Daniel Radcliffe, who played Harry Potter, affirming the supremacy of the reader:

> If these books taught you that love is the strongest force in the universe, capable of overcoming anything; if they taught you that strength is found in diversity, and that dogmatic ideas of pureness lead to the oppression of vulnerable groups; if you believe that a particular character is trans, nonbinary, or gender fluid, or that they are gay or bisexual; if you found anything in these stories that resonated with you and helped you at any time in your life—then that is between you and the book that you read, and it is sacred.[14]

Because the response was so immediate, so unanimous, and so typical of the *Harry Potter* community as it had evolved over the years, many observers missed the fact that these readers had just staged a pretty serious coup. The many ways that they had unabashedly claimed the books as their own culminated here in their separation of the texts from their author. They didn't need Rowling anymore because the books belonged fully to them, to the readers and the passionate fans. Some day we may mark this as the end of the literary criticism as most of us have known it—seeking a final authoritative interpretation, dominated by white male writers and critics, in the thrall of a few Great Books, and more than occasionally featuring bigotry both veiled and overt that we were invited to overlook. I like to think that it was the summer the New Criticism died. "These books are ours now," readers proclaimed. And Dumbledore's Army rose up and fought for them.

One more thing I would add about these revolutionary readers: I know them. Not all of these young women specifically, but the many women, and a few men, whom I've encountered in my *Harry Potter* classes—and a couple who grew up in my house. And I really like them. I have written elsewhere how they took me by surprise the first time I taught a *Harry Potter* course (at their request).[15] I didn't anticipate how much they would teach me or how the thinking I was doing about novels and how they live among us in the United States would be energized by (of all things) a multivolume fantasy series about a British schoolboy.

These inspiring readers and the multidimensional ways they connect with novels are forcing critics who are paying attention to rethink the relationship between reader and text in an age of expanding leadership by people of color and white women in the publishing industry, in our universities, and across the globe. They make me hopeful that this time, with these engaging novels, we literary professionals won't find an excuse to double down on the critical status quo by reinforcing the walls that marginalize popular texts and amateur readings, by shoring up the fences that forestall passionate engagement. If *Harry Potter* readers are any indication, studying literature will change. The texts we examine may be less sacred but more loved, their authors less revered but more alive (and more accountable), and leadership in the classroom and beyond will be more justice-centered, more aware of race and culture and more willing to speak truth to power.

Under the Bonnet

In this collection, we Potter professors aim to honor these active readers and to enact the hopeful vision of literary criticism that their passion inspires. In the following chapters we expand on concepts that often grew out of classroom conversations with undergraduate *Harry Potter* readers. Several of the writers assembled here have published book-length works on the novels, and several more are just beginning their careers as professors or critics, though they have been studying *Harry Potter* for most of their lives. Chapters representing various contemporary critical perspectives, both text and reader-centered, comprising postcolonial theory, feminist, queer and gender studies, digital and medical humanities, literary history, language and genre studies, eco-criticism, linguistic analysis, trauma studies and critical race theory, make up this collection, and it includes scholars from the United States, the United Kingdom, Germany, Portugal, Canada, and Syria.

The book is divided into two parts: "Horcruxes," highlighting seven text-centered close readings, and "Hallows," placing the novels in social and cultural contexts. Chapter 8, straddling the middle of the collection, examines the state of literary criticism itself and how the *Harry Potter* novels call it into question. I lead off the "Horcruxes" section with an essay authored jointly with Amy Mars, a St. Catherine University librarian, examining the generally accepted premise that the novels get increasingly more difficult as readers (and characters) progress through the series. This chapter also functions as introductory, in that we include a brief review of the key plot points of each of the novels as part of our study. Together, through close and distant reading, digital and textual analysis, and in conversation over our observations, Amy and I discover that the truth of progressive complexity isn't always a steady climb up a graph line; the novels' trajectory is more complex than we anticipated.

Emily Strand finds similar complexity in her interrogation of how "good" the novels actually are. Using the tools of aesthetic analysis, she approaches the texts from her perspectives as novel writer, scholar, and parent in chapter 2. What do we do, she asks, with Rowling's overuse of adverbs, the way she apparently flouts the rules of good writing as taught in creative writing classes? Strand's disarming answer involves rabbits and dandelions. Close attention to language characterizes Christina Phillips-Mattson's chapter as well, as she looks at the linguistic and literary roots of nonsense. She credits Rowling with manipulating that traditional mode of children's and folk literature by way of her magical spellwork. As she develops her unique language, Rowling also exemplifies how readers can transform their own reality through careful use of words. Using similar linguistic foundations, Jennifer M. Reeher approaches the novels through the discipline of medical humanities, comparing health care in Potter world and in our world of Muggles. Reeher, too, pays attention to spells and demonstrates how Harry consistently trusts Madame Pomfrey, a trained expert, to perform the Healing Spells—in effect, to say the words correctly.

Marie Schilling Grogan focuses intently on the epigraphs and (the controversial) epilogue that stretch the narrative boundaries of *Deathly Hallows* in her close reading, informed by structuralist narratology, in chapter 5. What do these paratexts demand from readers, she asks, and how does Rowling imagine her audience making use of them "nineteen years later" and beyond? Beatrice Groves, in chapter 6, has a related interest in the space where text and reader meet, as she puts interpretive communities, from gossip to libraries, up for intertextual comparison between Jane Austen novels and the *Harry Potter* series. Because Austen is Rowling's professed favorite author, their attitudes about what novels can do and how they do it are clearly related, Groves argues, as she uncovers a wealth of revealing connections among these well-loved books.

John Granger, our well-published "Dean of Potter Punditry," continues Professor Groves's line of questioning as he links Rowling's work with Vladimir Nabokov's, another author Rowling has disclosed in interviews that she admires. This admiration, argues Granger, leads her to practice a sort of Russian formalism in the plotting and development of the novels, which he outlines in chapter 7. Chapter 8 is, again, an interrogation of the nature of our literary critical work, written by Patrick McCauley, founder, with his colleague Karen Wendling, of the first (and most long-running) recurring academic conference on *Harry Potter* in the United States, at Chestnut Hill College.[16] McCauley has been teaching the novels in an interdisciplinary undergraduate seminar for years and contemplating how they move students beyond the standard questions of literary criticism. Standing on a hermeneutical foundation and responding to the interests of his students, McCauley urges more consistent engagement with the novels' meaning. He asks how such attention could shift the direction of literary studies, focused as the field has been on critique.

In chapter 9, Kate Glassman shines the spotlight on Minerva McGonagall in a feminist reading that places her (rightfully) center stage from the beginning to the end of the series. The only adult to consistently treat Harry fairly and impartially as the boy he is, she has earned his respect when, in *Deathly Hallows*, he wields his wand to defend her with his only successful use of the unforgiveable Cruciatus curse in the seven novels. The space where character study meets queer theory is the territory Jonathan A. Rose stakes out in his comparison of the werewolf characters Remus Lupin and Fenrir Greyback in chapter 10. Beginning with several critics who understand the werewolf as symbolically queer, Rose argues that their queerness comes from being "inherently uncategorizable." While "werewolf" may stand as a metaphor for homosexuality, Rose pushes that premise further toward insights about marginality and nonnormativity more generally.

Keridiana Chez also takes on characters who stand at the margins of the human in chapter 11, exploring where the novels invite our empathy and where they let the otherness stand uninterrogated. Chez's closer looks at Harry's relationships with these "others" reveals surprising shortcomings. Juliana Valadão Lopes's comparative study of nonhuman characters—centaurs, goblins and house-elves—and the collective stance their communities take in response to wizarding domination, follows Chez, and the two chapters together form a strong argument for a more attentive analysis of our own anthropocentricism, through observing its damaging variations in the wizarding world. Chez's conclusions challenge the foundational conception of a heroic, humane Harry, while Lopes's Marxist approach calls our attention to the place of subalterns in dominant political structures.

Recognizing rather than defeating evil is at the center of Lauren R. Camacci's study of the vestiges of the debunked science of physiognomy in the Potterverse in chapter 13. The effort to recognize the "bad guys" by how they look has deep cultural roots in a Western obsession with appearance, and Camacci demonstrates how this oversimplistic form of representation dances dangerously with eugenics and leads to the dehumanization of the novels' characters. Further complicating our understanding of who the bad guys are, Nusaiba Imady deploys postcolonial and gender theory toward a deeper understanding of what motivates the Slytherins' ideology, which, she argues, can be read as antiassimilationist rather than supremacist. Turning the commonly held Nazi comparison (with Voldemort as Hitler) on its head, she refigures the wizarding world as an oppressed minority in the context of a realistic frame of centuries of witch hunting and persecution from some of the world's major religions. A true Slytherin, she then opens the novel to a challenging and radical rereading, beyond Harry's controlling perspective.

In the final chapter, Tolonda Henderson returns our attention to the Boy Who Lived, homing in on Harry and his experience of trauma. Henderson's meticulous reading opens new avenues for understanding our central character, particularly as they visit "King's Cross Station" with Harry in the penultimate chapter of *Deathly Hallows*. Here, Henderson argues, Harry finds himself in a liminal space working hard to construct his own trauma narrative and to overcome the barriers that would prevent his defeating Voldemort. Henderson completes the collection with "A Coda:

She-Who-Must-Not-Be-Named," sorting through the challenges that Rowling's blatant and insistent antitrans arguments created for them and others in the Potterverse. "I am a genderqueer–which for me means nonbinary transgender–*Harry Potter* scholar, something that has grown increasingly difficult to be throughout the summer of 2020," they write. Henderson's decision to excise the author's name from chapter 15 creates a tiny space where a love of the wizarding world endures, for now, through the heartbreak and disappointment that the living author instigates.

While this collection is rich, showcasing creative analysis through a breadth of critical methods and a wealth of literary insight, it is certainly not definitive. So much good work on the *Harry Potter* novels can be found online and, increasingly, among our "legitimate" scholarly publications; we urge scholars of all ages and situations to seek it out. Our aim here is to honor the work that is circulating while inviting scholars to join us in opening the literary critical conversation in earnest here at the close of the series, at a moment when Rowling has insisted repeatedly that there will be no new *Harry Potter* novels. We aim, like the centaurs, to resist the dominant discourse, push back on easy dismissals, and find our own footing in the literary critical methodologies that serve us well in other contexts. We wish, again, to give back to these novels the careful attention and passionate readings they have inspired in this cultural moment, in our students and in our own work; while reveling in the playful responses they invite, we mean to take the *Harry Potter* novels seriously as literature, even "literature for the ages" (even as many of us energetically embrace Barthes's theoretical "Death of the Author"). In short, we accept the challenge of the Golden Snitch, to open at the close, to examine the words within, words that are, as Professor Dumbledore insists, "the most inexhaustible source of magic."

Notes

1. Though the word "muggle" is apparently an old one, it had fallen from use, and now the *OED* lists it as "Origin: 1990s: used in the *Harry Potter* books" in the online *Oxford Dictionary*, accessed 7.3.18. I would also note here that the nearly ten years the *Harry Potter* books have been on the series bestseller list doesn't include the many years each book spent on other *NY Times* Bestseller lists—first the general fiction list, then to a newly created Children's Books list and then to Children's Series (I last accessed the *NY Times* Bestseller list on 3.21.21. when it registered 622 weeks). See Kate Glassman's discussion of these moves in "The Harry Potter Phenomenon: Locating the Boy Wizard in the Tradition of the American Bestseller" in *A Wizard of Their Age*.

2. This is not to sideline the important work that children's literature scholars have done with these novels, most notably Giselle Liza Anatol's two volumes of essays *Reading Harry Potter* and *Reading Harry Potter Again*. They came early and have been indispensable both to my work with students and to my own study of the novels. I also have the privilege of working with Professor Sarah Park Dahlen, who is not only a leader in the movement to bring more diverse books to children, but she is also a Ravenclaw, an astute reader of the *Harry Potter* series, and an editor of a forthcoming collection of essays on diversity in *Harry Potter*.

3. The analysis that follows was presented in an earlier form as the keynote address for the Chestnut Hill Harry Potter Conference, 20 October 2017, at Chestnut Hill College, Chestnut Hill, PA, entitled "It's Complicated: The Relationship between the *Harry Potter* Novels and Their Avid Readers."

4. For further development of these reader-centered qualities of good literature see *The Ulysses Delusion: Rethinking Standards of Literary Merit* and *Reading Oprah: How Oprah's Book Club Changed the Way America Reads*.

5. I discuss, at greater length, the deeply intertwined history of women and novels—and the creation of the book club movement—in chapters 2 and 3 of *Reading Oprah*.

6. Relatable is in the dictionary, meaning easy to tell, but "relatabilty" hasn't yet arrived—even to spellcheck—though many have discovered and, generally, disdained it, conflating it with identification and the need for likeable characters. It is neither of those things. See, for example, the *New Yorker*'s "Forum on 'Likeablity,'" called "Would You Want to Be Friends with Humbert Humbert?" and including dismissive comments from Claire Messud and Margaret Atwood, among other writers of literary fiction (5.16.13).

7. See GoodReads, Shelfari, Whichbook, Litlovers, GoogleBooks, Oprah's Book Club (oprah.com/oprahsbookclub) and many listicles on "how to choose your next book" and "how to talk about books."

8. Again, chapter 3 of *Reading Oprah* outlines the history of the women's book club movement. I also addressed consciousness-raising readers, with Jaime Harker, in the "Introduction" to *This Book Is an Action: Feminist Print Culture and Activist Aesthetics*. For an excellent survey of Black women's participation in these movements, see Elizabeth McHenry's *Forgotten Readers: Recovering the Lost History of African American Literary Societies*. I also urge readers toward Nina Baym's still foundational *Novels, Readers, and Reviewers: Responses to Fiction in Antebellum America* among her other (life's) work on women readers and the novels they love.

9. Anne Jamison notes in *Fic* that the majority of fan fiction writing is by women "or if not by women, then by people who are willing to be (mis)taken for women." Given that "less than 30 percent of television writers are women; [and] in film, that figure is below 20 percent . . . those numbers mean there's a lot of variously talented women we haven't been hearing from. A great many of these women are writing fic" (19). Jamison's text also defines terms related to fanfiction which I use here, including AUs, Mary Sue, and ships (207, 118)

10. When Kate McManus last updated her article "Loading the Canon: Harry Potter and Fanfiction" for its 2015 publication in *A Wizard of Their Age*, her research had "over 645,000 Harry Potter stories archived on fanfiction.net alone." Here let me also insert a reminder that readership of novels, like authorship of fanfiction, continues to be overwhelmingly female.

11. Though I watched a video of this performance (along with the follow-up explanation that Rostad taped shortly after) several times over the past few years via Button Poetry and YouTube, it appears at last search, in February 2021, to be no longer available. At one point, in 2018, a transcript could be found on Rostad's Tumblr blog, and some pirated tapes of the performance were accessible, but it is no longer in the archives of Button Poetry or on

YouTube (marked "Private" and "unavailable"). Now none of these previous sources are available, and Rostad's performance seems to have vanished from the Internet.

12. Though I, too, hesitate to accuse Rowling of purposeful marginalization of Cho Chang, I was taken aback by a scrawled page in the British Library's Harry Potter: A History of Magic exhibition (on a visit in January 2018). It was a table, written in ink on loose leaf paper, on which Rowling had outlined the things she needed to pay attention to in *Order of the Phoenix*, chapter by chapter, along the left side. Among other key plot elements charted across the top of the table (DA, Prophesy, Hagrid and his brother) was this one: "Cho/Ginny." It was clear in the notations in the column that Rowling was focused on a purposeful contrast, one that characterized Ginny as, among other things, "practical" to Cho's "sad" and "dramatic." These words are from my notes; the reproductions of this table in the published exhibition catalogue don't include the same pages. These observations were confirmed by my colleague Sarah Park Dahlen in her visit to the New York leg of the exhibition in late 2018.

13. These participants from the St. Catherine Alumnae Book Club gave permission to use their posts in this essay. I would also like to point out that some readers made an altogether different choice, represented here by Sarah Molland, who tossed her books and exited the book club. With several others, she was done with J. K. Rowling and her problematic Tweets; her adult values overrode what she had enjoyed as a teen. She wrote:

> Idk if I can enjoy a book with little goblins who have big noses who love money; fat people who are only incompetent or evil; enslaved elves who claim to love their servitude; staircases that protect "real" women from men pretending to be women in order to sneak into their dorms; all women being sexless spinsters, moms, or cool sluts who must die; a character named cho chang; and a black character (one of 2? 3?) with "shackle" in his name. Tbh this list could go on forever. These books have some wonderful moments, but they are also harmful and mean. No amount of magic and escapism can really make the pain these depictions cause worth it. I really liked these books growing up, greatly enjoyed studying them in class, and I still have some fondness for them. I also know that their presentation of oppressed people isn't something I can overlook enough to enjoy them now.

14. A concise account of the events in the Potterverse in Summer 2020 can be found at: https://variety.com/2020/film/news/harry-potter-jk-rowling-mugglenet-leaky-cauldron-anti-trans-1234697127/#! There are good embedded links to related texts within this article—particularly JKR's anti-trans essay—but information on the fans' firm call to accountability can be found all over the Internet.

15. I tell the story of how I came to teach a *Harry Potter* course in the introduction to *A Wizard of Their Age*.

16. The Chestnut Hill Harry Potter Conference began in October, 2011. Amy McKeever writes about it in "The Magic of the Annual Harry Potter Conference" in *Pacific Standard Magazine* (November 9, 2015). McKeever focuses on the challenges of being a *Harry Potter* scholar in a context where elite critics like Harold Bloom, writing in the *Wall Street Journal* (July 11, 2000), called that work "another confirmation of the dumbing-down it leads and exemplifies." She quotes McCauley (with a statement I love): "As an academic, the one thing you can't afford is to get a reputation for being a goofball."

Works Cited

Anatol, Giselle Liza, ed. *Reading Harry Potter: Critical Essays.* Wesport, CT: Praeger, 2003. Print.

Anatol, Giselle Liza, ed. *Reading Harry Potter Again: New Critical Essays.* Westport CT: Praeger, 2009. Print.

Baym, Nina. *Novels, Readers, and Reviewers: Responses to Fiction in Antebellum America.* Ithaca NY: Cornell University Press, xxx. Print.

Bennet, Alanna. "What a 'Racebent' Hermione Granger Really Represents: The beauty of the *Harry Potter* character as a woman of color." *Buzzfeed*, 1 February 2015. https://www .buzzfeed.com/alannabennett/what-a-racebent-hermione-granger-really-represents. Accessed 7.3.2018.

Díaz, Junot. *Ledger Live* on nj.com (speaking with high school students in October 2009): https://www.nj.com/ledgerlive/index.ssf/2009/10/junot_diazs_new_jersey.html. Accessed 7.3.2018.

Felski, Rita. *The Uses of Literature.* Hoboken, NJ: Wiley-Blackwell, 2008. Print.

Glassman, Kate. "The Harry Potter Phenomenon: Locating the Boy Wizard in the Tradition of the American Bestseller" in *A Wizard of Their Age.* Albany NY: SUNY, 2015. 19–34. Print.

Jamison, Anne. *Fic: Why Fanfiction Is Taking Over the World.* Dallas TX: BenBella, 2013. Print.

Konchar Farr, Cecilia. *Reading Oprah: How Oprah's Book Club Changed the Way America Reads.* Albany NY: SUNY, 2007. Print.

Konchar Farr, Cecilia. *The Ulysses Delusion: Rethinking Standards of Literary Merit.* London: Palgrave, 2016. Print.

Konchar Farr, Cecilia, ed. *A Wizard of Their Age: Critical Essays from the Harry Potter Generation.* Albany NY: SUNY, 2015. Print.

Matthews, Carrie. "My Harry Potter Story" in *A Wizard of Their Age: Critical Essays from the Harry Potter Generation.* Albany NY: SUNY, 2015. 182–84. Print.

McHenry, Elizabeth. *Forgotten Readers: Recovering the Lost History of African American Literary Societies.* Durham NC: Duke University Press, 2002. Print.

McManus, Kate. "Loading the Canon: Harry Potter and Fanfiction" in *A Wizard of Their Age: Critical Essays from the Harry Potter Generation.* Albany NY: SUNY, 2015. 35–47. Print.

Radway, Janice A. *A Feeling for Books: The Book-of-the-Month Club, Literary Taste, and Middle-Class Desire.* Durham, NC: U of North Carolina P, 1997. Print.

Rowling, J. K., John Tiffany and Jack Thorne. *Harry Potter and the Cursed Child, Parts One and Two.* London: Levine, 2016. Print.

HORCRUXES

1

ASCENDIO
A Close and Distant Reading of
Progressive Complexity in the *Harry Potter* Series

Cecilia Konchar Farr and Amy Mars

It is a given in both scholarly and popular writing about the *Harry Potter* novels that this series increases in complexity as it progresses, paralleling the growth of its first readers. In this study we set out to test that widely accepted assumption.[1] A literature professor and a librarian, we use the tools of both of our disciplines, employing close and distant reading to investigate progressive complexity in the series.

What Is Close Reading?

Close reading, the central tool of literary analysis in today's college class-rooms and lecture halls, involves careful textual examination and critical evaluation. It assumes repeated rereading as it calls on its practitioners to go deeply into a book, to perceive recurrent themes, structures, and patterns, to capture symbolism and allusion, to recognize nuance, innovation, and complexity, and to pay attention to the details of language and word choice. Rooted in the practices of scriptural and classical studies, close reading has dominated literary analysis since the middle of the twentieth century, when the New Critics standardized textual practices for college students and teachers, directing "the reader's attention to the text itself." Close reading is now "a key requirement of the Common Core State Standards" for students at all grade levels, from primary to high school and on to college.[2]

What Can Close Reading Do?

There's a reason close reading has been the preferred method of literary analysis in secondary and higher education for so long. First, it is easy to teach and test (with multiple choice and even true or false questions). But also, its deference toward the text and its attention to detail draw out insights while honing perceptiveness. In today's skills-based assessments, it can be counted on to offer measurable results in critical reading and thinking. Perhaps most significantly for this study, it heightens our awareness to texts in productive ways. For example, in *Harry Potter and the Prisoner of Azkaban*, the third book in the series, we find this passage: "'How extraordinarily like your father you are, Potter,' Snape said suddenly, his eyes glinting" (284). Later, Professor Albus Dumbledore similarly notes, "I expect you'll tire of hearing it, but you do look *extraordinarily* like James" (427). Both characters use the same phrase, "extraordinarily like," with "*extraordinarily*" italicized in the text in the second occurrence. This could, with a single reading, be passed over as coincidence. But a careful rereading with attention to the details of word choice would recognize what we discover later, that Professor Severus Snape and Headmaster Dumbledore talk about Harry when he's not around, that they are bound to one another by their commitment to watch over Harry and keep him safe. The depth and authenticity of this commitment, originating with Harry's parents' death, is central to the seven-novel narrative. While Snape and Dumbledore experience their pledge to protect Harry differently—Snape heavily, as punitive and ultimately redemptive, and Dumbledore more lightly, as paternal and quite possibly self-serving—it drives their relationship with one another. As these passages remind us, Snape and Dumbledore are allies, and being "extraordinarily like" James Potter elicits opposing responses from them for a multitude of reasons that readers won't fully understand until book 7, reasons only suggested here in the repeated and nuanced phrase.

What Is Distant Reading?

"Distant reading" describes the use of quantitative, computational methods for analyzing patterns across texts.[3] Like other digital humanities methods of inquiry, it is interdisciplinary, combining the tools of computer scientists (programming languages like R and Python), the concepts and terminology of corpus linguists (lexical density, type/token ratio), the quantitative measures of statisticians (frequencies, correlations), and the critical lens of literary critics and discourse analysts. The goal of distant reading (and all digital humanities methods, we would argue) is not and should not be the uncritical adoption of digital tools for the sake of "doing something digital" or "keeping up with current trends." Rather, we maintain that digital tools should be employed in service of textual inquiry.

What Can Distant Reading Do?

Distant reading can work in tandem with close literary analysis in meaningful ways. It can lend quantitative evidence to support or contradict qualitative interpretations, deepening the discussion around a text. In one example, Sally Hunt, a professor of corpus linguistics, used word collocation and correlation to show how words signifying more passive bodily actions were more likely to be associated with female characters in the *Harry Potter* series, supporting her reading of gender disparity in the way agency is portrayed for male and female character.

In addition to buttressing the interpretations that arise from close reading, distant reading techniques can help discern patterns not observable through close reading—some not even humanly detectable. In a type of distant reading called stylometrics, scholars use quantitative text analysis to surface linguistic patterns that allow them to identify the authors of texts for whom authorship was previously unknown or disputed. This type of distant reading was used to reveal that crime novelist Robert Galbraith (author of *The Cuckoo's Calling*) was actually J. K. Rowling.[4] Distant reading can also be exploratory, revealing patterns that shift the direction of our research or raise new questions entirely. For example, Robert K. Nelson of the Digital Scholarship Lab at the University of Richmond digitized the *Richmond Daily Dispatch* and used topic modeling to unveil patterns in the headlines that dominated the period from 1860–1865 in this Southern, Civil War–era newspaper. Large digitization projects like this, in combination with the computational power of distant reading methods, allow scholars to detect linguistic and literary patterns at a scale that was previously not feasible through close reading alone.

Close and Distant Reading of the *Harry Potter* Series

In this study we used a combination of close and distant reading methods to investigate the generally recognized progressive complexity in the *Harry Potter* series. More specifically, our approach employs close reading to analyze complexity on three fronts: the increasing complication of the challenges and dilemmas that Harry and his friends face, the progressive development of character depth in the service of identity formation for Harry, and the gradual shift toward disruption of established narrative structures. We employ distant reading to uncover complexity at a more macro level, looking at measures such as word, sentence, and chapter length, word frequencies and mapping, readability, and lexical density.

Our hypothesis, again, was that the series increases in complexity with each novel, thus adapting to the development of the reader and underlining the age of the main characters. We find this quality of progressive complexity in *Harry Potter* unique in children's series books, and, of course, in novels aimed at adults, which most often remain static at one reading level. Though others have used distant reading techniques to analyze novels in the *Harry Potter* series, no one has yet used distant techniques to analyze the entire series with reference to this question of complexity, nor have they used a combination of online tools and programming methods for each measure to reduce margin of error in any particular tool or application as our project does.

We found the combination of close and distant reading methods fruitful in this inquiry. Most commonly, these methods are used in isolation, or distant reading is used only to validate a close reading interpretation. Our work was more collaborative, more dialogic and iterative. For example, a close reading that posits that decisions the characters make become more challenging and fraught prompted a distant reading that looks at frequencies of words like "decide," "decision," "choose," and "choice," as they are spread throughout each book in the series.

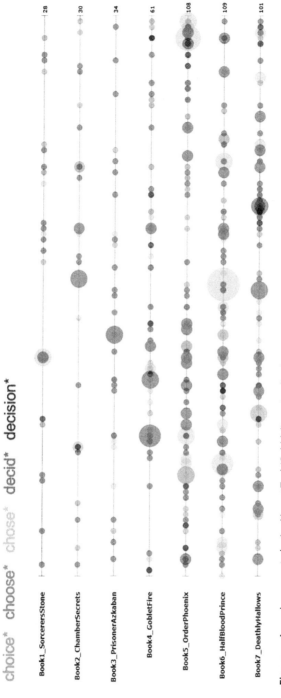

Figure 1.1 A word map created using Voyant Tools' Bubblelines visualization

Book	Flesch Kincaid Reading Ease	Flesch Kincaid Grade Level	Gunning Fog Score	Coleman Liau Index	SMOG Index	Automated Readability Index	Space Score	Dale-Chall Score	Lexile
Book 1: Sorcerer's Stone	81.1	4.7	6.2	9.5	7.3	4.3	362.7	4	880
Book 2: Chamber of Secrets	77.9	5.2	6.7	10.1	7.7	5	451.4	4.5	940
Book 3: Prisoner of Azkaban	76.9	5.2	6.6	10.3	7.8	4.8	494.2	4.5	880
Book 4: Goblet of Fire	76	5.5	5.9	10.2	6.8	5	688.3	4.5	880
Book 5: Order of the Phoenix	74.8	5.9	7.5	10.3	8.3	5.7	830	4.6	950
Book 6: Half-Blood Prince	74.8	5.9	8.8	10.3	9.5	5.7	699.2	4.5	1030
Book 7: Deathly Hallows	76	5.7	7.4	10.1	8.2	5.5	752.4	4.5	980
Min	81.1	4.7	5.9	9.5	6.8	4.3	362.7	4	8th–9th
Max	74.8	5.9	8.8	10.3	9.5	5.7	830	4.6	10th–12th
Max-Min	6.3	1.2	2.9	0.8	2.7	1.4	467.3	0.6	
	½ grade	1 grade	3 grades	1 grade	3 grades	1.5 grades		½ grade	

Figure 1.2 A matrix of readability scores for each book of the Harry Potter series. With the exception of Lexile score, each number indicates the grade level at which each book is scored.

The most revealing aspect of our study came when multiple distant reading measures uncovered complexity peaking in unexpected places, specifically in books 5 and 6 rather than 7. This prompted an investigation of our assumption at the close reading level. In our case, it led to a re-examination of our working hypothesis, that final book in the series as the most mature and complex, as you will observe below.

In this process of combining close and distant reading, we uncovered unexpected nuances unavailable in either approach on its own, and we concluded that the progressive complexity we expected to affirm was not, in fact, a straight trajectory. Different methods' points of attention revealed different peaks across the seven-novel series. This reinforced our final thesis: that close and distant reading together yield more informative results than either one alone.

Distant Reading and Crooked Lines

Lengths and Reading Levels

Perhaps the most obvious marker of increased complexity in the series is the one most easily surfaced through distant reading: the increasing length of words, sentences, chapters, and books as well as the progressive, though not completely linear, rise in reading challenge as measured by various readability scores.

Though the general trend is toward increasing length, there is a notable peak of sentence, chapter, and book length in the fifth book—a pattern we will see again in readability scores. Also notable is the way that chapter length increases gradually. Librarians who provide reader's advisory or work with struggling readers can attest that long chapters can be a stumbling block to engagement in a book. For emerging readers, shorter chapters provide much-needed breaks as well as the positive reinforcement of completing reading milestones, which can fuel confidence and create motivation to dive deeper into the story. The gradually increasing length of chapters allows readers to build their stamina, confidence, and engagement in the world the author built—perhaps one explanation for why the *Harry Potter* series is famous for appealing to struggling, emerging, and even non-readers (Garlick).

	Average Word Length	Average Sentence Length	Average Chapter Length	Book Length (in words)
Book 1: *Sorcerer's Stone*	4.11	12	4583	81,273
Book 2: *Chamber of Secrets*	4.21	12.5	4778	89,349
Book 3: *Prisoner of Azkaban*	4.24	11.8	4792	112,438
Book 4: *Goblet of Fire*	4.24	12.6	5218	199,150
Book 5: *Order of the Phoenix*	4.27	13.8	6846	268,391
Book 6: *Half-Blood Prince*	4.26	13.5	5704	176,721
Book 7: *Deathly Hallows*	4.31	12.5	5392	204,471

Figure 1.3 Average word and sentence lengths were calculated using R and the tm package

Readability scores employ various formulas to calculate reading difficulty based on measures of word, sentences, and syllables within a text. Using the Korpus package created by Meik Michalke and the programming language R, we applied readability measures to the *Harry Potter* series [see figure 1.2, above]. Though there is variability between the assorted measures, two patterns stand out: the way that reading difficulty gradually increases as one progresses through the series and the curious peak in the fifth book. The increasing reading difficulty supports our theory that the series' complexity grows in parallel with the reader but the gradual ease of readability after the fifth book is somewhat confounding. If the dilemmas faced by the characters become more complex as the series goes on, and the plot diverges from patterns in earlier books as we argue later, it stands to reason that a more "readable" text frees the reader to fully confront the level of sophistication presented in the last two books.

Vocabulary Density

Vocabulary or lexical density measures the percentage of unique words in a text. It asks what the proportion of different words to words used is overall. The simplest way to measure vocabulary density is to count the number of unique words (type) and divide it by the total number of words (tokens). This is called the type-token ratio. However, an issue arises as you begin to compare texts of different lengths: the longer the book, the higher the likelihood that words will be repeated, lowering the lexical density. To control for the skewing effects of length, the Moving Average Type-Token Ratio (MATTR)

	# of Unique Words	% of Unique Words	Type-Token Ratio (TTR)	Moving Average TTR	Mean Segmental TTR
Book 1: *Sorcerer's Stone*	6077	7%	.08	.76	.76
Book 2: *Chamber of Secrets*	7331	8%	.08	.76	.76
Book 3: *Prisoner of Azkaban*	7932	7%	.07	.76	.75
Book 4: *Goblet of Fire*	10968	5%	.06	.75	.75
Book 5: *Order of the Phoenix*	13072	5%	.05	.76	.75
Book 6: *Half-Blood Prince*	11023	6%	.06	.75	.75
Book 7: *Deathly Hallows*	10950	5%	.06	.73	.73

Figure 1.4 MATTR and MSTTR were calculated using R and the KoRpus package

and the Mean Segmental Text-Token Ratio (MSTTR) were formulated. Both use random sampling to calculate the Type-Token Ratio, thus controlling for the skewing effects of text length. We applied each of these measures to the *Harry Potter* series, and, as you can see in figure 1.4, there is only a slight difference in vocabulary density between books, and where there are variations they point to the vocabulary getting *less* dense as the series progresses.

How do we interpret these results? It is possible that the sampling techniques used in MATTR and MSTTR do not fully control for the skewing effects of length. Another explanation is that the higher vocabulary density in the early books is the result of the world-building required in series books, particularly in fantasy and other speculative genres. It is also important to remember that measures of vocabulary density are quantitative not qualitative. In other words, they reflect the number or unique words not the complexity of the concepts conveyed by the words. When we factor in sentence structure or use of literary devices such as metaphor, allusion, and imagery we are reminded that an author can write works of great complexity with a limited vocabulary.[5] Thus, while these results do not support our theory of increasing complexity in the series, they also do not refute it.

Word Mapping

Distant reading methods like word mapping allow us to get a birds-eye view of a text and to map its features. Using Voyant Tools' Bubblelines, we were able to map specific words and themes to see how their frequency changes throughout the series. Bubblelines is a visualization tool that maps a text along an x-axis and then shows where specific words appear and how often. The larger the bubble, the more mentions of that word.

We were able to put this distant reading technique in dialogue with close reading by selecting words (and their various forms and synonyms) to investigate whether concepts and themes that reflected the complexity seen at the close reading level were more frequent as the series progressed. Though this analysis will be taken up later in more depth, it is worth showing a couple of examples of how the various word forms for "choice" and "decision" as well as "death" become much more prevalent in the later books (see figure 1.1 on page 7 and figure 1.5 below). It is especially notable that the theme of death, though present at the end of the last four books, haunts almost the entirety of book 7, supporting the hypothesis that not only do the themes become more mature as the series progresses but that the seventh book is a dramatic departure in structure from the other six.

Taken together, these distant reading measures support our hypothesis that the series progresses in complexity. But that complexity is, well, complicated. What we weren't able to see until we employed these measures was that this progression is not a straightforward, linear trend, but rather shows a curious peak in sentence and chapter length, readability, and frequency of certain concepts related to plot complexity in the fifth book. We also discovered the limitation of one of our distant reading measures, lexical density. We found out that vocabulary density is particularly challenging to measure while controlling for the world-building that occurs earlier in the series. Not only that, we were reminded that the presence of novel words does not necessarily equal a measure of the complexity of *meaning* that can be conveyed with a relatively modest vocabulary, as in a Hemingway story for instance.

Distant reading helped us confirm our hypothesis as well as surface trends that were not visible by close reading alone. But it is by putting these two methods in conversation that we came to uncover a richer and more nuanced picture of complexity in the *Harry Potter* series. During the course of our analysis we met frequently to share our observations and incorporate our findings into new investigations. Themes and plot elements from close reading informed what words were input into the Bubblelines visualization, and the curious peaks in the fifth book gleaned from distant reading prompted second looks and new attention to the fifth and final novels.

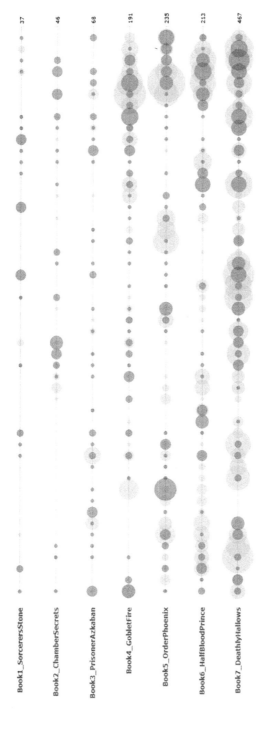

Figure 1.5 A word map created using Voyant Tools' Bubblelines visualization

Close Reading and Curious Peaks

Central Plot Dilemmas and Calls to Action

As with the distant reading, close reading of the series readily reveals some progressive complexity, most obviously in each book's central plot, but, again, this progression is not as straightforward as we expected. This is apparent as we trace Harry's focus, what formalist or archetypal theorists might call his "call to action" in each novel. While the narration throughout the series is consistently in third person, it is not a traditionally omniscient third person, but rather free indirect discourse—a third-person narrative almost always tied to Harry's perspective; that is, if Harry doesn't know something, the reader probably doesn't either. Even more, as Veronica L. Shanoes writes, it is "a form of narration that entices us into equating Harry's thoughts with our own" (134). Thus, tracing Harry's dilemmas allows us to identify the key plot elements of each novel. Not only is he the titular character, but readers are also invited to inhabit the stories from his perspective.

In the first book, *Harry Potter and the Sorcerer's Stone* (SS), Harry must simply get to the Sorcerer's Stone before Professor Quirinus Quirrell does (though Harry mistakenly thinks his opponent is Professor Snape). Meeting this challenge will keep the series' ultimate villain, Lord Voldemort or He-Who-Must-Not-Be-Named, from returning, thereby saving the Wizarding World. This challenge is articulated most clearly below, when Harry decides, in what will become typical form, that *he* must do something *right now*:

> Don't you understand? If Snape gets hold of the stone, Voldemort's coming back! Haven't you heard what it was like when he was trying to take over? There won't be any Hogwarts to get expelled from! He'll flatten it, or turn it into a school for the Dark Arts! Losing points doesn't matter anymore, can't you see? D'you think he'll leave you and your families alone if Gryffindor wins the house cup? If I get caught before I can get to the stone, well, I'll have to go back to the Dursleys and wait for Voldemort to find me there, it's only dying a bit later than I would have, because I'm never going over to the Dark Side! I'm going through that trap door tonight and nothing you two say is going to stop me. Voldemort killed my parents, remember? (270)

Harry's challenge is direct: Get there, get it done. His growing understanding of his past contributes to his urgency. But the stone itself isn't identified as his objective until well into the book (on page 220, with fewer than 90 pages to go). While other plot details are later revealed as clues for solving the puzzle of the stone—the Mirror of Erised, Rubeus Hagrid's dragon, detention in the forest—most of this first novel is taken up with the world-building characteristic of fantasy novels and with developing characters, setting patterns and staging interactions. There is, in short, little density to the plot itself.

There is also not much complexity in the dilemmas Harry confronts in this first novel. He works on figuring people out (Draco Malfoy, Hermione Granger, Snape, Quirrell, Voldemort, and Dumbledore) but his assessments are starkly black and white. Voldemort is set up as the very obvious bad guy, though he appears in this novel via Quirrell, and Dumbledore is already the good guy, Harry's grandfatherly mentor and wise advisor. By the end of the novel readers have learned to love "the Golden Trio" of Harry, Ron, and Hermione, and we delight in disliking Draco and his bullying sidekicks.

Harry Potter and the Chamber of Secrets (CS), though slightly longer, is similarly uncomplicated in plot structure. Harry must discover who opened the Chamber of Secrets and then stop them, this time saving Hogwarts and its literally and figuratively petrified students. His call to action comes earlier this time (at page 120 out of 341), when he first hears the basilisk and begins to understand the legend of the heir of Slytherin.

Dobby, the house-elf, is behind key story elements in this second novel, warning Harry as early as chapter 2 of "a plot to make most terrible things happen at Hogwarts" and engaging in antics clearly meant to appeal to a younger audience. Understanding Dobby, while uncovering the challenges of book 2, leads Harry to grasp more about the wizarding world and how it works, particularly the history of Hogwarts and the benefits of being true to your school and House. World building still claims much of the narrative space, such that this book could easily be read without the first one.

The Golden Trio, now cemented in their relationship, obsesses throughout *Chamber of Secrets* over their task of discovering the heir of Slytherin; first they wrongly suspect Draco and then Hagrid. Harry even suspects himself, but he never waivers in his mission to stop the heir. When Dobby tells him to go home, to leave Hogwarts, Harry replies, "I'm not going anywhere! . . . One of my best friends is Muggle-born; she'll be first in line if the Chamber really has been opened" (179). While the novel takes a few detours as Harry stumbles, suspecting people who aren't guilty, the plot is still straightforward: Find out who opened the Chamber and shut it down. Again, there is no gray area. And the bad guy is, again, Voldemort, though he appears as a memory and acts through Ginny Weasley.

Harry Potter and the Prisoner of Azkaban (*PA*) moves toward greater plot complication. It is only novel where Voldemort doesn't appear, even in memory or mind-melding vision. The bad guy throughout is Sirius Black, who, it turns out, is a good guy, while the real bad guy is not Voldemort, but one of his henchmen—Peter Pettigrew, disguised as Ron's rat. The intricacies of *Prisoner of Azkaban's* plot center on this idea of transformation, of things not being what they seem—werewolves, Animagi, and boggarts, as well as the introduction of the time turner and divination as a discipline. Harry's mission, then, is also less clear. He homes in on his pursuit of (and by) "the Grim" throughout, eventually seeking out Sirius to avenge his parents' death.

Harry's invitation to action comes much earlier in this novel, though he doesn't understand it at first. Arthur Weasley makes Harry swear, even before he leaves for Hogwarts, that he "won't go *looking* for Black" (73). Harry doesn't get it. "Why would I go looking for someone I know wants to kill me?" (74). Thus, even the central dilemma of the novel is unclear and then upended by false appearances. There is no simple mystery, unsolved puzzle, or obvious mission in this third novel.

The fourth novel, however, is the one most critics consider the turning point in the series, where the details get darker and the content more mature. Not only does the ending of *Harry Potter and the Goblet of Fire* (*GF*) involve the very disturbing death of a child, Cedric Diggory, but it also portrays the horrifying return to corporeality of Voldemort, who is now both named and embodied. His presence then looms over the final three novels, more malevolently than in the first three. No longer just a distant memory, as with Harry's parents, or an unfulfilled threat, as in the earlier novels, death is the climax of this novel. Mortality is thereafter a constant and painful fact of life for Harry and his readers, as illustrated in figure 1.5 on page 13.

Harry's primary purpose in the plot of *Goblet of Fire*, however, is not yet to seek out Voldemort or defeat evil, but merely to survive the Triwizard Tournament. Again, his call takes place well into the novel (this time on page 271 of 734) when Dumbledore decrees, "Both Cedric and Harry have been chosen to compete in the tournament. This, therefore, they will do."

But, as in the first two novels, an unexpected encounter with Voldemort becomes the climax of the story.

Similarly, this is the last novel where Harry has an unambiguous and explicit task assigned to him. The final three novels all hew to one overarching plot point—that Harry will, eventually, have to defeat Lord Voldemort. Analyzing the data we generated from distant reading analyses—on reading levels, average sentence, chapter and book length, and vocabulary density— also demonstrated for us that the end of the fourth novel sets up the final three, which trade places in surveys of grade level, maturity, or readability [see again figure 1.2].

In the aftermath of Voldemort's return to power, then, readers of book 5, *Harry Potter and the Order of the Phoenix (OP)*, observe the wizarding world coming to terms with dark forces—or avoiding the very idea of the inevitable confrontation ahead. Some students, believing Ministry and *Daily Prophet* propaganda, turn against Harry in their desire for comfort and normalcy. Others stand up and literally fight for their lives. The test for Harry in the final novels encompasses both the logical and physical challenges of the dilemma-based plots of the first novels and the more developmental questions, the central bildungsroman elements, of the last three. How will he react when his world, and not just his life or his status as a Hogwarts student, is threatened? What kind of man will Harry choose to become? While he strains at this complexity, things fall apart repeatedly in book 5, most movingly at the end, when his godfather is killed.

The plot dilemma of this novel is pushed toward a more intricate interiority as well, with Voldemort's at first accidental takeover of Harry's mind and Harry's response to it, made apparent in the graph below.

Much of the novel finds Harry vacillating between resisting and succumbing to Voldemort's incursions (with the repeated refrain "My scar is hurting again"). This is no series of puzzles unlocking a mystery here, but as with the puzzles, Harry is not alone in trying to resolve the plot's dilemmas. Loving communities surround him—his trio, the Weasley family (sans Percy), the Order, and the newly organized Dumbledore's Army (DA). The final battle is again with Voldemort, surpassing his forays into Harry's mind by literally taking over Harry's body. Side by side with Dumbledore, Harry triumphs in the Battle of the Department of Mysteries because he is full of love—repeatedly and increasingly reinforced as the most powerful force at work in this series and one of its chief concerns.

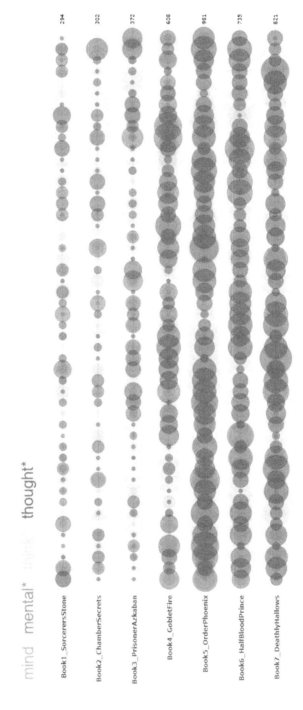

Figure 1.6 A word map created using Voyant Tools' Bubblelines visualization

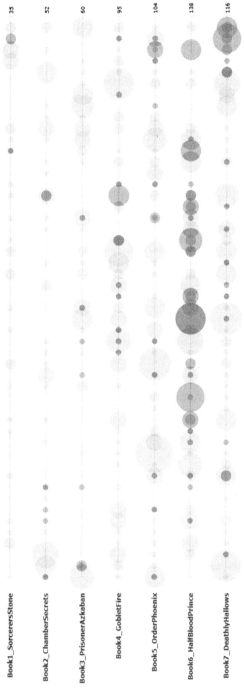

Figure 1.7 A word map created using Voyant Tools' Bubblelines visualization

The question of information—demanded, withheld, reliable or not—is again central in this novel, with Harry learning when to trust his own mind but also sorting through the lies and misdirection that accompany structural power struggles, as we see in this illustration.

Our attention often shifts from Harry's move toward adulthood to the wizarding world's tip toward fascism. Harry's principal task in this novel, however, is to control his own mind. Snape comes to Grimmauld Place, Headquarters of the Order, to tell him: "The headmaster has sent me to tell you, Potter, that it is his wish for you to study Occlumency this term. . . . Occlumency, Potter. The magical defense of the mind against external penetration" (518–19). Later, Dumbledore reaffirms this:

> "Listen to me, Harry," he said urgently, "you must study Occlumency as hard as you can, do you understand me? Do everything Professor Snape tells you and practice it particularly every night before sleeping so that you can close your mind to bad dreams—you will understand why soon enough, but you must promise me—(622).

These passages make clear that the larger plot, Harry's inevitable confrontation with Voldemort (and the salvation of the Wizaring World), has Dumbledore and Snape's full attention. Harry's part, in Hogwarts Year 5, is primarily to prepare himself, to manage his mind.

Harry's preparation continues to focus the plot of *Harry Potter and the Half-Blood Prince* (*HBP*), as well. Here, Dumbledore openly recruits Harry as his partner (but still pupil, not equal) in the war against Voldemort. Dumbledore also explicitly focuses the action of this novel when he begins in earnest to mentor Harry, telling him, "It is my wish that you take private lessons with me this year" (78). These lessons become the key concern of Year 6, as Harry works with Dumbledore to understand Voldemort and the concept of horcruxes in preparation for the final confrontation ahead. At the end of their last lesson, with Dumbledore weakened from their encounters with dark enchantments, Harry moves closer to becoming Dumbledore's successor. He tells Dumbledore not to worry, and Dumbledore replies, "I'm not worried, Harry. . . . I am with you" (578).

While at Hogwarts, Harry aims to become an auror, a professional resister of dark magic, and he excels at both Potions (with the Half Blood Prince's help) and Defense Against the Dark Arts. Because this novel leads so overtly

Figure 1.8 A word map created using Voyant Tools' Bubblelines visualization

to the climax that won't occur until book 7, the final confrontation is not with Voldemort but with his emissaries, who kill Dumbledore and leave Harry bereft. This book, like the third one, has no direct encounter between Harry and Voldemort. An important subplot, however, hearkens back to the puzzles and mysteries of the earlier novels: Who is the Half-Blood Prince? Through his Potions book, he mentors Harry—as Dumbledore does, as Horace Slughorn, Hagrid, Minerva McGonagall, and Remus Lupin do—urging him forward in the *bildung* plot.

It is also telling that the mission of book 7 is named most clearly at the end of book 6—hunting horcruxes. It was Dumbledore's work; it was what Dumbledore and Harry did together; and it's the work Harry must continue:

> "Then I've got to track down the rest of the Horcruxes, haven't I?" said Harry, his eyes upon Dumbledore's white tomb, reflected in the water on the other side of the lake. "That's what he wanted me to do, that's why he told me all about them." (651)

But, again, he doesn't continue alone. As we are repeatedly reminded, these novels aren't only about Harry's development; they are novels of friendship and community: "We're with you whatever happens," Ron says, and Harry "felt his heart lift at the thought that was still one last golden day of peace left to enjoy with Ron and Hermione" (652).

This is significant to the plot of the final novel, *Harry Potter and the Deathly Hallows* (*DH*), where the primary challenge is the completion of Harry's struggle for identity. The question gets posed variously as "Are you Dumbledore's man?" as a choice between "Hallows or Horcruxes," and as the constant query, spoken and unspoken, of "What do we do now?" Harry completes the plot in part by accomplishing the task first assigned to him in *Half-Blood Prince*, to find and destroy the horcruxes, more profoundly by accepting death and killing Voldemort, but, most significantly, by letting go of two of the Deathly Hallows. Standing with Ron and Hermione, he holds onto love and loyalty and lets go of power and the desire to defeat death. At the end of book 7, Harry completes the plot trajectory of the series by both destroying Voldemort and becoming himself.

While a close reading focused on Harry's development sees the trajectory of complexity continue to rise steadily (as we will demonstrate), this analysis of plot and its key dilemmas is not so apparently progressive. Pausing here to put our close and distant readings in conversation, examining the data from the first section ("Distant Reading and the Crooked Lines") and the textual interpretation from the second ("Close Reading and the Curious Peaks"), particularly in this section on central plot dilemmas, we come to understand the variance in these linear schemas, the blips in our proposed progressive complexity, as a function of what the final three novels have in common. In effect, they all share one plot; all three see Harry preparing for his ultimate encounter with Voldemort. Because we find these final novels more nuanced and complex overall, we also argue that book 5 marks the moment went they cross over, progressing roughly from children's literature (books 1 and 2) through young adult literature (books 3 and 4) to what we might categorize as "capital L" Literature or literary fiction in the final three. This textual shift between books 4 and 5 and the divergences it reveals in lines of complexity also lead us to affirm, again, that the conversation between these close and distant systems of analysis yields a more nuanced understanding of progressive complexity than either of these approaches would achieve alone.

Harry's Developing Identity

It is remarkable in repeated rereadings of this series how completely realized it appears even in its first scenes. Our first encounter with Professor McGonagall, from chapter 1 of book 1, has her exclaiming: "These people will never understand him! He'll be famous—a legend—I wouldn't be surprised if today was known as Harry Potter day in the future—there will be books written about Harry—every child in our world will know his name!" (13). This playful metafictionality is nonetheless revealing. There *will* be many books, and every child in our world *does* know his name. Building the character of Harry Potter, watching him grow up, make choices, and become a legend, is the primary work of what is essentially a seven-volume bildungsroman.[6] The who-am-I question Harry poses in the first novel is all simplicity—"How am I like my mum and my dad?" But Harry's identity questions are increasingly fraught novel to novel, until Hogwarts Year 7 when he must ask: "Am I, indeed, Dumbledore's man?" "What do my choices say about me?" and "Will I continue to exist when I die?"[7]

As we explore the progressive complexity of the series, the *bildung* plot, as we have seen, eventually becomes paramount. But its urgency is asserted even from the start, when, in *Sorcerer's Stone*, Harry's identity is presented as a series of simple "this or this" challenges. Harry first chooses to leave with Hagrid rather than stay with the Dursleys; he chooses to befriend Ron not Draco, and to be in Gryffindor not Slytherin. He fully trusts Dumbledore (who already shows signs to more mature observers of being manipulative or withholding, as in his socks answer to the challenge of the Mirror of Erised [214]), and, even given irrefutable evidence of Snape's caring assistance, Harry chooses to dislike and distrust the Potions professor.

In a developing and significant pattern for a genre traditionally characterized by a singular, independent hero, Harry's struggle for identity, like his problem solving, takes place mainly through relationships, as in his encounters, in the second novel, with Gilderoy Lockhart. As he sorts out who he wants to be, he loves Hagrid, admires Dumbledore, rejects Lockhart (and the limelight), and is compared with Tom Riddle (who, again, becomes the villainous Lord Voldemort). Riddle himself calls their similarity to Harry's attention: "There are strange likenesses between us, after all. Even you must have noticed. Both half-bloods, orphans, raised by Muggles. Probably the only two Parselmouths to come to Hogwarts since the great Slytherin himself. We even look something alike . . ." (317). But Harry, as we have noted, is already firmly ensconced in the Golden Trio and in the Weasley family; he suffers the admiration of Colin Creevey, frees Dobby, and saves Ginny. Per Dumbledore's advice, he has learned the primary lesson that "It is our choices, Harry, that show what we truly are, far more than our abilities" (333).

The focus of Harry's identity development in his third year at Hogwarts is on sorting out who he is and where he came from, primarily that he is his father's son. This understanding underpins his trust in Dumbledore and antipathy for Snape (as, again, they both remind him "how extraordinarily like" James Potter he is), but it also colors the information that he gets repeatedly, from several sources, that he has his "mother's eyes." Locating himself in a family that dissolved before he can remember, Harry pursues the basic identity work that compels every reflective child as they enter their teen-age years—how am I like and (oh please) unlike my father and my mother? In this pursuit, Professor Remus Lupin is a valuable mentor, having known and loved both of Harry's parents. He, too, reaffirms the novel's main lesson in the end (with different words): "You are—truly your father's son, Harry" (415).

But with his attention taken up with patriarchal lineage, Harry neglects the relationship building that has supported him in the first two novels (and, in effect, the mother's love that saved him). As Hermione and Ron fight over their pets, Hagrid finally has to take Harry and Ron aside and remind them what is most important: "I gotta tell yeh, I thought you two'd value yer friend more'n broomsticks or rats. That's all" (274). The important choice Harry makes at the end of *PA*, not to kill Peter Pettigrew, results from both of these insights about who he is and what he values. He explains to Pettigrew: "I don't reckon my dad would've wanted them to become killers—just for you" (376). Here Harry aims to save Lupin and Sirius, his father's best friends, from the damage that comes from killing another person.

After Harry's heroic progress in the first three novels, in Hogwarts Year 4 his identity seems to suffer some serious setbacks as he is often reduced to the too young, too inexperienced, too skinny boy thrown into the company of champions. His encounters with public opinion—with the Press through Rita Skeeter and with the Ministry of Magic via Cornelius Fudge—also place him as an outsider, vulnerable at first, then gaining in strength and self-confidence. He wrestles with how to assess people, especially self-interested or ambitious ones, and whom to trust, which is never an easy call but even less so when, like Mad-Eye Moody, people truly aren't what they seem. In the end, Harry again throws his lot in with Dumbledore with a preference for honesty, integrity and truth telling. As Dumbledore explains: "It is my belief, however, that the truth is generally preferable to lies, and that any attempt to pretend that Cedric died as the result of an accident, or some sort of blunder of his own, is an insult to his memory" (722). Dumbledore's guidance keeps Harry's identity quest from becoming overwhelming in these early novels, even in this more complex *GF*.

The matter of Cedric's death at the hands of Voldemort and Harry's commitment to being honest about it as he has learned to do from Dumbledore lead Harry to suffer both corporal and emotional punishment in *The Order of the Phoenix*, a high point of the *bildung* narrative. The increasingly absent Dumbledore now leaves Harry to his own devices, abandoning him to Dolores Umbridge's abuses and even to Snape's inept tutelage. And because Dumbledore has been Harry's touchstone for correct behavior, Harry seems particularly overwhelmed in *OP*.

Harry works to assert control—of his temper, of his reputation, of his feelings for Cho Chang, and of his mind. Through these challenges he encounters caregiving in many forms, from Molly Weasley's protectiveness to Sirius's sometimes reckless friendship, as in this exchange at Grimmauld Place:

"He's not your son," said Sirius quietly.

"He's as good as," said Mrs. Weasley fiercely. "Who else has he got?"

"He's got me." (90)

But Harry also has a more mature teenaged encounter with being his father's son when, seeing James through Snape's perspective, Harry realizes his father's imperfections and concludes that "he was a bit of an idiot" (670). If Harry is like his father, does he, too, have tendencies toward self-obsession or bullying? What are his real motives for speaking truth to power at Hogwarts, Harry wonders. And does he have "a saving-people-thing," a desire to act the hero (733–34)?

These are much more difficult identity questions, and they parallel other, deeper philosophical questions Harry begins to confront. This novel first addresses what happens after death, for example. It begins with Harry revisiting Cedric's death in his dreams and ends with Sirius taken from him so suddenly that Harry is completely unprepared and utterly done in by it. In his attempts to understand, Harry tries to see death from all sides; he talks to Luna, whose knowledge is always more intuitive than logic-based, and to Nearly Headless Nick, the Gryffindor ghost. "Wizards can leave an imprint of themselves upon the earth, to walk palely where their living selves once trod," Nick tells him ("miserably"). But Sirius, he says, will not come back. "He will have gone on" rather than choose, like Nick, to be "neither here nor there" (861). Again, as we have seen, the novels' attention to death hardly appears before the end of book 4 and becomes increasingly frequent throughout the last three books.

When Harry finally does get his moment with Dumbledore at the end of *Order of the Phoenix*, Dumbledore first lets Harry rant like the injured, angry boy he is and then begins, for the first time, to treat him like an adult who needs to hear the whole truth. This scene is pivotal to Harry's self-understanding, to his developing self-definition, as he comes to see how he is, indeed, "the chosen one," chosen by a prophecy and then by Voldemort to kill or be killed. Like Sirius and Cedric, like his parents before him, Harry will encounter the inexplicable.

This new insight places Harry in closer alliance with Dumbledore in book 6, as he trains to understand the enemy he is now called to face. Dumbledore schools him throughout *Half-Blood Prince*, but in the "Horcruxes" chapter, the headmaster memorable explains Harry's agency. Harry's fate,

Dumbledore says, was constructed by Voldemort (rather than "the gods" or the prophecy) and by Harry's own response to Voldemort's singling him out; Harry's continued innocence, his growing capacity to love, fueled Voldemort's determination that Harry was, indeed, his nemesis. But that doesn't have to dictate Harry's choices. "You see, the prophecy does not mean you *have* to do anything! But the prophecy caused Lord Voldemort to *mark you as his equal*. . . . In other words, you are free to choose your way, quite free to turn your back on the prophecy!" (512). Harry understands, then:

> the difference between being dragged into the arena to face a battle to the death and walking into the arena with your head held high. Some people, perhaps, would say that there was little to choose between the two ways, but Dumbledore knew—*and so do I*, thought Harry with a rush of fierce pride, and *so did my parents*—that there was all the difference in the world. (512)

This is another apex in Harry's growing self-understanding, one that offers him clarity as his encounters the most difficult challenges of the bildungsroman plot in book 7.

It is in this final novel that Harry completes an archetypal hero's cycle by, finally, returning to his community as a mature man, with new knowledge and leadership skills. His months in the wilderness hold mythic value, as do the many helpful encounters on his picaresque journey. But as we will see below, this final novel breaks nearly every comfortable narrative pattern of the first seven books as Harry removes himself from Hogwarts and undergoes a mostly solitary struggle with what he will become. He returns to Grimmauld Place (actually his own home), where he once felt nurtured and safe; he visits his parents' graves for the first time; he repeatedly second-guesses his understanding of Dumbledore; and he exposes himself to his best friends as utterly lost and confused—after which one walks away and one stays, breaking up the Golden Trio.

And throughout the novel, Harry fixates constantly on which choices to make, choices that now there is no help for. These aren't puzzles or either/or propositions. They don't involve clear-cut tasks or obvious rewards. With no guiding voices left to him, no mentors who can answer the questions meant only for him, he struggles mightily for meaning throughout *Deathly Hallows*, while violence rages, for the most part, just beyond the reader's view. The final chapters, where he experiences mortality and rebirth, close out the story cycle in canonical Western literary fashion. These chapters leave many questions unanswered and truth ultimately unattainable, but they feature choices affirmed, agency celebrated, integrity established, and love, particularly *philia* or the love of friends, upheld. Here Rowling is reaching well beyond the boundaries of a simple, didactic fantasy for children into the more intricate realms of literary fiction. This final novel of development is certainly the most complex of the series.

Disrupted Narrative Structures

One reason that the final novel appears more complex in a close reading than in a distant one is that its structure departs so markedly from the novels preceding it. Picking up a *Harry Potter* novel offers avid readers a sense of familiarity, with recurring patterns easily discernable and repeated plot points comfortably pointing the way through an often-unfamiliar fantasy landscape. Each novel visits 4 Privet Drive and Diagon Alley early on, and most spend some time at the Weasleys' Burrow; nearly all of them find Harry, Ron, and Hermione at King's Cross Station, where they board the *Hogwarts Express*, arrive at Hogwarts, greet Hagrid, and watch the sorting; in every novel, Harry attends classes, faces off with Draco, plays Quidditch or flies his broom, and celebrates Christmas with Ron or Hermione; in the final chapters, Dumbledore inevitably explains everything, and Harry heads back to the Muggle world through King's Cross Station, often steeling himself with a bit of humor or a mischievous encounter. The table below illustrates the patterns the novels establish throughout, and how many of them are left behind in *Deathly Hallows*—beginning in fact, with ending of book 6.

We should also note that these patterns are reinforced in repeat readings by glimpses of what comes later. For example, in *Sorcerer's Stone*, Dedalus Diggle "a little man in a top hat" (68) greets Harry at the entryway to the wizarding realm, in Diagon Alley. But he first appears in the Muggle world—"a tiny man in a violet top hat had bowed to him once while out shopping with Aunt Petunia and Dudley" (30). In book 2 Moaning Myrtle floats by at the Death Day Party, Snape gives the "impression of being able to read minds," the trio begin to think the Dark Arts position is cursed, the vanishing cabinet appears, Cornelius Fudge demonstrates the Ministry's incompetence, and Tom Riddle's diary acts like the horcrux it is.

Total plot consistencies	1: SS	2: CS	3: PA	4: GF	5: OP	6: HBP	7: DH
	10	10	11	11	11	9	5
HP at Dursleys	x	x	x	x	x	x	x
Visits the Weasleys			x	x	Grimmauld Place	x	x
Diagon Alley King's Cross	x	x	x	x	x	x	
Hogwarts Express	x	Ford Anglia	x	x	x	x	
The Sorting	x	Harry misses it	Harry misses it	x	x	Harry misses it	
School: Classes	x	x	x	x	x	x	
Quidditch	x	x	x	Triwizard	x	x	
Christmas at Hogwarts	x	x	x	x	Grimmauld Place	The Burrow	Godric's Hollow
Dumbledore explains everything	x	x	x	x	x	x (earlier)	x (but is it real?)
King's Cross	x	x	x	x	x		x (or in his head?)
(Humorous) Encounters w/Muggles	x	x	x	x	x		

Notes: Even when Harry misses it, the sorting is a plot point; the Triwizard is introduced as taking the place of Quidditch; Christmas is always celebrated, but in the last three books, it is not at Hogwarts.

Figure 1.9 A table comparing repeated plot elements in the novels of the series

The repetition invites familiarity, even as it cues changes in the storyline to come. Take, for example, the trio's return to King's Cross Station at the end of each novel. King's Cross serves a key function, as the text makes clear in *Chamber of Secrets*: "And together they walked back through the gateway to the Muggle world" (341). At the end of each of the first five novels, Harry's encounters with the Dursleys are comic relief, and he himself is often full of mischief. It's Harry, for example, who points out that Dudley doesn't know he's not allowed to use magic at home, not Hagrid as in the film (*SS* 309). Even the ending of *Goblet of Fire*, after Voldemort's return, has a comic turn, as the *Hogwarts Express* pulls into King's Cross, and Harry casually steps over Malfoy, Crabbe, and Goyle, "covered in hex marks," to threaten Fred and George with hexes if they didn't take his money for their joke shop. "We could all do with a few laughs," he tells them (734).[8] When the trio arrives at King's Cross at the end of *Order of the Phoenix*, after Sirius's death and the Battle of the Department of Mysteries, they are greeted by Fred and George in "lurid green" dragon skin jackets, and they observe the Order comically enforcing their authority over the cringing Dursleys.[9] In this dark moment of the story, Harry is notably warmed "to see them all ranged there, on his side" as he heads "toward the sunlit street" (870).

It comes as a complete disruption when the sixth novel ends at Dumbledore's funeral with Hagrid wailing in the background—no *Hogwarts Express*, no King's Cross Station. Everything has changed. And the final novel, from start to finish, reaffirms that disruption. The first chapter seems a true gateway to this novel in that it is dark and violent, a meeting of Voldemort with his Death Eaters, where he abuses and tortures his friends and enemies and then kills a Hogwarts teacher and feeds her to his snake. You may want to proceed no further.[10]

But the second chapter finds us back at 4 Privet Drive, with Harry preparing to say goodbye to a place he has little love for just before his seventeenth birthday—the age of maturity for wizards. However, this introduction, like the previous chapter, is not inviting for new readers. There is little description of Harry or the Dursleys, little allowance for readers who might not know the story or its characters. Following an almost tender scene with (the heretofore irredeemable) Dudley, Harry leaves for the last time, just as he came for the first time sixteen years earlier, with Hagrid on Sirius's motorcycle. But this time, he leaves right into the "Battle of the Seven Potters." He celebrates his birthday at the Burrow, but he, Ron, and Hermione aren't going to Diagon

Alley or on to Hogwarts. They set off, amid the rising threat of Voldemort's forces, armed with Dumbledore's final bequests to each of them, to seek horcruxes as he charged them to do.

The intervening chapters read like an adventure novel, as the trio (sometimes minus one) move through the British landscape and through a series of riddles and puzzles, often lost, often stumbling blindly, and sometimes barely escaping alive (at the Ministry, in Godric's Hollow, at Xenophilius Lovegood's house, and at Malfoy Manor). There is no sorting hat, no classes, no Quidditch. As the dark forces of terrorism envelop the wizarding world with violence, fear, chaos, and scapegoating, readers are left without their usual touchstones, so they, too, experience a measure of disorder. The novel offers pockets of resistance and surprising shifts of loyalties, as when Lupin briefly abandons Tonks, Ron leaves for sixty pages, and Xenophilius Lovegood sells them out. Along the way, everyone, readers and characters alike, must take a side.

The ending, however, is firmly lodged in Hogwarts, with one more episode of Dumbledore Explains Everything, this time from beyond the grave in the "King's Cross Station" chapter and via his portrait in the headmaster's office. There is no anticipated return to the Muggle world, though the epilogue takes us, nineteen years later, back to King's Cross Station.

Again, most patterns are broken in *Deathly Hallows*, but enough familiarity remains to confirm that this novel is the culmination of all of the others, particularly the final three. Book 7, however, exceeds their reach and confirms its themes as weightier, more profound, and, ultimately, more complex.

Rather than offering a definitive conclusion about the trajectory of progressive complexity in the novels, what we offer here, in conclusion, is more like a "choose your own adventure." Are the novels plot-driven adventures inviting children to be better readers? Then the complexity peaks in books 4 and 5, leveling off or decreasing slightly through the end. Are they "a seven-volume bildungsroman," located easily in traditions of (capital-L) literature? Then the complexity seems to rise progressively, peaking in the final three novels but more so in the disruptive seventh book. Together we looked at the language of these novels, their structures and form, their style, themes, and repetitions, and came up with various answers to our original question: Does this series indeed increase in complexity as it progresses? In the end, our most solid response to that question is a definitive "Yes and. . . ." But as we wrap up this analysis, we can say without equivocation that the *Harry*

Potter novels are worth studying, worth the attention we brought to them across our different disciplines, worth the conversations they initiated about the mutual benefit of close and distant reading in literary analysis.

Notes

1. See Hopkins, Whited, Shanoes, Meiden, Nikolajev, and Wolosky, among others.

2. From NIA: Newspapers in Education which circulates curriculum ideas and teaching materials for elementary and high school teachers. Last accessed 2.2021 http://nieonline.com/tbtimes/downloads/CCSS_reading.pdf.

3. "Distant reading" is a term coined by literary historian and theorist Franco Moretti in his 2000 article "Conjectures in World Literature" and further elaborated on in his 2013 monograph, *Distant Reading*.

4. Stylometry uses programming to compare vocabulary, use of function words, punctuation, and sentence length to a corpus of texts from various authors to look for a match. Computer scientist Patrick Juola used this technique to reveal the identity of Robert Galbraith as J. K. Rowling.

5. Journalist Shane Snow measured the readability of bestsellers and classic works using the Flesch-Kincaid reading formula and found that some of the most popular works and novels deemed "literary" by critics over the decades came out at a reading level from 4th through 6th grade. The Flesch-Kincaid measures word frequency and sentence length to determine reading level.

6. John Granger, our "Dean of Potter Pundits" (see chapter 7 in this volume) writes often of the connections between Harry Potter and other epic heroes of literature, of the Hero Cycle via Joseph Campbell, and the bildungsroman patterns across the seven novels. See *Unlocking Harry Potter*.

Michiko Kakutani famously (in the world of *Harry Potter* scholars) wrote in her review of *The Cursed Child* in the *New York Times*: "J. K. Rowling's magical seven-volume Harry Potter series is the ultimate bildungsroman, tracing that young wizard's coming of age, as he not only battles evil but also struggles to come to terms with the responsibilities, losses and burdens of adulthood. In the course of those books, we see a plucky schoolboy, torn by adolescent doubts and confusions, grow into an epic hero, kin to King Arthur, Luke Skywalker and Spider-Man."

7. *Harry Potter* critics frequently discuss the series as bildungsroman; Patrick McCauley, in several chapters of his *Into the Pensieve: The Philosophy and Theology of Harry Potter*, does it very effectively, for example. See also his chapter 8 in this volume.

8. It's notable that Hermione kisses Harry on the cheek for the first time here at King's Cross, and it's clearly not sexual (in a book where teenaged sexuality distracts everyone). They are deeply connected as friends; they are both fierce fighters, truth-tellers and crusaders even at this point in the series. (For further confirmation of the significance of this alliance, see McCauley's discussion in chapter 8 of this volume.)

9. While Fred and George are the classic comic relief and often a distraction for Harry in books that might be overwhelmingly dark without them (*OP*, for example), they also allow the novels to assert that disruption is not the primary problem the wizarding world confronts in the age of Voldemort. The twins' mischief and creative mayhem are

distinctively different from the destruction and darkness that Umbridge and the Death Eaters bring to Hogwarts that year.

10. In fact, when friends ask me [Cecilia] if their children are mature enough readers for the *Harry Potter* novels, I tell them the novels often set up gateways like this one to let them decide for themselves if the books are too complex, boring, violent or scary.

Works Cited

Anatol, Giselle Liza, Ed. *Reading Harry Potter*. Connecticut: Praeger, 2003. Print.

Garlick, Shayna. "Harry Potter and the Magic of Reading. *The Christian Science Monitor*, 2 May 2007, https://www.csmonitor.com/2007/0502/p13s01-legn.html.

Granger, John. *Unlocking Harry Potter: Five Keys for the Serious Reader*. Unlocking Press, 2007.

Hopkins, Lisa. "Harry Potter and the Acquisition of Knowledge" in *Reading Harry Potter*, edited by Giselle Liza Anatol. Connecticut: Praeger, 2003. 25–34. Print.

Hunt, Sally. "Representations of Gender and Agency in the Harry Potter series" in *Corpora and Discourse Studies*, edited by Paul Baker and Tony McEnery. Palgrave Macmillan, 2015. 266–84.

Juola, Patrick. "How a Computer Program Helped Show J. K. Rowling Write [sic] A Cuckoo's Calling." *Scientific American*, 20 Aug. 2013, https://www.scientificamerican.com/article/how-a-computer-program-helped-show-jk-rowling-write-a-cuckoos-calling/.

Kakutani, Michiko. "An Epic Showdown as Harry Potter Is Initiated Into Adulthood," review of *Harry Potter and the Deathly Hallows*. New York Times, 7.19.2007. www.nytimes.com/2007/07/19/books/19potter.html.

Kakutani, Michiko. "*Harry Potter and the Cursed Child* Explores the Power of Time," review of *Harry Potter and the Cursed Child* (Jack Thorne, based on an original story by J. K. Rowling, John Tiffany and Thorne). New York Times, 8.2.2016. https://www.nytimes.com/2016/08/02/books/harry-potter-and-the-cursed-child-review.html.

McCauley, Patrick M. *Into the Pensieve: The Philosophy and Theology of Harry Potter*. Atglen PA: Schiffer, 2015.

Michalke, Meik. *koRpus: Text Analysis with Emphasis on POS Tagging, Readability, and Lexical Diversity*. (Version 0.13–5), 2021. https://reaktanz.de/?c=hacking&s=koRpus.

Mieden, Tricia, "Choosing a Moral Compass: The Journey towards Moral Maturity in Harry Potter" (2017). *Masters Theses*. 441. https://digitalcommons.liberty.edu/masters/441.

Nelson, Robert K. *Mining the Dispatch*. The Digital Scholarship Lab at University of Richmond, 2020, https://dsl.richmond.edu/dispatch/. Accessed 18 Mar. 2021.

Nikolajeva, Maria. "Harry Potter and the Secrets of Children's Literature." *Critical Perspectives on Harry Potter* (2008): 225–43.

Shanoes, Veronica L. "Cruel Heroes and Treacherous Texts: Educating the Reader in Moral Complexity and Critical Reading in J. K. Rowling's *Harry Potter* Books" in *Reading Harry Potter*, edited by Giselle Liza Anatol. Connecticut: Praeger, 2003. 131–46. Print.

Sinclair, Stéfan and Geoffrey Rockwell, 2016. *Voyant Tools*. 2016, http://voyant-tools.org/. Accessed 18 Mar. 2021.

Snow, Shane. "This Surprising Reading Level Analysis Will Change the Way You Write." *The Content Strategist*, 28 Jan. 2015, https://contently.com/2015/01/28/this-surprising-reading-level-analysis-will-change-the-way-you-write/.

Whited, Lana A., ed. *The Ivory Tower and Harry Potter: Perspectives on a Literary Phenomenon*. Colombia, MO: 2002.

Whited, Lana A., with M. Katherine Grimes. "What Would Harry Do? J. K. Rowling and Lawrence Kohlberg's Theories of Moral Development" in *The Ivory Tower and Harry Potter: Perspectives on a Literary Phenomenon*. Colombia, MO: 2002. 182–210.

Wolosky, Shira. *The Riddles of Harry Potter: Secret Passages and Interpretive Quests*. New York: Palgrave Macmillan US, 2010.

2

SAID HERMIONE EARNESTLY
Harry Potter's Prose, and Why It Doesn't Matter

Emily Strand

It was a proud day, sparkling with May sunshine and the promise of vicarious adventure, the day I began to read *Harry Potter and the Sorcerer's Stone* to my then five-year-old son. I had longed for this day, dreamed of it since he'd been born. If I'm being honest, I conceived of and bore the child in question in no small part in order to experience this glorious day. On this day, I would share with my beloved boy not just a book, but a gateway to an imaginative world that I just knew would engage and engross his young mind, perhaps even more than it had my own.

Even better, it had been a few years since I had read the *Harry Potter* books straight through, start-to-finish, because I had been absorbed in writing and editing my own first novel. And absence makes the heart grow fonder . . . right?

Still in our jammies on a lazy Saturday morning, we grabbed mug and sippy cup (respectively) and settled in on his twin bed to meet the Boy Who Lived. How I wish someone had read *me* these books when I was his age. Alas! I was born too soon; I'd had to wait until adulthood to encounter Rowling's magic. But that arbitrary injustice of timing would soon be rectified. The stage was set: reading my son *Harry Potter* was going to be *perfect*.

I have long had the first line of *Sorcerer's Stone* memorized, the one about the Dursleys being perfectly normal, thank-you-very-much, so we started off easily enough. Then things got weird. *Wait, are we in Dursley's point of view?* No, it can't be. The narrator mocks the Dursleys—Vernon especially, with his boring neckties—even as it reveals them with seeming objectivity, recording things they don't see (mostly owls) and events that take place after they fall asleep. This was unlimited omniscience: a point-of-view choice that, I had recently been informed by the experienced writers in my fiction critique group, was not a good option for anyone attempting to publish a novel these days. It's so nineteenth century! It lacks intimacy! It's emotionless and hard to relate to! (Browne and King 50–62) And yet, here it was, laying its omniscient claims over chapter 1 of *Harry Potter*.

Huh. It was particularly weird since I knew that the bulk of the series is written in Harry's limited third-person omniscient point of view. So why the inconsistency? Is this the mark of a first-time author or sloppy editing?

I glanced at my son, shaking myself from this writerly reverie. His little legs had ceased swinging under him and now dangled serenely off the bed. His head nuzzled my shoulder, his blue eyes wide with interest as they glanced up at me. I smiled at him and kept reading.

Then something even more troubling than omniscient point of view presented itself. An information dump! A big, fat one, three paragraphs long, slowing the narrative pace and—gasp!—telling instead of showing! What's all this about Mr. Dursley's wife's dead, unDursleyish sister? Whatever it is, can't she show it to us *in a scene*, or in dialogue, or tell us later on, when we're invested enough to stomach some backstory? *How dare she?* said I, the reader-turned-writer-turned-back-to-reader (but-unable-to-ignore-the-writer).

Yes, you do detect a twinge of jealousy in my reaction. I had personally tried the whole backstory dump in the first chapter of my own novel, the very first piece I'd submitted to my local writing critique group. My cheeks grow warm even now remembering their knowing expressions around the table at the Chinese restaurant where we'd met, patient in their pity for my ignorance. All heads nodded in agreement as each member exposed this worst flaw (of many) in my chapter. "You're doing a lot of telling," said one. "Novels these days start pretty quickly," said another. "Try giving us your main character in a compelling scene," a third added, at pains to be constructive. Finally, driving the point home with devastating honesty, a senior member advised, "If you want to hook me, don't start your story like this."

But *why*? I'd cried inside, scribbling their comments dutifully. Why can't I start my story by telling you several hundred words of stuff you *really, really* need to know? It's important to the story, I swear!

"Backstory has its place in a story, but that place isn't *usually* at the very beginning," says Les Edgerton in his book *Hooked* (86). He maintains that opening scenes of books should not start with "long boring explanations of the protagonists' past." (By inference, boring explanations of the protagonist's uber-dull uncle's past are also ruled out.) Rather, opening scenes should engage the reader on an emotional level, compelling them to read on (Jodie Rhodes qtd. in Edgerton 87). Renni Brown and Dave King, in their book *Self-Editing for Fiction Writers*, argue that the influence of movies and television on today's readers have made them "accustomed to seeing a story as a series of immediate scenes," and this shift has gradually evacuated narrative summary of its power to engage modern readers (8). Perhaps most importantly, says Noah Lukeman in *The First Five Pages*, narrative summary can take away a reader's power to reckon his own interpretations of what he reads; in short, it inhibits readers from making the text their own (120).

Since we're on the subject of allowing the reader to make the text her own (or not, as the case may be), as my son and I continued to read Chapter One of *Harry Potter*, I noticed something even worse than narrative summary, something that made the recently-awoken fiction writer within quiver in revulsion: a damnable surfeit of –ly adverbs, especially to describe dialogue. *Who put all these here?* I wondered in amazement. How can they be filling the pages of this book that I thought I knew so well, seeming to multiply as we read, as if the first one had been hit by a Gemini charm? They were so numerous, I actually counted; no fewer than twenty adverbs to describe dialogue delivery mar the pages of *Harry Potter and the Sorcerer's Stone*'s first chapter.

What's worse is they're not needed. Dialogue is one of Rowling's greatest strengths as a writer; through dialogue, she paints evocative pictures of her characters, their personalities and motivations. Hers does not suffer from the weaknesses that often prompt writers to prop up their language with these "helper" words. The dialogue of Chapter One clearly and cleverly reveals marks of Professor McGonagall's character; she (cat form) sits more stiffly than most cats and she's opted to sit on a brick wall all day instead of celebrating Voldemort's defeat with every other magical being in Britain. Thus, there is no need to tell us, in the next breath, that she sniffs "angrily" at Dumbledore's arrival (plus, I'm not even sure how one can sniff *angrily*;

try it and then tell me if I'm wrong). And when she responds "I know," to his reminder that there's been precious little to celebrate for eleven years, the reader does not need to be told that she says this "irritably" (12–13). We already know she's irritable with Dumbledore (and likely with people in general), because *we've been paying attention*. Adding adverbs that heap on unneeded description makes our close attention to the text all but unnecessary. Soon, if the unneeded adverbs persist, we may put the book down, ostensibly out of boredom but really for not respecting our investment in it.

But the funny thing is, with *Harry Potter*, we don't.

As my son and I finished Chapter One of *Sorcerer's Stone*, I shook my head and made to close the book, disturbed at what this re-read had revealed to me, the aspiring fiction writer.

But my son stuck his chubby hand into the paperback to stop me. "Mom!" he said, bouncing on the bed. "Can't we *pleeeeeeeease* read some more?"

I smiled at him, checked the time (ten more minutes until lights out) and resolved to quit counting adverbs. "Sure, kiddo," I said. "This next chapter is one of my favorites."

How does *Harry Potter* get away with the flaws in its prose style? Despite what the experts on fiction writing have to say, nothing has held readers back from making *Harry Potter* their own. Millions of readers world-wide continue to engross themselves in the now twenty-year-old books, despite Rowling's unconventional narrative opening, her inconsistencies in point of view and her free-wheeling and use of –ly adverbs. So what's the deal? Are the defining books of a generation poorly written? Are more than 30 million book buyers, as *New York Times* book critic Harold Bloom once averred in his now-infamous pan of *Sorcerer's Stone*, simply "wrong"?

This essay focuses on *Harry Potter*'s prose style, setting aside the rose-colored glasses of the fan in favor of the fiction editor's blue pencil. As we've seen above, Rowling's prose, by professional standards, is occasionally weak and unconventional, making rumors that her manuscript was rejected by twelve publishers less surprising than media reports would have us believe (Flood). And yet the injustice, the preposterousness of these rumors lingers—that were it not for one reader's ability to look beyond such surface-level flaws, the world might never have met the Boy Who Lived (No Adverb Necessary). That's how most of us fans see it, anyway.

But what of the critics? The surface-level flaws discussed above, while irrelevant to most readers' enjoyment of the *Harry Potter* books, have left them vulnerable to a prejudicial dismissal by literary critics, who often fail to notice their more sublime aspects in their haste to decry Rowling's bad literary habits. The remainder of this essay will examine some negative reviews of Potter, noting the content of their critiques and interrogating an important subtext for their dismissals of Rowling (and even of her fans) in their scorn for the books' popularity. Employing alternative standards of literary merit, those articulated by Cecilia Konchar Farr in *The Ulysses Delusion*, which attempt to help readers pry the way we judge books from the stranglehold of the literary establishment, this essay will address what Rowling gets right in *Harry Potter*: vibrant characters, sparkling dialogue, keen humor and intricate, seamless plots. Finally, one seeming "flaw" of Rowling's prose, inconsistency in narrative point-of-view, will be examined and revealed as an essential (and likely intentional) way in which Rowling achieves the same breathtaking twists of narrative misdirection as her literary hero, Jane Austen.

Nicholas Lezard, writing for the *Guardian's* books blog in July 2007 (a month full of praise for *Potter* in most quarters, if you recall), provocatively titles his piece "*Harry Potter's* big con is the prose." He begins by admitting the futility of making "a stand" against Potter, given "the vast, unstoppable juggernaut of popular acclaim" which the books enjoy. Lezard then launches a juggernaut of his own, first lamenting the demise of independent booksellers (for which he blames *Harry Potter*, indirectly) and then the "toxic," "flat," and "pedestrian" prose style of the *Potter* books themselves. His main problem is with Rowling's overuse of adverbs, especially to describe the way characters deliver dialogue, but Lezard also touches on Rowling's overuse of cliché as well.

Lezard is clearly writing for an elite audience. After citing a particularly adverb-heavy passage of *Order of the Phoenix* as evidence, Lezard asks, "Do I need to explain why that is such second-rate writing?" The question is rhetorical; he does not go on to explain why it is second-rate writing to his readers (the elite). Instead, he insults those who *would* need this explanation: Rowling's readership.

> If I do, then that means you're one of the many adults who don't have a problem with the retreat into infantilism that your willing immersion in the *Potter* books represents. It doesn't make you a bad or silly person. But if you have the patience to read it without noticing how plodding it is, then you are self-evidently someone on whom the possibilities of the English language are largely lost. (Lezard)

The insult is as poignant as it is sweeping. According to Lezard, reading *Harry Potter* without reviling its prose is a sign the reader is stunted, dull, obtuse when it comes to language. *Harry Potter* readers simply read for the plot then. Rest assured, it doesn't make us bad or silly (even when we retreat into "infantilism"[1]); we're just dim-witted. Recall that Lezard has established, from the opening of his brief piece, that his "stand" against *Harry Potter* will be "futile" before the "vast juggernaut" of popular opinion. Thus, he positions himself (with his elite readership) as the lone voice for aesthetic taste on the vast battlefield in the war for books. Note also that Lezard insults Rowling's readers far more brutally and directly than he insults the writer herself. Sure, he calls her writing "the kind of prose that reasonably intelligent nine-year-olds consider pretty hot stuff, if they're producing it themselves," but throughout the piece (especially, by inference, in his diatribe on the role of popular purchasing habits in the demise of independent booksellers), Lezard directs the blame for the sad state of affairs that has made *Harry Potter* so successful primarily on book buyers and only secondarily on book authors.

Let's turn to another review from the *Guardian*'s books blog, this one written in 2000 by Anthony Holden, who had judged the 1999 Whitbread Award for books, which Rowling won in the Children's category for *Prisoner of Azkaban*. Holden's piece shares some striking similarities with Lezard's, especially in its anti-populist bent. He advises his readers to stay home a week from Saturday (the book's release date) to avoid being "mobbed by parents and children stampeding to obtain not the latest faddish toy or computer game . . . but a book," one he claims is "less a book and more a . . . marketing phenomenon" with "advance hype worthy of a Wonderbra" (Holden).

Still on the subject of the media hype surrounding *Potter* book launches, Holden wonders whether the publishers have "no faith in their product's ability to sell on its own merits?" Here Holden roots himself firmly in the literary elite (if his endorsements of Seamus Heaney and David Cairns don't do the job) and shows he's somewhat out of touch with the *Potter* phenomenon. Everything about *Harry Potter*'s publication and rise to popularity tells a story of books succeeding *entirely* on their own merit: unpublished, impoverished author writes book, persevering in publishing it despite early rejections; book sweeps not only nation but globe, promoted by children's librarians. Hasn't Holden been paying attention to this popular story, one that actually supports the metanarrative of the meritocracy?

Of course, the meritocracy is a populist narrative, one Holden likely regrets, perhaps even fears. Holden, like Lezard, predicts that for his own good taste in denouncing the *Potter* books, he, too, will be martyred at the hands of popular opinion. "I brave the wrath of millions by daring to say so, but it really doesn't take a high-minded killjoy to worry what these books are doing to the literary taste of millions of potential young readers." In this statement, Holden lends urgency to the issue: the popular embrace of *Potter* is not merely to be lamented for what Lezard and others have called the "infantilism" of adult culture these days, but for its warping effect on the young. For Holden, the *Potter* phenomenon is not just annoying—it's worrisome.

Case in point, he says, is what happened with the 1999 Whitbread award. *Prisoner* squeaked by (Holden claims, after a "mid-meeting" change in the rules) with the Children's category award and threatened to take the overall award as well. But Holden put a stop to that, threatening to take his football and go home (he actually used far more elitist terms; they were French, and I had to resort to Google to understand them). In reaction to his ultimatum, he says, "All populist hell broke loose." (Translation: he was called a "pompous prat" on television the next day.)

Interestingly, the focus of Holden's ire in the piece is not *Harry Potter's* prose. He exhausts far more words complaining about the popularity of *Harry Potter* than on its prose flaws, and those he does mention are in passing, almost as an assumption. He calls the language of Heaney's translation of *Beowulf* "much more exciting" than *Potter's*, and he calls Rowling's writing first clunky, then "pedestrian," "ungrammatical," and "unadorned." He uses up more words insulting Rowling's adult readership than he does her prose: "As for the 150,000 adults who paid extra to buy the same books in grown-up dustjackets, to avoid embarrassment when reading them in public (or perhaps even at home), well, get a life." From there he implies that adult *Potter* readers are funny-pages-reading clutchers of comfort blankets who refuse to adult. It is clear from the way Holden spends his word count that, among the many regrettable aspects of *Potter*, the most deplorable is its popularity.[2]

Harold Bloom, in his review of *Harry Potter and the Sorcerer's Stone* for the *Wall Street Journal*, continues the antipopulist critical campaign against *Potter*, opening (predictably, by now), with the acknowledgment that voicing criticism of *Potter* is futile. Ironically, Bloom references Shakespeare to do so, another writer whose popularity may have blinded critics of his day to his genius. "Taking arms against *Harry Potter*, at this moment," says Bloom, "is to emulate Hamlet taking arms against a sea of troubles. By opposing the sea, you won't end it." Bloom calls *Potter* an "epiphenomenon," a symptom of a wider dumbing down of popular culture. Like Lezard's and Holden's, Bloom's remarks on Rowling's prose are sweeping yet brief in the context of his critique. Bloom says, in his only direct critique of Rowling's language, "Her prose style, heavy on cliché, makes no demands upon her readers. In an arbitrarily chosen single page—page 4—of the first *Harry Potter* book, I count seven clichés, all of the 'stretch his legs' variety." For Bloom, as for Lezard and Holden, *Potter*'s aesthetic weaknesses are not the focus; they provide a gateway into a much broader complaint against the dumbing down of culture in general and of those perceived to be leading that movement. (For Bloom, it's less Rowling herself and more the *New York Times* with its "not very literate book review.")

It's understandable for *Harry Potter* fans to feel offended at the way these critical reviews of our favorite books impugn and insult us, directly and implicitly. I certainly do. And yet I can't help but share, to some degree, their critical view of Rowling's prose style, if not their other complaints. I know I earlier promised to stop counting adverbs, but as a conscientious fiction reader and writer, it's my duty to point out that Hermione says things "earnestly" five times in *Prisoner of Azkaban* alone—and that's just one needless adverb in a sea of others. I was asked recently, in an interview for the podcast *Reading, Writing, Rowling*, whether Rowling's overreliance on adverbs isn't simply a stylistic cue that she's primarily an author of *children's* literature. To this same point, Barfield observes that the language of the *Harry Potter* novels matches Harry's "vocabulary and linguistic structures, as well as his perspective, rather than the adult third person omniscient narrator" (187). Maybe there are just too many adverbs in Harry's head, and that's why they're scattered so liberally throughout his story?

Hmm, says the writer, with eyebrow raised. Foregoing the debate about aesthetic standards and whether they apply to children's as well as adult literature (short answer from C. S. Lewis: "A book worth reading only in childhood is not worth reading even then" [47]), the thinking behind this notion of copious adverbs as a hallmark of "children's literature" might otherwise hold up if Rowling's use and abuse of adverbs did not stretch into the novels she has written for adults as well, such as *The Casual Vacancy* and her pseudonymous Cormoran Strike mysteries (spoiler alert: the needless adverbs are in those books, too).

So what's a literarily minded *Harry Potter* fan to do? Give the books up like a bad habit? Hardly. But it is worth the effort of looking critically at just about anything we love, especially something that so many have loved and admired. When we do, we find issues at work that are far more interesting than a debate over adverbs and clichés, info dumps and narrative points of view. Konchar Farr, in *The Ulysses Delusion*, articulates what's at work in the debate between fans who love popular fiction and critics who love to hate it. "[T]he literary establishment is, in effect, holding the novel for ransom, circumscribing this popular form with the language and concerns of the Academy. But the joke is on the professors, because instead of paying the required respect to a high art version of the novel, American readers are walking away, settling for less exclusive facsimiles" (Konchar Farr xv). Konchar Farr points out that the late-Enlightenment origins of the novel itself are "feminine, populist and diverse," and yet they have been, in subsequent eras, subjected to aesthetic judgments that are masculine and elitist, emphasizing disinterested artistry (25) over the engrossing fictionality that forms the essence, the distinguishing feature of the novel as a literary form (12–13). Barfield concurs in his study of Rowling's critics, pointing out that "the necessity of good style and the well-turned phrase, which seems a somewhat Formalist conception, has never been as inevitable (or indeed objectively described) a hallmark of literary quality as Rowling's detractors would like to imply it is" (178–79).

Konchar Farr advocates instead for reader-centered criteria by which to judge novels, such as readers' ability to relate to the story and characters, the level of absorption with which we read a novel and its "discussability," which implies the level to which it connects a reader with other readers ("It's Complicated"). When we judge *Harry Potter* by such standards, we begin to understand what critics like Lezard, Holden, and Bloom do not: that, as NPR book critic Alan Cheuse once said, "a novel isn't (only) an aesthetic object but (also) a cultural intervention, and (even more) a conversation with readers" (qtd. in Konchar Farr 22). The conversation between *Harry Potter* and its readers has been riveting from the start and continues to grow and deepen as the academy slowly embraces *Potter* not for the perfection of its prose style (some, Konchar Farr notes, will always have *Ulysses* to cling to for that), but for the questions it raises about everything from the way we encounter books to the ways in which we are free or not free to the age-old question of human mortality and what's to be done about it. It's a conversation readers of most ages and backgrounds can and do join, and it's a lot more interesting than talking about adverbs.

Real fruit bears out from refusing to judge Rowling's writing purely by aesthetic standards. For instance, take a second look at the inconsistencies in her narrative point of view. First, we must acknowledge the great debt Rowling's work owes to the author she has called her favorite of all time, Jane Austen (Rowling, 2000; See also Groves in this volume). Interestingly, what Rowling says she loves about Austen reveals much about what readers love about Rowling: "Her characters are vividly alive, she had a wonderful facility for dialogue, a dry and sometimes scathing sense of humour and she crafted seamless plots with such lightness of touch it appears effortless" (qtd. in Groves 97). But it is Rowling's manipulation of narrative point of view that links her most markedly to Austen. John Granger, in his many works,[3] and Beatrice Groves, in *Literary Allusion in Harry Potter*, observe that both Austen and Rowling "employ a narrative voice (known as 'third person limited omniscient view') that is partial in its knowledge, yet appears omniscient to the reader caught up in the story" (Groves 100). Citing the research of H. Dry, Groves observes that Austen's *Emma* "begins with an omniscient narrator but this 'objective' narrator becomes less and less present as the novel progresses" (101). By the novel's second half, Emma tells her own (limited third omniscient) story, having effectively and yet quite subtly usurped the narrative perspective. Thus, the reader is subjected to the same twists of narrative misdirection that sweep Emma off her feet. It makes a thrilling ride of a story that's mostly about manners and marriage, just as Rowling, through the same technique, makes something Harry has been carrying around on his forehead since he was a baby the very object that requires his destruction and the very thing that allows him to return from death: his scar.

When we observe this same subtle shift from unlimited omniscience ("Mr. and Mrs. Dursley of number four, Privet Drive, were proud to say that they were perfectly normal, thank you very much") to Harry's limited point of view, occurring across the first half of *Sorcerer's Stone*, it is tempting to judge from standards that emphasize pristine aesthetics of language. In doing so, we may dismiss Rowling's point-of-view inconsistencies as "cutesy" (Holden), convenient, or simply as lacking diligence. But it's more complicated, more nuanced, more intentional than that. "Both [Austen and Rowling]," says Groves, "progressively replace the omniscient narrative voice with one that draws the reader inexorably into the protagonist's world" (101). This intentional manipulation of perspective "is a brilliant device both for making a reader identify with the protagonist, and for springing surprises on them" (Groves 101). Writing about prose style, Browne and King call this narrative technique "in effect the literary equivalent of a camera moving from a long shot to gradually close the distance from the actor" (62). Far from a flaw in her writing, Rowling's manipulation of narrative point of view, upon further examination, is revealed as a sophisticated element of her prose style.

Alas, reinterpreting Rowling's overuse of adverbs as a mark of literary brilliance is not as easy. Stephen King famously said that for writers, the road to hell is paved with adverbs. "To put it another way, they're like dandelions. If you have one on your lawn, it looks pretty and unique. If you fail to root it out, however, you find five the next day . . . fifty the day after that . . . and then, my brothers and sisters, your lawn is totally, completely, and profligately covered with dandelions. By then you see them for the weeds they really are, but by then it's—*GASP!!*—too late" (125).

Surely King is right. Yet I can't help but hear his dandelion metaphor in a different way, having just read another beloved book to my son: Richard Adams's 1972 classic *Watership Down*, the only book that's ever made me wish I were a rabbit. Every time I read it, it immerses me so totally in the rabbits' perspective that for a long time afterward, when I see a rabbit in my yard, nibbling at my husband's lettuces, I think I know it, can relate to it, can understand something about its private life. (Also, I no longer want to set the cat on it.) *Watership Down*, like *Harry Potter*—like all the very best books—gives its readers the ability to put ourselves, wholly and completely, into another point of view.

In *Watership*, this new perspective is much lower to the ground.

We humans, rarified creatures of taste and privilege, owners of elaborate dwellings with lush, green lawns, see the dandelion as nothing but a pest, a nuisance, a sign of laziness or lack of concern for landscape aesthetics. We spend our time lamenting them, as the critics do adverbs, rooting them out so they won't multiply. But the rabbit, perhaps more like the average reader, sees them differently as he lopes along, close to the earth. He is not at all concerned with the integrity or exclusivity of grass in a lawn. Why should he be? Each dandelion is welcome variety, making his daily diet more interesting, more colorful, more fiber-rich and delicious. He does not observe how the dandelions multiply into a constellation of untidiness from above. If he could, he would cheer them on! Instead, his nose guides him, and each buttery yellow flower leads him to the next.

Sometimes it helps to think like a rabbit. I don't mean to imply, necessarily, that this means thinking in an unsophisticated fashion. My favorite aspect of *Watership Down* is Adams's careful, convincing construction of an intricate linguistic, cultural, and religious system for his rabbits. The popularity of Rowling's books, which emphasize story over prose, isn't the "dumbing down" of human culture, just as rabbit life is not all *silflay* (eating) and *hraka* (pooping), though it is those things too. At its core, rabbit life is built of myth and mystery, terror and daring, faith and friendship; in short, rabbit life makes for a damned good story. And in the story, dandelions are not weeds, but quite good fare, if you can get them.

Notes

1. Rowling's prose is only one aspect of the debate about the supposed "infantilism" of contemporary culture and *Harry Potter*'s role in it. See Steven Barfield's essay, "Of Young Magicians and Growing Up: J. K. Rowling, Her Critics and the 'Cultural Infantilism' Debate," in *Scholarly Studies in Harry Potter*, edited by Cynthia Whitney Hallett. Lewiston (NY: Edwin Mellen Press, 2005).

2. Most of Holden's other complaints have to do with Rowling's appropriation of the British boarding-school setting, and the nostalgic conservatism of the books, and this, by Barfield's assessment (see footnote 1), is the consensus of critics who envision *Harry Potter* as primarily a school-days story. Barfield points out that the school story, post 1945, is one of the most maligned literary genres, usually panned for seeming old-fashioned and socially regressive (Barfield 184). Cartmell and Whelehan also make the claim that *Potter* is inherently conservative, in their essay "Harry Potter and the Fidelity Debate," in *Books in Motion: Adaptation, Intertextuality, Authorship*, edited by Mireia Aragay (Amsterdam: Rodopi, 2005). But they provide far more compelling justification for it than Holden and the other critics Barfield studies in his essay. Holden also complains of the books' one-dimensionality, but cites evidence for it that would have failed him were he to have judged from all seven books (e.g., the unequivocal goodness of Harry's parents).

3. See especially John Granger, *Harry Potter's Bookshelf* (New York: Berkley Books, 2009), 25–31.

Works Cited

Barfield, Steven, "Of Young Magicians and Growing Up: J. K. Rowling, Her Critics and the 'Cultural Infantilism' Debate" in *Scholarly Studies in Harry Potter*, edited by Cynthia Whitney Hallett. Lewiston, NY: Edwin Mellen Press, 2005.

Bloom, Harold. "Can 30 Million Book Buyers Be Wrong? Yes." *The Wall Street Journal*, 11 July 2000, www.wsj.com/articles/SB963270836801555352.

Browne, Renni and Dave King. *Self-Editing for Fiction Writers*. New York: HarperCollins, 2004.

Edgerton, Les. *Hooked*. Cincinnati, OH: Writer's Digest Books, 2007.

"Episode Six: 2017 Chestnut Hill Harry Potter Conference." *Reading, Writing, Rowling* from MuggleNet, 8 January 2018, http://www.mugglenet.com/specialty-site/reading-writing -rowling/.

Flood, Alison. "J. K. Rowling says she received 'loads' of rejections before Harry Potter success." *The Guardian*, 24 March 2015, www.theguardian.com/books/2015/. mar/24/jk -rowling-tells-fans-twitter-loads-rejections-before-harry-potter-success.

Groves, Beatrice. *Literary Allusion in Harry Potter*. London: Routledge, 2017.

Holden, Anthony. "Why Harry Potter doesn't cast a spell over me." *The Guardian*, 25 June 2000, www.theguardian.com/books/2000/jun/25/booksforchildrenandteenagers. guardianchildrensfictionprize2000.

King, Stephen. *On Writing: A Memoir of the Craft*. New York: Pocket Books, 2000.

Konchar Farr, Cecilia. "It's Complicated: The Relationship between the Harry Potter Novels and Their Avid Readers." Chestnut Hill Harry Potter Conference, 20 October 2017, Chestnut Hill College, Chestnut Hill, PA. Keynote Address.

Konchar Farr, Cecilia. *The Ulysses Delusion*. New York: Palgrave Macmillan, 2016.

Lewis, C. S. "Sometimes Fairy Stories May Say Best What's to Be Said" in *On Stories*. New York: Harcourt, Inc., 1982.

Lezard, Nicholas. "Harry Potter's big con is the prose." *The Guardian*, 17 July 2007, www.the guardian.com/books/booksblog/2007/jul/17/harrypottersbigconisthep.

Lukeman, Noah. *The First Five Pages*. New York: Simon and Schuster, 2000.

Rowling, J. K. "From Mr. Darcy to Harry Potter by way of Lolita." *The Sunday Herald*, 21 May 2000. www.accio-quote.org/articles/2000/autobiography.html.

3

SAY THE MAGIC WORD
Spellwork and the Legacy of Nonsense

Christina Phillips-Mattson

Nearly one hundred and fifty years had passed since Edward Lear's *Nonsense Songs and Stories* when the resident sage of Hogwarts School puzzled his listeners and readers by announcing to his child audience: "Welcome to a new year at Hogwarts! Before we begin our banquet, I would like to say a few words. And here they are: Nitwit! Blubber! Oddment! Tweak! Thank you!" (*SS* 92). With this nonsensical speech, and by privileging language play throughout her seven-part series, Rowling joins the long line of writers from sixteenth-century John Redford (*Wit and Science*), to seventeenth-century John Taylor, to eighteenth-century Samuel Foote (*The Great Panjandrum* speech), to nineteenth-century poet Edward Lear and novelist Lewis Carroll, to twentieth-century modernist James Joyce and postmodernist Spike Milligan, who all wrote in the mode of literary nonsense.

That the *Harry Potter* series belongs to this prestigious lineage may still come as a surprise because, in large part due to the popularity of Lewis Carroll's *Alice* books, literary nonsense has long been most closely associated with children's literature. Indeed, in his book, *An Anatomy of Literary Nonsense*, scholar Wim Tigges employs Carroll and Lear as the standard by which to measure the nonsense genre. Attracted to nonsense for both personal and perhaps political reasons, Carroll and Lear, who incorporated nonsense devices like nonsequiturs, parallelisms, parodies, lexical exhibitionism, neologisms, puzzles, codes, incongruity, and portmanteau words into their novels and poems, were seen to conspire with the child in an effort to expose the illogical, bewildering, and at times ridiculous rules imposed by adult society. Because the most successful writers of nonsense literature wrote for children and employed poems and rhymes for children in their works, there is a common assumption that we can draw a straight line from oral tales and nursery rhymes to Victorian nonsense poems and novels. However, as scholars Kimberley Reynolds and Noel Malcolm explain, literary nonsense instead finds its earliest roots in literature for adults. It was first created to be performed at the Inns of Court and targeted an elite, educated audience.

Thus, we find that nonsense has a double heritage: on one hand, nonsense was first written for a sophisticated audience to which children were denied access, while on the other hand, nonsense was also found in oral folk tales and nursery rhymes, and, later, in children's novels. Tigges affirms that the creation of nonsense in any genre requires immense technical skill and a meticulous attention to opposing forces, but he also implies that literary nonsense in children's literature has not been as complex or revolutionary as it has been in adult literature, nor has it displayed an aesthetic philosophy since Carroll and Lear in the Victorian era.

J. K. Rowling, followed by many of her contemporaries such as Catherynne Valente, Lemony Snicket, and Trenton Lee Stewart, has challenged that assumption, repurposing nonsense as a device in contemporary children's literature, capitalizing on literary nonsense's heritage in a new way and revealing its sophistication and complexity. While Rowling's *Harry Potter* series is assuredly not a purely nonsense text, it does often privilege language in the same way. Rowling retains many of the so-called "childish" characteristics of Carrollian and Learian nonsense—its playful puzzles, codes, and improbabilities, its allusions to fantastic creatures, and its child-oriented vision—but her nonsense also incorporates the tension between meaning and its absence. Additionally, Rowling reworks the nonsense mode in children's literature by employing nonsense language not only to create an effective and aesthetically pleasing reality similar to Carroll's Wonderland, but also to examine the tension that exists between the interior self and external action. In this way, by employing a sophisticated aesthetic philosophy that recalls their legacy, Rowling's nonsense displays a simultaneous commitment to nonsense's most acclaimed literary antecedents and to nonsense's often playful place in more recent children's and adult literature.

Like Carroll and Lear before her, Rowling employs the nonsense mode to resist the grip of convention, but also to express a particular sense of playful and delightfully unpredictable reality within her novels.[1] From the first pages, the reader is plunged into a universe in which objects like a "deluminator,"[2] transportation systems like the Floo Network and Knight Bus, and rumor-mongers like an Animagus beetle[3] exist alongside the "normal" world's ordinary torches/flashlights, London Underground and night buses, and electronic bugging. Rowling cross breeds signifiers and purposefully pluralizes denotations to create a reality that is at once familiar, yet wholly unique. Indeed, the wizarding world is overrun with anagrams, puns, portmanteau words, symbolic names, and incongruities, many of which indicate the simultaneous realism and fantasy that these novels inherited from Carrollian and Learian nonsense. When we come across these whimsical magical alternatives in Rowling's text, we recall Alice's encounters with flamingo croquet sticks and run-ins with playing cards employed as guardsmen. For example, in *Deathly Hallows*, newly planted flutterby bushes dot the garden of the Burrow (the Weasley home). Not only are the flutterby bushes an anagram and play on butterfly bushes (they resemble butterflies perched on shrubbery), but the name "The Burrow," is itself also a pun: the ramshackle house has been magically modified so that the structure can bear the load of the numerous additions required to house all of the Weasley family, resulting in a home that resembles the above-ground brick-and-mortar equivalent of a weasel's burrow.

Like Carroll's "Jabberwocky" poem and *The Hunting of the Snark*, whose plots and creatures derive inspiration from knightly heroic quests and mythological or legendary creatures, Rowling's nonsense objects, characters, and creatures also at times recall fairy tales, myths, and legends that continue to permeate contemporary texts for children. In this way, Rowling circles back to the earliest texts that belong to the tradition of common readership and reworks them to create something new. For example, the Mirror of Erised, upon whose frame is inscribed "Erised stra ehru oyt ube cafru oyt on wohsi," is one of the first dangerous magical objects with which Harry comes into contact (SS 152). Though initially this inscription resembles the nonsense language Carroll created in "Jabberwocky," when reflected in a mirror with the separations rearranged, Rowling's nonsense words spell out "I show not your face but your heart's desire." Here, then, Rowling displays the tension between meaning and meaninglessness that mirrors Harry's confusion as to what is dream and what is reality. Harry, who during his nightly vigils sees his deceased parents and extended family reflected back at him, becomes listless and apathetic during the day, consumed by his longing for the people he sees in the mirror, but whom he can never truly join. Rowling's Erised anagram thus recalls not only the mirror in *Snow White* that reveals her stepmother's obsessive desire for beauty, which, in turn, inspired her murderous hatred, but also the sad fate of the mythological character Narcissus, whose all-consuming desire for what he saw reflected in still water caused his death. Dumbledore further suggests this connection, warning Harry of his unhealthy attraction to the mirror: "It does not do to dwell on dreams and forget to live, remember that" (*SS* 152).

Additionally, Rowling plays with impossibilities by making the mirror a vehicle through which to bestow another magical object, the Philosopher's Stone, or, in the US editions, the Sorcerer's Stone. Again, Rowling fuses the legendary with the fantastic because in the "real" past, the creation of the Philosopher's Stone was the most sought-after goal in Western alchemy. The stone itself is yet another nonsense object because its existence is based upon an impossibility, namely, the science of alchemy. Here, Rowling incorporates the real history of the stone into her fictional reality, taking something impossible and making it possible. The maker of the stone is identified as Nicolas Flamel, who, in Rowling's universe, is a highly skilled wizard, but who, in reality, was a successful French scribe and manuscript seller as well as a rumored alchemist during the late fourteenth and early fifteenth centuries. In this way, the two worlds collide in Flamel's and his identity becomes a possible impossibility.[4]

In the chapter "The Man with Two Faces," both the mirror and Harry's knowledge of how it works become crucial to the plot. Incidentally, Rowling again plays with multiple meanings as "The Man with Two Faces" can allude to Professor Quirrell, whose body is being inhabited by Lord Voldemort and thus has another face behind his own; it can also allude to Quirrell's two-facedness because he pretends to be one thing but is really another; or it can mean a reflection, the second face seen in a mirror. When Voldemort commands Quirrell, who is unaware of how the mirror operates, to use Harry as a means of taking the stone, Harry looks into the mirror and lies about what he sees: "'I see myself shaking hands with Dumbledore,' he invented. 'I—I've won the House Cup for Gryffindor'" (*SS* 212). In reality, Harry sees

his reflection, pale and scared-looking at first. But a moment later, the
reflection smiled at him. It put its hand into its pocket and pulled out a
blood-red stone. It winked and put the Stone back into its pocket—and as
it did so, Harry felt something heavy drop into his real pocket. Somehow—
incredibly—*he'd got the Stone.* (SS 212)

Here, the tension between reality and unreality is momentarily suspended
as Harry and his mirror-self collide, bringing an object from nonbeing into
being. Not only do we remember the magical appearance of the cake, bottle,
and key in *Alice in Wonderland*, but this moment summons similar images
in previous fairy-tale texts like *Rumpelstiltskin, Cinderella,* and *The Emperor's
New Clothes,* where characters conjure something out of nothing. Additionally, throughout the series, we learn that Rowling sometimes employs the
nonsense mode to connect episodes from the earlier *Harry Potter* novels
with situations that occur later in the series. As a result, the "rules" of magic
become apparent to the reader. For example, in another nonsensical moment
in *Deathly Hallows,* Professor McGonagall answers a question posed by the
Ravenclaw doorknocker:

> There was a genteel tap of the knocker and the musical voice asked, again,
> "Where do vanished objects go?"
> "Into non-being, which is to say, everything," replied Professor McGonagall.
> "Nicely phrased," [5] replied the eagle doorknocker and the door swung open.
> (476)

In this scene, the reader is reminded of the earlier moment when a magical object (the mirror) interacted with a character (Harry) and produced
a moment of tension between meaning and its absence. Because we first
witnessed the way the stone appeared in Harry's pocket out of nowhere, and
because we also know Dumbledore enchanted the mirror, we realize that
Dumbledore must have vanished the stone into nonbeing, meaning that it
was in everything, thus making it possible for the mirror to act as a vehicle
for its reappearance. As a result, this moment with Professor McGonagall,
which again operates in the nonsense mode, reveals the deeply layered fictional reality that Rowling has created through words.

Character names in *Harry Potter* also reveal nonsense's legacy in contemporary fiction for children; by choosing symbolic names for her characters,

Rowling creates codes that the reader must decipher in order to discover the selfhood or identity of each character, a practice that challenges the reader's knowledge of literary history and etymology and helps the reader to become an active participant in the creation of meaning. Rowling's name symbolism is both expansive and comprehensive. Indeed, almost every magical character name incorporates some clue to his or her selfhood.[6] A notable example is Lucius Malfoy, whose first name suggests Lucifer, and whose surname is a portmanteau word from the French *mal* (bad) and *foi* (faith). As Lucius Malfoy is one of Voldemort's inner circle, his name's alliance with evil comes as no surprise. However, additionally, with Lucius's allegorical surname, Rowling, like Spenser before her, gives us a clue as to Lucius's character and fate: Malfoy almost always acts in "bad faith," abusing his servants, manipulating government officials in order to pursue his own ends, persecuting Muggle-borns, and even at times bullying his own family. But his name also suggests that Lucius puts his faith in the wrong people. Lucius falls from Voldemort's favor when he fails both to collect the prophesy at the Ministry of Magic and to capture Harry Potter. He is consequently severely punished by Voldemort, who gives Lucius's son, Draco, what is essentially a suicide mission as revenge for his father's failure.[7]

Finally, the most Wonderlandish and Learian example of nonsense can perhaps be found by examining the magical creatures who inhabit the wizarding world. Like Alice, who encounters Cheshire cats, dodo birds, mock turtles, and March hares through her increasingly nonsensical journey, Harry comes across numerous magical fauna during his seven-year epic. Familiar mythological creatures like centaurs, sphinx, basilisks, unicorns, merpeople, dragons, and chimaeras exist in Rowling's universe, but the true word play occurs with the creatures of her own invention. For example, the Acromantula is a species of giant spider created by wizards before the 1965 Ban on Experimental Breeding. The etymology of this fictional creature's name comes from the Greek *acros*, meaning "peak" or "high point" and suggests "arachnid" and "tarantula." Another original creature is a beast identified as an Erumpent. Erumpents are native to Africa and resemble the rhinoceros in their size, coloring, thick hides, and sharp horns. "Erumpent" suggests elephant, trumpet, and, indeed, "erumpet"—to grow or burst through a surface. Humorously, Rowling's erumpent horns contain a deadly fluid that causes whatever is injected with it to explode.

Adding yet another layer of complexity, Rowling indicates that it is possible for wizards to believe in legendary or imaginary creatures within their own magical universe. Xenophilius Lovegood lamentably mistakes an erumpent horn for that of a Crumple-Horned Snorkack, a legendary creature who is most definitely an homage to Carroll's Snark. Xenophilius and his daughter Luna spend their holidays "hunting" the Snorkack, who like the Snark is very difficult to find and capture. The other characters and the reader know the reason for this difficulty because, despite the earnest belief of the Lovegoods, the Snorkack exists neither in the real world nor the wizarding world. This similarity to our own world's diverse mythological creatures that pepper our literary history and the belief/disbelief in their existence displayed by different factions of people at various points in time is further explored in the *Fantastic Beasts* films, where convincing the wizarding community of the possibility of impossible creatures like the parasitic Obscurus becomes crucial to the plot.

Rowling is thus indebted to the legacy of nonsense literature in the creation of her fantastically inventive fictional reality, but at the same time, she manipulates the nonsense mode in a new way to promote a more complex understanding of her magical universe that we do not have of Wonderland. Rowling famously created a spell language for her wizarding world, allying herself with yet another tradition of literary nonsense, the invention of language, which dates as far back as even the fifteenth century. Noel Malcolm calls attention to a tradition from that historical period called "macaronics" (commonly called "dog-Latin" or "kitchen-Latin") in which a Latin surface layer is added to a vernacular substratum to produce a comic effect (103–4). The basic strategy of macaronics is to exploit our assumption that the more Latinate and formal-looking a word is, the more rationally abstract its meaning. Rowling's spell language employs Latin in a similar way, constructing neologisms that take advantage of our assumptions about its complexity based on its Latinate appearance, but, for the most part, she does not aim for the same comic effect. Instead, Rowling's spell language is privileged above the vernacular, much in the same way that modernist nonsense poetry and prose reveal serious concern beneath the nonsense motifs, as in the works of Franz Kafka and Samuel Beckett. For these writers, Tigges tells us that the nonsense language has an undeniable point (218–19).

The underlying meaning of spell language is illuminated both by the breakdown of the neologism and by the manifestation of the spell-word's intention in reality. In this way, it creates a new kind of nonsense device, serving not only to delight but also to instruct, and through which we come to a greater understanding of characters in *Harry Potter*. In particular, spell language, which I will refer to as "spellwork," operates as a means to examine their education and moral development. Rowling employs spellwork to demonstrate the relationship between the interior self and external action. In many cases of fantasy fiction, spells are merely an interesting by-product of a magical world and exist only to differentiate those learned in the magical arts from ordinary mortals. However, in her series, Rowling uses the discipline of spellwork as a key indicator of Harry's growth throughout his seven years in the magical community, both in his education and in his humanity. As Harry learns how to channel his magic through spells, we see him begin to transform himself from the passive "Boy Who Lived" and "Chosen One" to the active defender of his community.

First, it is important to understand how spellwork operates in the series as a language that must be studied and mastered. Rowling shows us throughout the series that possession of a weapon and an intention are not enough for Harry to defeat the forces of evil. It is the spell, articulated verbally or nonverbally, but performed with accuracy and deliberation, that seals the deal. From the first book, Rowling intimates that spellwork is a tricky business when the students start their lessons, although initially mistakes of spellwork were mostly amusing. In *Chamber of Secrets*, for example, we witness the fiasco that occurred as a result of Gilderoy Lockhart's ludicrous psychobabble. Here, nonsense language is just that: nonsense. When Lockhart mispronounces and inaccurately performs the spell to subdue a horde of Cornish pixies, his mistake is supposed to be humorous, but it also indicates to the reader that manipulating this specialized language and achieving the creative potential of words takes work, understanding, and practice. As we progress deeper into the series, Rowling intimates that incorrect spellwork—whether it is by mispronunciation, misuse, or misdirection—is not always comical. For example, in his sixth year, when Harry uses a spell (*Sectumsempra*) that he found scribbled in his Potions textbook against his bully and almost fatally wounds Draco, Harry feels the power of magical language with full force. He learns in this scene that words can be dangerous, even lethal, and that spells can betray you if you neglect to divine their deeper meaning through careful study.

Thus, as he continues his magical education, Harry learns that spellwork is not just stringing words together, but that it includes both semantics *and* semiotics. As Bellatrix Lestrange tells Harry, to successfully cast spells, one has to mean them. J. L. Austin's *How to Do Things with Words* is helpful in understanding Rowling's purpose in creating this magical language. Austin asserts that "words do not have meaning in and of themselves; they are affected by the situation, the speaker, and the listener" (6–7). He also tells us that speech is not passive; it can actively change the reality it is describing. Austin claims that "the issuing of the utterance is the performing of an action—it is not normally thought of as *just saying something*" (6–7). By this, he means that our words reflect our inner conditions or modes of being. What is interesting for Rowling's purposes about this power of words is that their abstract creative potential lends itself wonderfully to magic because as we read *Harry Potter*, we witness how performative utterances directly translate themselves into actions in the story. When Harry performs a spell, it is not merely an utterance, but also an act of meaning-making.

As the creator of a magical world, Rowling differentiates her spell language to make it seem like it possesses a direct power not associated with ordinary, day-to-day language. This language, like nonsense, creates reality and, in so doing, reveals the tension that exists between meaning and its absence. Thus, ordinary language, even if it is manipulated into verse or a string of alliterative imperatives, will not do.[8] Rowling, therefore, uses Latin as the base for her spells because Latin is archaic, and, as there are no longer any native speakers of Latin, it is estranged from our common parlance. Yet because it is so often at the core of our modern vernacular, it is still comprehensible to us. As a result, similar to Lewis Carroll's nonsense poems like "Jabberwocky," what at first seems like nonsense is actually, upon closer analysis, somewhat understandable. But Carrollian nonsense lacks a coherence that allows for its words to be understood in isolation. While "'Twas brillig, and the slithy toves / Did gyre and gimble in the wabe: / All mimsy were the borogroves, / And the mome raths outgrabe" can be deciphered when the reader or listener hears the words in succession, when they are isolated, "brillig," "slithy," "mome," and "outgrabe" may hint at a definition due to their phonetics, but they are not part of an established lexicon (187). Rather, these are nonce words, lexemes created for a particular occasion to solve a problem of communication. Indeed, Carroll not only creates nonce words, but he demonstrates how and why they are employed with the dialogue that occurs between Alice and Humpty Dumpty:

> "That's enough to being with," Humpty Dumpty interrupted: "there are plenty of hard words there. '*Brillig*' means four o'clock in the afternoon—the time when you begin *broiling* things for dinner."
>
> "That'll do very well," said Alice: "and '*slithy*'?"

"Well '*slithy*' means 'lithe and slimy.' 'Lithe' is the same as 'active.' You see it's like a portmanteau—there are two meanings packed up into one word." (187)

Here, by giving his definition of each "hard word" in the poem, Humpty Dumpty inadvertently demonstrates that nonce words are essentially meaningless and disposable. For example, when he claims "slithy" is like a portmanteau word, which combines the words "lithe" and "slimy" and their morphemes and meanings into a new word, he reveals that it is merely an invented linguistic form, as "slithy" was not part of the Victorian English lexicon and had no meaning outside the text. The word "slithy" in isolation and without Humpty Dumpty's definition may thus *hint* at meaning, but the word itself does not have meaning in our language.

By contrast, having Latin (and, on occasion, other real/operative languages) at its root, Rowling's spell language achieves a complexity that surpasses previous nonsense language. Like Carroll's nonce words, and, indeed, like her own "Muggle," "Squib," and "kneazle," Rowling's spells are indeed neologisms, but Rowling's formulation of this particular kind of neolexia is meticulously prescribed to instill each word with a creative authority that has the power to actually change the reality of her fictional world. For example, let us examine the spell *Expelliarmus*. This spell magically disarms another wizard by expelling the wand, the deadliest weapon in the wizarding world, out of the opponent's hand. In Latin, *expello* refers to the act of driving out or thrusting away; *arma* means weapons; and the ending, -*mus*, while not an ending for nouns, *is* an ending used for verbs in first person, plural, active forms. So, if we put them all together, we realize Rowling has cleverly fashioned a new verb for her spell. The *mus* gives us the "we," the *expel* gives us the "drive or thrust away" and the *arm* gives us the "weapons." So "*Expelliarmus!*" becomes "We thrust or drive away the weapons!"

But what makes Rowling's language of enchantment even more meaningful, what elevates it still further above previous nonsense languages in children's literature, is how the employment of certain spells is related to her characters' actions and decisions. For example, for her deadliest villain, Rowling creates a deadly spell. *Avada Kedavra*, the killing curse, is one of only three curses in the wizarding that are labeled Unforgiveable, and it is Lord Voldemort's signature spell.[9] Interestingly, *Avada Kedavra* is one of the only incantations without a Latin derivation. Instead, it seems to come from a play on "*Abracadabra*," but further probing leads us to "*ebra kidbara*," an ancient Hebrew-Aramaic expression for, "I will create with words," "I create like the word," or "I create as I speak" (Conley 66). By contrast, it is perhaps ironic that Rowling's *Avada Kedavra* is the ultimate spell of destruction. However, if we look closer at the words, we see that Rowling has changed the "b's" to "v's" making *cadabra* sound more like *cadaver*, linking the word to death. So instead of "I will create with words" it means, in this series, "I will destroy with words." During an audience interview at the Edinburgh Book Festival, Rowling confirmed the spell's Aramaic origins and translated it as "let the thing be destroyed."

This historical connection of spell and object is repeated in Rowling's series. In *Half-Blood Prince*, we learn that Voldemort used the killing curse for the first time when he was a teenager, killing Moaning Myrtle. In so doing, he used the spell to create his first Horcrux, an object in which a Dark witch or wizard encases a fragment of his soul in order to achieve immortality. Therefore, not only does Voldemort destroy with the words of this spell, but he also creates destructive objects with them. As a result, *Avada Kedavra* becomes the defining incantation of Voldemort's life, not only because he often employs it, but because his life and identity become so irrevocably intertwined with its meaning. As Voldemort continues to employ the killing curse, fragmenting his soul for each "significant"[10] death, we witness the simultaneous dissolution of his humanity. Voldemort not only becomes physically disfigured, but he also becomes emotionally less human.[11] Fittingly, in his last battle with Harry, Rowling again indicates that Voldemort's identity and destiny are closely related to this spell, as, this time, with no Horcruxes remaining to him, Voldemort is killed by his own rebounding *Avada Kedavra* curse.

Another example of this connection between spell word and inner life in Rowling's series occurs with the spell *Sectumsempra*. The result of this spell is to wound the opponent with deep cuts into the body that cannot be healed with ordinary magic. The first part of the spell comes from the Latin *sectum*, which means "having been cut" (comparable to "section" or "segmented"), while *sempra* is derived from *semper*, which means "always." Thus, the spell can be translated as "always cutting" or "sever forever," which also points toward the spell's creator, Severus Snape. Snape created this spell when he was a student and, judging from the book, *Advanced Potion Making for N.E.W.T.*-level students, during his sixth at Hogwarts School.[12] This timing is significant, because it means that the year Snape created the spell was when he was planning on joining Voldemort's Death Eaters and, most significantly, it was also the year after which he irrevocably severed his relationship with

Lily Potter. In a scene Harry witnesses in the Pensieve, Snape fights with James Potter after his O.W.L. exams, and, when Lily Potter (Lily Evans at this time) comes to his aid, in his embarrassment and fury, Snape calls her "Mudblood," the most offensive term for someone who is Muggle-born. Up until this point in Snape's life, his love for Lily had always conquered his prejudice against Muggle-born wizards. Here, however, the other influences in Snape's life momentarily override his love for Lily, and his underlying prejudice against her blood status becomes his instinctive retaliation. Though Snape pleads for her forgiveness, Lily remains immovable, not believing him when he says it was an accident.

In this scene, as we witness how one word destroys a relationship, we also come to understand the intimate connection between Snape and his spell, *Sectumsempra*. Because he was unable to deny Lily's claims about his intentions regarding the Dark Lord and his followers, and because he could not bring himself to tell Lily that he loved her, he became "severed forever" from the person he treasured most in the world, the one he would love, as he famously told Dumbledore, "always." In the year that followed, Snape also adopted the moniker "The Half-Blood Prince," further allying himself to Voldemort because, like his master, he wished to reject his own name in order to cut ties with his Muggle lineage. In this way, his new name tethered him even more closely to the deeper meaning of his spell. By changing his name from Severus Snape, the boy who was once Lily's friend and companion and who once had the conscience and autonomy to struggle with moral evaluation, to the Half-Blood Prince, the servant of Voldemort, prince to his king, whose own beliefs and will were subservient to those of the Dark Lord, Snape lost the moral agency that he once had as the boy Severus. It is only later, when he realizes the information he passed to Voldemort would cause Lily's death, that Snape rejects his self-generated sobriquet, his pride, and his prejudice and regains his moral agency. Snape's ultimate decision to turn spy for Dumbledore therefore reestablishes his previous identity, which was centered around his love for Lily. From this point onward, we learn that all of Snape's actions have been to atone for his accidental but fatal betrayal of her, which began with his calling her Mudblood and severing their friendship. Therefore, when Dumbledore questions Snape's loyalty, Snape demonstrates through his doe Patronus that his allegiance has never wavered since he took his oath after Lily's death, because his entire selfhood depends upon this desire to reestablish his relationship to her.

It follows, then, that spells are the translation of a wizard's very core. Spell-work is the way one takes the power, desires, and meanings within oneself and transmits them outward. As Plutarch once wrote, and as J. K. Rowling repeated in her commencement address to Harvard University: "What we achieve inwardly will change outer reality." In *Harry Potter*, spellwork demonstrates the process of Harry's education as the hero of Rowling's series. As the novels progress, Harry's growth as a moral agent is reflected in his acquisition of spell language, specifically his mastery of certain spells and his choice as to which spells he employs. Two incantations in particular come to be directly associated with him: *Expecto Patronum* and *Expelliarmus*.

Obeying Rowling's rules for spell language, *Expecto* (or *exspecto*) is appropriated from the Latin verb meaning "to await" or "to expect." Yet the word's roots reveal a profounder meaning: *Ex* is a preposition meaning "out from," and the noun *pectus* refers to the "chest," "breast," "heart," or "soul." Thus, *Expecto* intimates the literal, physical center and figurative, emotional core of a person. *Patronum* is appropriately declined as the direct object of a verb— the spell caster expects (v.) a Patronus (d.o.)—and the word itself comes from the Latin *pater* or "father." In Ancient Roman society, a *patronus* was a protector and benefactor, especially in terms of providing legal representation, loaning money, influencing marriages, or supporting a candidacy for political office. In return, the client was expected to perform various services for their patron whenever necessary. Consequently, when they utter the phrase *Expecto Patronum*, Rowling's characters (here the casters of spells are in the position of the clients), generate their own, unique Patronuses or protectors with their words. Thus, when Harry performs the *Expecto Patronum* spell, he invokes a silvery, not-quite-opaque, stag guardian who bursts from the core of his wand in order to protect him from dementors.[13] What is more, to successfully cast a Patronus, the wizard must think of a moment in which he or she was truly happy, and often the Patronus reflects that memory in some way, further tethering the words and the wizard together.[14]

Harry's Patronus and his ability to cast it become crucial to his survival and also to his identity. In *Prisoner of Azkaban*, Harry learns for the first time some of the details surrounding his parents' death at the hands of Voldemort and, at the climax of the novel, when he finally realizes that their true traitor was Peter Pettigrew, he also gains a guardian and paternal figure in Sirius Black. At the end of *Prisoner of Azkaban*, when he and Sirius Black are under a near-fatal attack from the Dementors, it is of course *Expecto Patronum* that comes to Harry's aid. Harry, who returns from the future to help prevent Sirius's capture, realizes that the caster of the Patronus that saved their lives in the past was not his father returned to life or in ghostly form, but himself, Harry-in-the-future. Thus, in conjuring his Patronus, Harry recovers his legal guardian and remembers his parental guardian, but he also discovers a guardian within himself. In the books that follow, Harry becomes known throughout the wizarding community for his ability to conjure a corporeal Patronus, illegally employing *Expecto Patronum* in the Muggle world to save his cousin Dudley and defying Dolores Umbridge to teach the Patronus charm to the members of Dumbledore's Army. Harry's essence as a defender and a leader is therefore linked to this spell.

As he learns how to master one spell after another during the seven years of his education, Harry also learns how to decipher which spells feel the truest for him. These spells are not unforgivable, offensive spells like the *Cruciatus* or *Avada Kedavra* curse, but defensive spells, like *Expecto Patronum*, the stunning spell *Stupefy*, and, of course, *Expelliarmus*, the disarming spell. In this way, Rowling shows us that Harry is a morally courageous character who uses defensive spells to distinguish himself from his destructive enemy and to show that, at his core, he is the defender and savior of his community. It is notoriously the *Expelliarmus* spell in particular that Harry relies upon, even in both instances when he faces his mortal enemy at a disadvantage.[15] Harry identifies with this spell because it is the closest translation of his inner self and his role in the wizarding world. In the misty "King's Cross Station" chapter of *Deathly Hallows*, Dumbledore asserts that Harry is the ultimate defender of love, loyalty, and innocence, things of which Voldemort is completely ignorant. He also reveals that Harry's choice to sacrifice himself as a last resort to defend his community rather than to fight Voldemort in the forest has made all the difference. Throughout Harry's story, as others died to defend him, Harry, in turn, picked up their mantles and felt responsible for defending their beliefs and continuing their common mission. And with this assumption of responsibility also came a kind of instinct in his spellwork, as if at the most crucial moments of his life, his very essence as this defender manifests itself in his incantations; casting spells is the way he communicates the unique magic within himself to the outside world. Harry is almost like an athlete in the way the lessons that he has learned throughout his magical education have seeped into his core and mingled with his own nature; as a result, his choice of defensive spell over offensive spell is like a reflex.

This is why when Harry could seriously injure or kill Stan Shunpike in the beginning of *The Deathly Hallows*, he reacts by disarming him instead of cursing him as he did Draco Malfoy in *The Half-Blood Prince*. His previous (mis)use of offensive language taught him restraint; the kind of wizard and person he wants to be does not intentionally harm anyone. This code of honor manifests itself outwardly in what Lupin calls Harry's "signature spell," *Expelliarmus*, which he employs even in his last battle against Voldemort. In the final scene, when Harry yells "*Expelliarmus*" as Voldemort cries his own signature spell, the text tells us that Harry is casting his "best hope" to the heavens. He is driving away the fiercest weapon, "*Avada Kedavra*," or destruction through words.

Finally, I would argue that what Harry discovers is his "best hope" is this deep respect for language that, in this series, is tied so closely and so irrevocably to life. Harry's signature spell is intimately bound to his essence as a defender and to his cultivated respect for every human (and nonhuman) life. Therefore, as we witness Harry's wizarding education, we also watch him make moral choices about what to do with his power. Which is why, in the final battle, he refuses to kill Lord Voldemort outright. Instead, he allows Voldemort be the destroyer and to use destructive language against himself. In this way, Rowling revolutionizes the nonsense mode in literature by employing nonsense language not only to create an effective and aesthetically pleasing reality, but also as a device for a moral education of the self. She therefore capitalizes on literary nonsense's double heritage in a new way, revealing its sophistication with her technical skill and elevating her novels above previous works of children's fiction by showing us the profound power of the simple expression of complex thought. Ultimately, we could make the argument that this whole series is about how to do things with words or how to actively transform our reality through our careful use of language.

This chapter is adapted, with permission of the author, from her previously published work, *Children's Literature Grows Up: Harry Potter and the Children's Literature Revolution*, 2017.

Notes

1. This unpredictability is especially the case in the first three novels, when Harry is plunged into the wizarding world and must acclimatize himself to what might as well be an alternate universe. As he becomes accustomed to life as a wizard, he becomes less and less surprised by its unique idiosyncrasies. This differs from Alice's journey through Wonderland because though she navigates her way through the alternate world, she never becomes accustomed to it (though, of course, Alice's journey occurred in one afternoon, while Harry's spans more than seven years).

2. A unique magical object, of Dumbledore's invention, which is capable of absorbing any and all light from the user's surroundings as well as bestowing it. Additionally, it acts as a sort of homing device, leading the possessor via a light through his/her heart to his/her most treasured people. "Where your treasure is, there will your heart be also" is the epitaph Dumbledore selected for the graves of his mother and sister, which perhaps inspired the idea behind this object.

3. Rita Skeeter is both a rumormonger reporter and an unreported beetle Animagus.

4. Ironically, as in Rowling's book, Flamel actually did marry a woman named Perenelle in 1368, whose name, of course, suggests "perennial."

5. Additionally, the doorknocker's response "nicely phrased" demonstrates the privileging of language that occurs when operating in the nonsense mode (McGonagall is successful in opening the magical door because she correctly employed the right words).

6. If a character's name doesn't reveal anything about his or her identity, often Rowling will mention something about the witch or wizard that recalls another character in literature, thereby giving the reader a hint at his or her personality. For example, Mafalda Hopkirk's Polyjuice Potion turns a "pleasant heliotrope colour" (*DH* 195) and Hermione-as-Mafalda shakes a bag of pastilles at Mr. Cattermole. The color of the potion (which, after all, helps transform the taker into the person whose hair is added to it) and the episode with the sweets reminds the reader of old-fashioned and pragmatic Miss Heliotrope with her peppermints in Elizabeth Goudge's *The Little White Horse*, one of Rowling's favorite childhood novels.

7. In turn, Draco Malfoy, whose first name is derived from the Latin *draco* (dragon), and which also refers to the constellation, does indeed believe he is the star of his family when Voldemort selects him to kill Albus Dumbledore. He, too, consistently acts in bad faith and puts his faith in the wrong people, from his attempt to get Harry expelled by standing him up for a duel in *Philosopher's Stone* to his actions in the Room of Requirement in *Deathly Hallows*.

8. Rowling demonstrates to us that ordinary language cannot operate in the same way as her spell language when Ron attempts a fake spell given to him by his brother (a known prankster): Sunshine, daisies, butter mellow, turn this great big fat rat yellow! Not only does the spell not work because Scabbers is not truly a rat, but also because Ron attempts magic with ordinary vernacular.

9. The three Unforgiveable Curses are *Avada Kedavra* (the killing curse), the *Cruciatus* Curse or *Crucio* (the torture curse), and the *Imperius* Curse or *Imperio* (the curse by which the castor assumes complete control over the victim).

10. We know from Dumbledore that Voldemort originally intended to reserve his Horcrux creation for particularly significant deaths. For example, the Horcrux diary was made to mark the first time he killed; the Horcrux ring was made when he murdered

his father and grandparents, thus eradicating his connection with his Muggle lineage; he intended to make a Horcrux after he killed Harry because Harry was prophesied to be the one threat to his power.

11. We witness in the Pensieve as, from memory to memory, his once-handsome face becomes first "hollow-cheeked," then blurred and burned, looking and pale as wax, and then snake-like with slits for nostrils and red eyes.

12. *Advanced Potion Making* by Libatius Borage is a potions spellbook used for N.E.W.T. students, which are students in their sixth year at Hogwarts.

13. Harry has the same Patronus as his father, the male counterpart to Lily's doe.

14. For example, Severus Snape's Patronus is a doe, the representation of Lily Potter, which indicates that his happiest memories were those he spent with her. Likewise, Nymphadora Tonks's Patronus changes in book 6 into a form that resembles the werewolf, revealing her love for Remus Lupin.

15. Harry faces Voldemort in the graveyard of Little Hangleton in *The Goblet of Fire* and again in the Forbidden Forest in *The Deathly Hallows*.

Works Cited

Austin, J. L. *How to Do Things with Words*. Cambridge: Harvard University Press, 1975.
Carroll, Lewis. *Through the Looking-Glass*. New York: Penguin, 1998.
Conley, Craig. *Magical Words: A Dictionary*. 3rd ed. San Francisco: Weiser Books, 2008.
Malcolm, Noel. *The Origins of English Nonsense*. London: Fontana Press, 1998.

4

MAGICAL MEDICINE
Healers, Healing Spells, and Medical Humanities

Jennifer M. Reeher

Much of the magical medicine in the *Harry Potter* series reflects aspects of Western medicine throughout our history. Whether considering the healing power of bezoars and mandrakes, both used in European medicine in the medieval and early modern periods, or the similarities between dementors, which "suck the happiness out of a place," and human experiences with depression, the parallels cover a wide range of medical beliefs and practices (*PA* 97). Generally, the medicine of the *Harry Potter* universe mirrors current medical practices in ways that allow us to reflect on those practices and on the wider impact of medical humanities—including the ethical use of medical rhetoric and the appreciation for patients' lived experiences—through an examination of this fictional series.

However, the wizard medicine of Harry Potter's world also challenges the power of contemporary Western medicine by favoring "old-wives'-tale" treatments—including chocolate to comfort and heal—while marking Muggle medical technologies, such as stitches, as barbaric. In this chapter, I am particularly interested in the dissonances and the harmonies Rowling creates between magical and Muggle sociomedical practices. Specifically, I am concerned with three primary ways that language is tied to medicine in the series: (1) through the power of Healing Spells to physically mend the body and mind, as Christina Phillips-Mattson notes in the previous chapter; (2) through the power of curses or misused Healing Spells to physically harm the body and mind; and, finally, (3) through the power of medical rhetorics of health and disease to affect reality, thus uncovering parallels that allow readers to recognize the dangers of medicine misused for prejudiced and hateful purposes.[1]

As Phillips-Mattson notes, all spells, regardless of their specialty, require a certain mastery of a particular set of signifiers; through Healing Spells specifically, we can also begin to question the complications that arise whenever language has the power to affect some of the most intimate parts of our reality—our bodies and our health. This particular linguistic examination follows in the tradition of linguists such as George W. Grace, among many others, who argue that language doesn't merely *map* reality but that it actually has the power to *construct* reality.[2] Considered in the context of spells in the *Harry Potter* universe, this linguistic argument takes on a new form, allowing readers to see immediate, tangible changes that language—and, more specifically, spells—has the power to create in the physical world.

While witches and wizards do not rely exclusively on spells to treat illnesses, wounds, and other medical concerns, this linguistic power manifests itself significantly in the world of medicine within the *Harry Potter* universe. In the cases where spells and charms are applicable to magical medicine, knowing and using the correct sign in the correct way has the power to literally and physically heal the body and the mind; while there are some near-equivalents in Muggle medicine (such as narrative medicine and some psychotherapy techniques), this healing process is shown more explicitly in the *Harry Potter* universe, where language and magic replace the technology of the Muggle world.

Healing Spells in the Hands of Nonexperts

However, not all witches and wizards are comfortable, skilled, or knowledgeable with Healing Spells; this is one of the places where questions of privilege and experience—at least linguistically speaking—come into play in the *Harry Potter* canon. For example, when Tonks heals Harry's broken nose in *Harry Potter and the Half-Blood Prince*, Harry is initially nervous. When the often-clumsy Tonks offers to help, Harry "did not think much of this idea; he had been intending to visit Madam Pomfrey, the matron, in whom he had a little more confidence when it came to Healing Spells," but he ultimately does let Tonks heal his nose using the *Episkey* spell (157). While Tonks is able to successfully mend his nose using this spell, Harry is keenly aware that not all people are equally positioned in terms of their power to use Healing Spells effectively.

We also see a similar concern when Lupin bandages Ron's leg in *Harry Potter and the Prisoner of Azkaban*, except in this example the concern comes from the executer of the spell. Lupin says, "I can't mend bones nearly as well as Madam Pomfrey, so I think it's best if we just strap your leg up until we can get you to the hospital wing" (376). Lupin recognizes his own limitations and feels that someone more skilled with this particular type of magic, in this case, Madam Pomfrey, is likely to have better results. Rather than mending Ron's broken leg, then, Lupin uses the *Ferula* spell, which causes bandages to spin around Ron's leg and splint it (376–77). Lupin chooses to apply a temporary fix rather than attempting a more permanent spell.

In each case, with Tonks and Lupin, acting in ignorance could cause further danger. When Tonks heals Harry's nose, Harry is aware of the dangers of her potential ignorance; when Lupin cares for Ron, Lupin is aware of his own ignorance and the further pain and damage he could cause for Ron if he misused a more permanent spell. However, not all witches and wizards are so quick to recognize and respect their limitations. We see this perhaps most memorably in the character of Gilderoy Lockhart.

When Harry breaks his arm during the Quidditch match in *Harry Potter and the Chamber of Secrets*, Lockhart insists that he can mend Harry's arm right there on the Quidditch pitch. Lockhart proceeds even though Harry is reluctant to have Lockhart perform this spell, and he ultimately ends up removing the bones from Harry's arm rather than mending them (173). In this instance, ignorance and inexperience lead to a misuse of the spell, and it does not have the intended effect; instead, as Lupin feared when Ron broke his leg, ignorance leads to further danger and pain for the patient. As Madam Pomfrey notes when Harry is finally taken to the hospital wing, "I can mend bones in a second—but growing them back—[. . .] it will be painful" (174). Lockhart, however, attempts to dismiss the additional danger and pain he causes by noting, "But the point is, the bones are no longer broken," as if to suggest that, though this was not the exact *method* in which he intended to address the problem, the problem had, in fact, been addressed (173).[3]

Healers—Becoming the Expert

Each of the preceding examples allows the reader to see the concrete power of spells—and, therefore, language—in the wizarding world. Language has great power, but, again, only for those who know how to use it. In that regard, we can also see how healing can go right, especially when concerns about knowledge and experience are taken into consideration, as well as the ways that healing can go incredibly wrong when such concerns are ignored or overlooked.

The confidence that many characters place in a person to perform Healing Spells is based largely on experience, especially *successful* experience. For that reason, witches and wizards who have made their careers in magical medicine, such as Madam Pomfrey and the employees at St. Mungo's Hospital for Magical Maladies and Injuries, are often the preferred administrators of Healing Spells. These specially trained witches and wizards are known as Healers. While Harry sees an immediate connection between the Healers at St. Mungo's and doctors from the Muggle world, Ron is quick to correct him: "'Doctors?' said Ron, looking startled. 'Those Muggle nutters that cut people up? Nah, they're Healers'" (*OP* 484). While there are key differences that separate Muggle doctors from magical Healers, particularly in how treatments are administered, they share many similarities, including the need for specialized training, establishing healing experience, and the importance of treating patients as people—a factor that often results in the physician taking action beyond a hospital or infirmary setting.

Like other professions, such as the Aurors, Healers must undergo specific training for this position. While the exact process for completing wizarding medical school is not outlined in the *Harry Potter* novels, we do get a glimpse at a step of that training in *Harry Potter and the Order of the Phoenix*. When Arthur Weasley is in St. Mungo's, there are two named Healers on his ward: Hippocrates Smethwyck, the Healer-in-Charge, and Augustus Pye, the Trainee Healer. While we know that Pye is a trainee, we don't know his exact level of experience; however, we may infer (or at least *hope*) that he is fairly new to his trainee position given his suggestion that Mr. Weasley use stitches to treat his snake bites. While Mr. Weasley is eager to try a Muggle remedy—as he is enthralled by all things Muggle—Mrs. Weasley is far from pleased, especially when the stitches fail. As Hermione points out, stitches work quite well for nonmagical injuries (507); however, magical injuries require magical treatment. It is ultimately Smethwyck, the Healer-in-Charge, who "worked his magic in the end [and] found an antidote to whatever that snake's got in its fangs" (522). Smethwyck, with experience, succeeded where the Trainee Healer failed; we can also assume that Pye learned from this experience as well and will likely not be treating other magical injuries with stitches from this point on.[4]

Because of the specialized training required, it is important to consider the role that privilege plays in being able to execute spells properly as well as being able to heal properly. Madam Pomfrey is, in the vast majority of cases, the expert on healing in the *Harry Potter* series. As such, she is usually the character whom others look to when they are ill, wounded, or otherwise in pain. Her privileges come not only from having access to magic, as the magical characters in the series are a privileged class of their own, but from having specialized training in healing. While other witches and wizards may be able to address more minor injuries and health concerns (such as a broken nose), the major concerns are best addressed by the experts in the field who have a better command of this category of spells.

Her specialized knowledge—and the invaluable nature of that knowledge—also puts Madam Pomfrey in a position of privilege. In fact, with the power to heal patients, many medical professionals gain additional power and prestige. For Madam Pomfrey, this includes the power to make demands about how the school is run, the power to tell patients how to behave when in the hospital wing, and the power to forbid certain visitors and topics of conversation she sees as detrimental to the patient's healing process. This dynamic is also common in Muggle medicine. Doctors are trusted to identify what is wrong and treat or cure the issue accordingly. This is a relationship that often works well when that trust is well-earned. However, this puts patients in a potentially precarious position when things to go awry, as they do with Lockhart; it is often difficult, if not impossible, for the patient to seize power in the doctor-patient hierarchy, should the need arise.

However, even Madam Pomfrey is not able to heal all wounds. When Bill Weasley is attacked by the werewolf Fenrir Greyback in *Harry Potter and the Half-Blood Prince*, Harry asks Madam Pomfrey if she can fix Bill's wounds with a charm, to which she responds, "No charm will work on these . . . I've tried everything I know, but there is no cure for werewolf bites" (613). This limitation shows what happens when the language needed to affect a particular reality does not exist; no spells exist to affect the reality of Bill's wounds in the way that his friends and family would hope. As long as the power to name something doesn't exist, as long as the spells don't exist, the reality can't be changed. In this case, it does not matter if Madam Pomfrey has a specialized education in Healing Spells; even her knowledgeable state does not combat the absence of the necessary signs.

This, then, also allows us to consider the ways that the field of medicine in the Muggle world is not absolute; there are conditions and concerns that cannot be addressed or cured with current medical knowledge. We might also consider, then, the future of medicine, both magical and Muggle. While new spells can be created in the magical world (which we can see with the *Sectumsempra* spell that Snape creates) and new technologies can be developed in the Muggle world, we must also consider what *fuels* those developments. In both cases, power and privilege, paired with need, dictate where resources can and will be spent, and the influence that social stigmas and prejudices have on such decisions cannot be ignored. To consider how prejudices make their way into medicine, we should consider, then, both the administrators of medicine and the general public and their concern about personal and public health.

Bridging the Gap: Diagnosis, Stigma, and the Rhetoric of Health

Building on the work of literary and medical scholars, including Ann Jurecic and Arthur Kleinman,[5] we recognize that an important part of medicine and health is appreciating not only the expertise of medical professionals but also the lived experience of patients. This is particularly important when considering the power of medical rhetorics of health and disease to affect reality. The patient is the person directly affected by these rhetorics, the one who will face ostracism, questions of self-worth, and violence, so when we consider the implications of medicine in these novels, we must also consider how the characters who face illness, injury, or questions of genetic "viability" within that universe are affected by these factors in their daily lives.

While the use of Healing Spells in the *Harry Potter* canon allows us to see the healing (and, when misused, harmful) powers of the sign in particularly concrete and tangible ways, our own practices of Western medicine are not without examples of linguistic powers and their constructions of reality. A doctor's diagnosis, for example, boasts a significant amount of rhetorical power and authority; a diagnosis can change the way that we think about ourselves as well as the way that society thinks of us. In this way, a certain diagnosis can affect our reality after our condition has been named, both in terms of the ways that we proceed with treatments as well as in terms of the stigmas and discriminations attached to a number of conditions.

We also see this happen with Lupin in the *Harry Potter* universe, so it is not, by any means, a strictly realist phenomenon. Lupin's diagnosis of lycanthropy—or, in other words, being a werewolf—affects how he lives his life, not only in terms of needing Snape to cover his classes during the full moon but also in terms of his hesitation to begin a relationship with Tonks. In fact, Lupin is so defined by his diagnosis that even his name is tied to his condition; "Remus" is a reference to one of the mythical founders of Rome who was raised by a wolf, and "Lupin" comes directly from the Latin *lupus* meaning "wolf."[6] The burden of lycanthropy permeates his entire character in a way that suggests that Lupin as a person cannot exist separate from the diagnosed condition.

There are also similarities between the ways medical dangers are discussed in the *Harry Potter* universe and in the contemporary culture. A key example of this is Lupin's rhetoric of "contamination" after Bill is bitten by Greyback: "I don't think Bill will be a true werewolf . . . but that does not mean that there won't be some contamination. Those are cursed wounds. They are unlikely ever to heal fully" (*HBP* 613). Lupin also repeats that there "will probably be some contamination" when Mr. Weasley later asks about Bill's condition (622). This rhetoric of contamination is one that is not unfamiliar in our world. When we are risking contamination or there is a fear of contamination, we immediately associate this with both dirt and danger. [See also Rose's discussion of Lupin's condition in chapter 10.] In this way, the connotations of the term "contamination" influence the way that we understand the reality around us and the reality around Bill as we read this passage.

It is also important to note the difference between contamination and infection. When considering lycanthropy, contamination, as in Bill's case from a nontransformed werewolf attacker, means danger, but it does not result in an absolute or full transformation. When the attacker is a transformed werewolf, however, the contamination *becomes* absolute, resulting in the lycanthropy infection, as in Lupin's case. This is why Bill and Fleur can still have a relationship, but Lupin insists that he cannot have a similar relationship with Tonks, despite both of their desires: "It's different, . . . Bill will not be a full werewolf," he argues (*HBP* 624). Here we can see not only the difference between Bill's contamination and Lupin's infection, but we can also see the importance of the diagnosis again; Lupin lives his life based on his understanding of himself in relation to his diagnosis.

This rhetoric of contamination is dangerous, however, as it creates damaging stigmas that can disrupt or even destroy the lives of patients in ways outside of the scope of the actual medical condition. This rhetoric becomes a kind of disease itself as it infects social and personal relationships and can create toxic attitudes towards groups of people in ways that are entirely undeserved. Lupin is also no stranger to stigma and discrimination based on his condition, and his awareness of this stigma, like his awareness of the diagnosis itself, influences his personal and professional options and choices. Not only does Lupin initially reject Tonks's affection because of his condition and how he fears it will affect their life together, but, in *Prisoner of Azkaban*, he also resigns from his post as Defense Against the Dark Arts teacher because Snape publicizes his diagnosis. Lupin says he must resign because "this time tomorrow, the owls will start arriving from parents. . . . They will not want a werewolf teaching their children" (423). Lupin is anticipating a response to his condition based on the stigma that surrounds it, that werewolves are dangerous and will infect the people around them, and, therefore, deserve to be ostracized.

Lupin goes on to explain, "And after last night, I see their point. I could have bitten any one of you. . . . That must never happen again" (423). This demonstrates how Lupin has actually been taught to fear *himself* based on this diagnosis, a fear that can be tied to his rejection of Tonks as well. Connected to this fear is also the belief that ostracism is deserved, Lupin believes that Dumbledore would be right to fire him after parents complain and that Tonks should be with someone healthy who wouldn't put her in danger. It isn't just society at large that buys into the stigma around his condition. It's a stigma that Lupin internalizes to the point that he believes himself to be dangerous, damaged, and detestable, despite the many precautions that he is careful to take.[7] From both of these perspectives—internally believed and externally imposed—we can see the power of naming, diagnosis, and linguistics to affect reality in highly significant ways.

However, instances of lycanthropy are not the only place where we see the rhetoric of dirt or contamination in the *Harry Potter* universe. Another significant example is in the prejudice against Muggle-born ("Mudblood") characters. Though being Muggle-born is certainly not a disease, illness, or injury, as in the other examples that I've examined thus far, it is treated with similar rhetoric. As Ron points out in *Harry Potter and the Chamber of Secrets*, "Mudblood" literally *means* "dirty blood" (116). For characters who possess the racist beliefs that Muggle-born characters are "filthy" (a term often associated with "Mudblood" references in the series), there is a fear that "pureblood" wizards are being contaminated by nonwizarding blood. (We might also look to Hagrid in this example, as he tries to keep his half-giant parentage a secret for the majority of the series.) When considering this link between rhetorics of filth, dirt, and contamination, we must also consider how eugenics can be and has been used to justify the inhumane treatment of people deemed a threat to "pure" or "clean" bloodlines. When considering this appalling tradition, we can find examples (though certainly not an exhaustive list) in Nazi medical experiments, racist twentieth-century American medical and social hierarchies, and other historical and present-day beliefs, traditions, and policies that frame people of color, people living in lower socioeconomic classes, and people with diverse abilities, among others, as second-class citizens or worse. By providing false scientific "proof" of their inferiority, these rhetorics allow for and support social prejudices, discrimination, and violence against the individuals and populations that are stigmatized, all while masking these prejudices as "unbiased" science.

In *Harry Potter*, by linking these beliefs predominantly to Slytherin House, Rowling signifies her judgment of people who accept beliefs like this. However, even within this fictional universe, we see these beliefs permeate into a wider culture, even into characters whom we might otherwise accept as heroes of the series. While many Slytherins support "the purification of the Wizarding race, getting rid of Muggle-borns and having purebloods in charge" and see "anyone of Muggle descent [as] second-class," many other magical characters see Muggles as dumb, backwards, or otherwise lesser than (*OP* 112; *GF* 102). For example, Ron refers to doctors as "Muggle nutters" and, when Ron's Great-Aunt Muriel says of Hermione, "Oh dear, is this the Muggle-born? [...] Bad posture and skinny ankles," Ron tells Hermione not to take the comment personally (*OP* 484; *DH* 142). So, while the most violent anti-Muggle impulses might come predominantly from characters associated with Slytherin House and/or with Voldemort, prejudice permeates the wizarding world, supported by rhetorics of health and fueled by fears of being contaminated by the Other. We can see many examples of this in our own world. Whether the prejudice is based on race, ability, or any other of a number of factors, the rhetoric of contamination or genetic inferiority is not uncommon to us,[8] and we must contend with the ways that supposedly unbiased fields such as science and medicine come to be used for these obviously prejudiced purposes, both historically and in the present day.

The Muggle Value of Magical Medicine

As this chapter has demonstrated, an examination of the *Harry Potter* canon through the perspectives of linguistic theory and medical humanities encourages us to question how we use language—particularly language associated with health, purity, and contamination—and the ways that language is tied to privilege and power, as well as the ways that this in turn can truly alter the reality that we live in.

Further, by critically examining this fictional universe, we can also question and critique elements of our own world. Questioning the use of "contamination" and "filth" in the *Harry Potter* universe—and the inescapable implications these terms have for personal and public health—encourages us to also question similar rhetorical strategies in our world and to similarly critique the resulting, real-life stigmas and discriminations tied to this use of language. Similarly, we can question the relationship between real-life diagnoses and real-life treatments of patients, considering especially the benefits not only of expert physicians but also physicians who are invested in patients as individuals and as people. In other words, though we are mere Muggles, we too can find the value in magical signs, Healing Spells, and the power to combat curses and hate, not just as literary constructions but as valuable and eye-opening parallels to our own sociolinguistic, cultural, and medical practices.

Notes

1. The first two connections I've outlined here deal with the power of language to create a physical, tangible change in the world; the final deals with the sociocultural implications of rhetorical choices. While all three examples constitute the power of language to affect reality, it is important to understand that the realities being affected, and the ways in which they are affected, are not the same across all three categories.

2. In his work *The Linguistic Construction of Reality*, Grace explores the implications of viewing language as a reality mapper rather than a reality constructor. He ultimately concludes that language does more than simply *map* reality; he further argues that, by understanding that language can actually create or change reality/-ies, we can appreciate the different constructions of reality that are possible through different languages and, by extension, different cultural lenses and experiences. This also opens doors to questions of linguistic privilege. What language(s) are privileged in a particular area or among a particular group? Who has access to that language? Who is excluded? How does access to a particular language affect a person's experience, both personally and socially, in a specific area or with a specific group of people? How is a description of reality influenced by the language and culture describing said reality?

3. It is also worth noting the role that the patient's consent plays here. Harry does ultimately give consent to Tonks in *Harry Potter and the Half-Blood Prince*; however, he never consents to be treated by Lockhart in *Harry Potter and the Chamber of Secrets*. (In fact, it may be this earlier experience with Lockhart that makes Harry initially reluctant to let Tonks treat him later in the series.) When considering magical and Muggle medicine, this disregard for patient consent becomes even more alarming when we consider it outside of a fictional setting. Lockhart's comment that Harry "doesn't know what he's saying" when Lockhart is in the more powerful, expert position also speaks to problems of real-life physicians who may be dismissive of their patients' discomfort and concerns (172). This is one instance in which paying close attention to the patient/illness narrative can shed more light on the experience. Though we, as readers, know that Harry doesn't want to be treated by Lockhart, other characters within the story see Lockhart as an experienced professional (though that opinion is predominantly short-lived) and see Harry as a possibly disoriented, certainly inexperienced student. This is a power dynamic that, in this case, must be disrupted for the sake of the patient.

4. While this method of apprenticeship follows a common literary trope (younger, inexperienced magical character learns through shadowing someone with more experience), it is also reflective of many Muggle medical training programs, which often require young physicians to shadow established professionals, including completing their clinical rotations, which, in many programs, take place during the last two years, with the earlier years focusing more heavily on classroom study.

5. In his work *The Illness Narratives: Suffering, Healing, and the Human Condition*, Kleinman argues that it is important for physicians and other medical professionals to be invested in their patients' personal experiences; he suggests that an important part of this investment must come from listening to and valuing the narratives that patients can share about their personal experience with illness or injury. Kleinman argues that physicians, after becoming invested in their patients' personal experiences, are more likely to recognize their patients as people who live lives beyond the clinical setting. While the present field of medical humanities recognizes the importance of patient/illness narratives, this is not necessarily the case in literary analysis and criticism. As Ann Jurecic argues in her work *Illness as Narrative*, the field of literary scholarship still too often disregards these narratives as "victim art" or "misery memoirs," quick to dismiss them as sentimental and untrustworthy narratives (10–11). While both Kleinman and Jurecic focus on real-life patients and their illness narratives, I argue that the importance of valuing a patient's personal experience can also be transferred to fictional works; in the *Harry Potter* series, for example, this focus

will allow the reader to better understand, analyze, and question the deep, complicated, and inescapable connection between medical diagnoses and personal experience.

6. The power of naming doesn't just apply to the diagnosis here; Rowling uses language to hint at Lupin's condition through his name, a name that he has had since before he contracted lycanthropy. This then begs the question: Was he named Lupin because he would eventually be bitten? Was he eventually bitten because he was named Lupin? The linguistic cause and effect, especially considering the magical power of words within the *Harry Potter* universe, creates a chicken-and-egg type of interrogation where we are forced to wonder if Lupin was *destined* to become a werewolf, was *destined* to contract lycanthropy, because of *who he is*. This also opens doors for us to consider prejudice and medicine in our own Muggle world, particularly with medical conditions that are associated with specific types of bodies or behaviors. We are compelled to ask: Does anyone deserve to be sick simply because of who they are?

7. In her *Pottermore* article "Illness and Disability," Rowling writes about her intention to have Lupin's condition and the stigma surrounding it specifically reflect aspects of the Muggle world: "Remus Lupin's affliction was a conscious reference to blood-borne diseases such as the HIV infection, with the attendant stigma. The potion Snape brews him is akin to the antiretroviral that will keep him from developing the 'full-blown' version of his illness. The sense of 'apartness' that the management of a chronic condition can impose on its sufferers was an important part of Lupin's character" ("Illness and Disability").

8. For example, consider antimiscegenation laws and the one-drop rule.

Works Cited

Grace, George W. *The Linguistic Construction of Reality*. Croom Helm, 1987.

Jurecic, Ann. *Illness as Narrative*. University of Pittsburgh Press, 2012.

Kleinman, Arthur. *The Illness Narratives: Suffering, Healing, and the Human Condition*. Oxford University Press, 1988.

Rowling, J. K. "Illness and Disability." *Pottermore*, n.d., https://www.pottermore.com/writing-by-jk-rowling/illness-and-disability.

5

ROWLING'S PARATEXTUAL GIFTS
Thresholds to Community in *Harry Potter* and the *Deathly Hallows*

Marie Schilling Grogan

Harry Potter and the Deathly Hallows begins with two epigraphs, short quotations from other authors, and concludes with an epilogue, a few pages relating what has happened to the characters since the action of the final chapter. Like the protective charms the three protagonists cast each time they set up camp in the long chapters of wandering at the heart of the novel, the epigraphs and the epilogue appear to encircle the narrative with the author's own spell, aiming to protect her story from misinterpretation. J. K. Rowling does not add these paratextual features to any other book in the series, so here, at the close of her epic, their deployment might betray an author reinforcing a "proper" interpretation of her story. By the time she writes book 7, Rowling is certainly aware that the vast audience whose misreadings she might wish to forestall ranges from those who will track down the intertextual implications of the epigraphs to those who will simply turn that page to get to the story; from those who will find profound satisfaction in the domesticity of the epilogue to those who will reject its predictable pairings and its heteronormativity.

As the story itself affirms, however, even the best of protective spells is subject to breach. Focusing, then, not on a text to be protected, but rather on a readership to be guided, we could instead see Rowling's use of these framing devices as evidence of her attention to the particular readerly community that she imagines as her audience. It may be useful to recast the epigraphs and epilogue not as protective charms creating boundaries around the text, but rather as gifts from author to readers—freely offered but operating outside of the story's boundaries, outside of a commercial economy of coercive contracts. As with any gift, Rowling's final bequests of the epigraphs and epilogue may be rejected; true reciprocity between the author and her readers requires the freedom of that refusal. In these "extra" liminal spaces appended only to the last *Harry Potter* book, Rowling offers thresholds to the text across which author and reader encounter each other in the give and take of genuine human interdependence. Indeed, I argue in this essay that with these particular authorial interventions, Rowling models the belief in an enduring human community, one that transcends time and place, that is at the heart of her literary project.

To talk of Rowling's desires to guide or direct her readers' encounters with her novels and her audience's resistance to or rejection of the readings she encourages reveals the lens of structuralist narratology I bring to bear on this text. This critical approach, which names the distinction between the "story" (that is the sequence of events) and the "discourse" (the manner in which the story is told) and which incorporates the insights of both structuralism and reader-response theory, is well-suited for interrogating the rhetorical complexity of this novel. As the final installment in an internationally beloved series of books, *Harry Potter and the Deathly Hallows* was written under the intense scrutiny of a highly diverse global audience that, in the age of websites and social media platforms, communicated a dizzying panoply of desires this longed-for story might address. In his most recent book, *Somebody Telling Somebody Else: A Rhetorical Poetics of Narrative*, James Phelan points to Rowling's work in his introduction to illustrate some of the distinctions he makes about "audience" as he argues for a shift to a "rhetorical paradigm" in postclassical structuralism (7–8). Although I conclude this chapter with some discussion of the various audiences *Deathly Hallows* may address, I will not employ all of Phelan's terminology for the four categories of audience.[1] I do, however, share with him the core belief that meaning is made of this or any story at the intersections of "authorial agency, textual phenomena (including intertextual relations), and reader response" (6).[2]

To begin with, the "textual phenomena" of the epigraphs and epilogue are, in the taxonomy of Gerard Genette, "paratexts," which Genette defines as "functional elements" surrounding the text, including the titles, prefaces, publisher's blurbs, dedications, epilogues, footnotes, some provided by the author, some attached to a text by a publisher or later editor, but all "dedicated to the service of something other than itself that constitutes its *raison d'etre*. This something is the text" (12). I have already suggested, however, that the *raison d'etre* for some paratexts may rather be the author-reader relationship; this shift in function is possible because a subspecies of the paratext that Genette calls the "epitext" is increasingly significant in a world where Rowling continues to add commentary to her texts in interviews, on Twitter, and at Pottermore. Genette divides "paratexts" into two main types: "peritexts" including (but not limited to) all of the elements mentioned above, which are "spatially" appended to the material text,[3] and "epitexts," which are elements "not materially appended to the text within the same volume but circulating, as it were, freely, in a virtually limitless physical and social space" in author interviews, author comments at colloquia, and private correspondence (344). In an age when fraught discussions of the *Potter* canon can parse the degree of authenticity and reliability that the Black family tree used in the fifth *Harry Potter* movie may have, Genette's illustrations of epitexts, letters by Proust, for example, seem limited and quaint. But writing just as the Internet came into being and well before social media existed, Genette presciently identified the "limitless . . . social space" where textual meaning is also made. Genette's exercise of distinguishing when, where and in what form the author creates thresholds across which the reader will encounter her text continues to illuminate those liminal spaces where narrative meaning is made.[4]

As quotations from other works, epigraphs are a species of allusion. Beatrice Groves has written about the many allusions that Rowling weaves through the *Harry Potter* corpus and rightly notes that the effect of this body of allusions is to evoke an audience of fellow readers (xi) [See also chapter 6 in this volume.] Epigraphs do not merely allude to other texts, but directly. quote them; here at the outset of book 7, Rowling quotes a drama by Aeschylus and a collection of maxims by William Penn. As Groves observes, such direct quotations are both "self-effacing and authoritative" (xiii); they announce the author's debt to a master and assert the new text's place in an exalted literary pantheon. As Genette suggests, the most canonical function of an epigraph is to provide a commentary on the text it precedes, commentary which may be clear from the outset, but which "more often . . . is puzzling, has a significance that will not be clear or confirmed until the whole book is read" (158). Rowling's epigraphs fall into the latter category; the middle play of the *Oresteia* and a seventeenth century collection of pithy sayings are not widely familiar texts. What audience does Rowling imagine encountering these epigraphs? As suggested above, some readers may skip them; others will make what they can of the plain sense of the words. But Rowling seems to have hoped for more. In an interview just after the release of *Deathly Hallows*, she revealed, "I'd known it was going to be those two passages since *Chamber* was published. I always knew [that] if I could use them at the beginning of book seven, then I'd cued up the ending perfectly. If they were relevant, then I went where I needed to go.... They just say it all to me, they really do." Rowling's telling conditionals ("if I could use them"; "if they were relevant") evoke the contingency of any author's control over a narrative as it develops—new ideas emerge, characters develop in unforeseen ways, readers make demands. To Rowling's apparent delight, when she writes book 7, the quotes are still appropriate, and the threshold she believes they provide to her narrative's meaning ("they just say it all") can be opened for readers who care to dwell in those spaces. I will comment briefly, then, on the themes these quotations might suggest to readers interested in the intertextuality they offer: that is readers already familiar with the texts they reference or willing to seek out the quoted works to understand their significance for the novel. I will move on then to consider how the particular genre of each epigraph functions to reinforce the thematic concerns.

For those familiar (or who come to be familiar) with the fifth century BCE *The Libation Bearers*, the quotation chosen for the first epigraph calls the entire story to mind. Groves, Granger, and Spencer are among those who have thoughtfully reflected on the ways that the story of Orestes parallels and may be used by Rowling to comment on Harry's story. Like Orestes charged with avenging his father's death, Harry seems fated to avenge the death of his parents. The life histories of the two protagonists also include parallels: sent away from home at birth, they return as adolescents to face their destinies; each bears a scar by which he can be recognized; both will undertake their challenges with the crucial support of comrades—Electra and Pylades for Orestes, Hermione and Ron for Harry.[5] But notwithstanding these points of confluence at the narrative level, it is also possible that this particular hymnos from *The Libation Bearers* functions to raise dissonant themes, evoking a species of human dilemma and worldview that is *unlike* the one the novel portrays. The lines are a prayer offered by the chorus asking that the children of the family of Atreus (those "in the House") will be able to cure the torment of that family, whose multigenerational cycle of crime and vengeance is "an inherited disease" (Fagles and Stanford 17).

The translation Rowling reproduces here is by Robert Fagles. In this edition, the noted classicist W. B. Stanford collaborated with Fagles on a well-known introductory essay, which explores how the *Oresteia* dramatizes humanity's "passage from savagery to civilization" (Fagles and Stanford 21). In its focus on characters' responses to suffering, this trilogy portrays a deeply human world and the nobility of embracing one's duty even if the "cure" involves actions "more horrific than the crime" (Marshall 1). But while marked by some optimism, the vision of civil order that concludes the trilogy is not the same as the Christian consolation the second epigraph from Penn offers, whose particular contours will be discussed below. Rowling herself remarked on the differences in the worldviews noting of her epigraphs, "one is pagan, of course, and one is from a Christian tradition" ("Interview"). Especially as the middle play in the *Oresteia* trilogy, *The Libation Bearers* grapples with evil, but ultimately provides "no certain answer to the questions posed. There is only the problem, and a recognition that human institutions struggled with it" (Marshall 13). The speakers of these lines are the chorus comprised of female palace slaves who bear libations, liquid offerings, to pour on the grave of Agamemnon in the hope of appeasing his dishonored spirit. Both the chorus and the children who must act to avenge Agamemnon are under obligation to the memory and honor of those who have died, but in the ancient Greek cosmos, the relationship of those who still live with those who have died is not envisioned as the loving communion of Christian tradition. In many ways, a central concern of the *Harry Potter* series, and of *Deathly Hallows* especially, is the nature of the relationship of the living and the dead. Certainly, the epigraph from *The Libation Bearers* poses questions about that relationship that the second epigraph will likewise take up, and that the novel itself is poised to answer.

But beyond the parallels to plot points and character and the more important thematic orientation suggested by the first epigraph, the very nature of the epigraph as a quotation from a classical narrative is also significant. As Richard Spencer notes, Rowling's quotations from the classics suggest that her own narrative meditations on life and death are a form of "rediscovery of a human treasure which belongs to the ages, but which is now re-set for a new time and a new age" (92). And even more tellingly, he imagines that such allusions "put us in tune with the souls and experiences of people of the ages" (92). Choosing an epigraph that is abstracted from another story, in this case an ancient drama, which was itself a piece in an intertextual web of ancient narratives about Orestes and his family, is to place the new work into a complicated nexus of stories, readers, and tellers that does indeed stretch across the ages. Contemporary readers who want to puzzle out the relationship between *The Libation Bearers* and *Deathly Hallows*, whether they already know or are prompted to learn the source texts, are, in effect being handed a story before the story, one whose exact relevance cannot possibly be clear, given that the *Deathly Hallows* narrative has yet to begin. First-time readers are asked to carry this epigraph, and by extension the story from which it is excerpted, into the novel, pondering the words as they go, waiting to see how *The Libation Bearers'* plot, characters, or themes might unlock some mysteries within the world of *Deathly Hallows*. In this sense, we might compare the textual offering of this deeply allusive epigraph with the bequest of the collection of fairy tales, another type of "human treasure which belongs to the ages," given to Hermione at the outset of her journey. Stories from *The Tales of Beedle the Bard* are familiar to Ron, whose memories of hearing them from his mother represent the wizarding world's continued guardianship of its own ancient wisdom, but Hermione and Harry encounter them as uninitiated readers; with their varying degrees of textual familiarity, all three will discuss the tales and work out the keys they offer to the mysteries the protagonists face.

The second epigraph, taken from *More Fruits of Solitude* by the early Quaker William Penn represents a generically different kind of intertext. This epigraph is a compilation of four short maxims. A maxim, or aphorism, is a pithy sentence that expresses wisdom. The seventeenth century prized the genre of the maxim, and in addition to Penn, many authors wrote collections of short, wise sayings. John Granger delves fully into the Quaker beliefs that Penn's maxims convey and examines Rowling's alteration of Penn's work.

As Granger points out, Rowling has altered the format of the maxims as they are found in the Harvard Classics edition cited on the copyright page as her source, combining what were four separate sentences into a single paragraph, removing their numbers, and removing capitalization as well:

Death is but crossing the world, as friends do the seas; they live in one another still. For they must needs be present, that love and live in that which is omnipresent. In this divine glass, they see face to face; and their con-verse is free, as well as pure. This is the comfort of friends, that though they may be said to die, yet their friendship and society are, in the best sense, ever present, because immortal.

Granger suggests that the capitalized "Friends" of Penn's text referred to the Society of Friends, that is the Quakers, who had at this time quite literally crossed the seas to live in the New World; given the conventions of seventeenth-century capitalization, which govern all of the maxims in the collection and dictate the capitalization of almost all nouns, this is not necessarily Penn's meaning. But although Rowling's emendation to the lowercase "f" and "s" does familiarize the text for contemporary readers and universalizes the meanings of these words, Granger is certainly correct to suggest that "friends," "friendship," and "society" mean something for both Penn and Rowling that is deeper and more binding than our casual use of these words today suggests. The four-sentence epigraph proclaims that "friendship and society," that is our relationships with our loved ones and companions, are in fact immortal, even after friends die. This theme of enduring "friendship and society" is insistently played throughout the novel, in answer to the essential question, noted above, of what happens to the relationships formed in life when friends die.

One lovely image from the novel that captures the importance of the theme of enduring friendship is the circle of portraits Luna has painted on her bedroom ceiling. As the narrator reports:

> Luna had decorated her bedroom ceiling with five beautifully painted faces: Harry, Ron, Hermione, Ginny and Neville. They were not moving as the portraits at Hogwarts moved, but there was a certain magic to them all the same: Harry thought they breathed. What appeared to be fine golden chains wove around the pictures, linking them together, but after examining them for a minute or so, Harry realized that the chains were actually one word, repeated a thousand times in golden ink: *friends . . . friends . . . friends . . .*" (417)

It is unclear when Luna painted her ceiling, though one feels it may have been while she was last home, before being taken by the Ministry. There are long months in the story when separated friends do not know who is still alive and who may have died. Lee Jordan runs *Potterwatch*, a radio program on which the disembodied, distant voices of members of the resistance offer news and hope to friends they cannot see, but whose presence they still affirm in their faithful broadcast. Luna's ceiling feels like an emblem of the same stubborn hope: friends she may no longer see each day are with her, in her remote tower bedroom. The "magic" of these portraits is their promise of life: "Harry thought they breathed" (417). In the words of the Penn epigraph, although the earthly fate of Luna's friends may not be known, "their friendship and society are, in the best sense, ever present, because immortal."

However, as the maxims also suggest, in an allusion to the writings of the apostle Paul, we can only truly see "face to face," truly know each other, in the "divine glass" of life lived in the presence of "that which is omnipresent," that is, God. A "glass" is a "mirror," and, of course, worldly mirrors, which in Pauline terms reflect the sublime only dimly or partially, are symbolic motifs throughout the series, including in this final book where the fragment of Sirius's mirror reflects only confusion and mystery to Harry.[6] Throughout *The Deathly Hallows*, mists swirl, darknesses obscure; characters disguised, cloaked, voiced-but-not seen, are frequently unable to see each other "face to face." The maxims here at the beginning of the book make hopeful promises about what will unfold ahead, but they encapsulate a wisdom that is not yet available to the characters within the story, nor to the readers who begin it, uncertain how it will turn out.

The genre of the maxim is structurally quite distinct from the genre of a choral speech excerpted from a classical drama. Unlike an epigraph from a narrative, which pulls one story into dialogue with another, a maxim, or even a paragraph comprised of four maxims on a common theme, is more self-contained. The French structuralist critic Roland Barthes, in considering the maxim as a form, talks about its "closed" nature. Barthes posits a maxim as a "hard object," comparing it to the armor of an insect, noting, "the maxim is armed *because* it is closed" (5). Barthes suggests that in their brevity and the "plenitude" of their substantives, words such as "love," "passion," and "pride" that have "eternal, in fact autarchic meaning," maxims are not open to the play of meaning that other forms of discourse invite (5). Each of the maxims, when considered separately, is a discrete "unit" of wisdom, meant for contemplation, but not pointing allusively outward to other stories or intertexts.

As Rowling has altered the four separate sentences into a small, fully justified paragraph, it takes on in aggregate the characteristics Barthes attributes to individual maxims. This textual block is still brief; it is characterized by a fullness of substance in the wisdom it encapsulates. In its closed, self-contained nature, this little epigraph might well be compared to a hard object, even an insect's "corselet," in Barthes's metaphor,[7] which certainly makes me think of a snitch. Here, before her readers know what it will be good for or how it might be used, Rowling offers a second gift: an interpretive key that will break open most fully at the end of the story. The first epigraph invites readers to bring a story into the story, to call upon an ancient community of meaning makers and seekers for guidance; this koanic gift calls for more solitary contemplation. We carry this little epigraph, its paradoxical words buzzing and whirring about us as we read, but it will only really "open at the close."

Which brings us to the epilogue. Rowling's final chapter, "Nineteen Years Later," has been controversial since the book's publication. It finds Harry and Ginny, Ron and Hermione back on Platform 9¾ sending their own children off to Hogwarts. Over seven pages we learn what has happened to many of the principal characters of the series. The brief chapter brims with details and allusions to delight fans. It is a "scenic," not "summative" epilogue, offering a glimpse of the characters' on-going lives, but not an exhaustive rehearsal of their lives until death. We might say that beyond the boundaries of the main narrative, one brief episode in the characters' future lives has been illuminated for the reader before the final "lights out" of the last page, rather like a deluminator at work. Certainly, many readers feel this epilogue is another gift from Rowling, offering emotional satisfaction; but others suggest that it mars the artistry of the series. In her original *New York Times* review of the book, Michiko Kakutani praised Rowling for offering her readers "good old-fashioned closure" in "an epilogue that clearly lays out people's fates" (para 2). Kakutani calls the use of an epilogue "old fashioned" because, although epilogues were popular for centuries, the modernist and pos-modern preference for ambiguity has degraded the value of this literary device.

Except, as Mike Cadden notes, in the genre of children's literature. There, epilogues remain a common feature, providing not just closure to the narrative proper, but also a sense of comforting emotional completeness for the child reader. Cadden explores the ethics of authorship for the writers of children's literature, who seem to feel a responsibility to protect their young readers' hearts. He concludes that in opting for the closure of "happy endings" and the "completeness" of epilogues, children's authors, like Rowling, have privileged their own desires "that the reader be comforted at all literary costs" (355). In other words, for Cadden and many others, Rowling's epilogue is a literary or aesthetic failure; an artist truer to the logic of the narrative would have seen that Harry must die.

Susan Johnston disagrees. Using the term "eucatastrophe," coined by Tolkien to refer to the deeply joyous turn with which fairy stories conclude, she suggests that the epilogue of the *Deathly Hallows*, in the tradition of fantasy literature, proposes "that the miraculous grace of the happy ending is neither unworldly nor an affront to the mimetic demands of realism" (xx). Johnston argues that both Tolkien's and Rowling's books are Christian not because of allegorical structures, Christ-like characters, or ethical underpinnings, but rather in the "deep structure of the hope," a "communal hope," that infuses the stories and does lead "logically" to their conclusions. According to Johnston, the earthly unity of Rowling's homely gathering on Platform 9¾ points to the ultimate unity of the eternal kingdom described in Augustine's *City of God*. Earthly communities are living signs of the "kingdom of good" that transcend the present time.

Johnston's identification of "communal hope" as the linchpin to the narrative—and her assessment of the communal gathering in the epilogue as a sign of that hope—is apt. Indeed, Rowling's final scene evokes another figure for that eternal communion taken from the words of St. Paul's letter to the Hebrews: those who accompany us from beyond the grave are the "great cloud of witnesses."

Rowling asserts that it was her desire for the epilogue to be "nebulous," something "poetic," and that she wanted the readers to feel as if they were looking at Platform 9¾ through the mist, unable to make out exactly who was there and who was not. This is, indeed, the effect, as voices float out from the "thick white steam" pouring from the train, while "indistinct figures were swarming through the mist" (754); some voices remain disembodied (Percy may or may not be there). Beyond the characters standing on the platform, those who have gone before, the beloved dead, are present in the children named for them, and in memory, as evoked when Harry glances at the watch that once belonged to a Weasely uncle. Generations yet to come are suggested in the burgeoning romance of Teddy and Victoire. And even the Malfoys are there because, as Johnston notes, true communion does not erase differences, but embraces them. The Hogwarts Houses will not disappear, but in the figure of Albus Severus or in the possibility of a friendship (or more) between Rose and Scorpius, divisions can be healed.

This veritable "cloud of witnesses" gathered on the train platform evokes the core Christian tenet that believers are, every day in their ordinary lives, members of a timeless communion; this is the definition of the Christian theological term, "the communion of saints." Theologian Elizabeth Johnson writes that "together the living form with the dead one community of memory and hope, a holy people touched with the fire of the Spirit, summoned to go forth as companions bringing the face of divine compassion into everyday life and the great struggles of history" (18). The great struggles of history include the classical world's engagement with human suffering as expressed in the *Oresteia*, evoked in the first epigraph. And while *The Libation Bearers* does not offer the same vision of the "one community of memory and hope," the very presence of a classical quotation puts *Deathly Hallows* readers "in tune with the souls and experiences of people of the ages" who likewise pondered the durability of human connection. In the swirling mists of the King's Cross platform *and* in the midst of the here and now, individuals separated by space, time, and death may not yet see each other "face to face," but the promise of such converse, "free as well as pure" in the divine presence is that held out by that small, closed object, the aphoristic second epigraph, which opens here to affirm that though friends do die, "their friendship and society are, in the best sense, ever present, because immortal." The nebulous, poetic epilogue points to a euchatastrophic vision of human communion beyond death to which the hopeful gestures of the Potterwatch broadcasts and Luna's ceiling painting also bear witness. Intriguingly, there are illusionistic ceiling frescoes found in churches throughout the world that depict the cloud of witnesses, the communion of saints. Portraits of heavenly "friends," saints, and angels often gathered together in circles that spiral up through cumulus clouds, share those sacred spaces with the living congregations gathered below them. [8] Could Luna's ceiling, described at the midpoint of the novel, be an ekphrastic emblem that gains meaning when viewed across the paratextual thresholds that emphasize communion?

Vantage points from outside the main text, offering such vistas ahead or back into the story that have the power to alter readers' responses to the central narrative are created in book 7 alone. I have compared the textual phenomena of these "extra bits," these instances of Rowling's authorial agency, to gifts, because I think it is precisely their paratextual nature that makes them sites of author-reader exchange. You may take them or leave them and still have a very good story. But their very presence with the text has meaning that must be acknowledged whether readers care to accept the textual commentary and thematic resonances they offer.

The actual audience (Booth's "flesh-and-blood readers") for Rowling's books was growing exponentially as she wrote, and this audience includes resistant readers, who, for instance, have already critiqued the world of Hogwarts as misogynistic or oppressively heteronormative. Resisting readers, as described decades ago by Judith Fetterley, are those who call into question any belief that literature is apolitical; the worlds shaped by authors inescapably have their own political biases and architecture whose hegemony some readers will choose to resist. There are also "rebellious readers," a category of reader carefully theorized by Leslie Goodman, who are willing to enter an author's fictional world, but from within that readerly position, reject some of the author's judgment, for instance of a particular character. Rowling's rebellious readers would include, then, devoted fans who feel Cho Chang is unfairly characterized and judged. The actual author Rowling knows these actual readers exist; she acknowledges their complaints in interviews. But does Rowling's authorial audience include such readers? I would argue that the presence of the epigraphs and epilogue functioning as "gifts" rather than "protective spells" suggests an author who imagines an expansive authorial audience, one that may include resistant and rebellious readers. An author bent on coercing readings rather than inviting them could have done things otherwise: worked the quotes she loved into the narrative itself or written an even more summative epilogue. But as they are presented, the epigraphs and epilogue work to invite community.

One last look at the epilogue helps illustrate the way it functions as a threshold where the author and readers encounter each other to make meaning, together. In the epigrammatic very last line of the book, "All was well," many have noted that Rowling echoes the medieval English mystic Julian of Norwich's assertion that "all shall be well, and all manner of things shall be well." But rather than Julian's "shall," foreclosing challenges for the future, the past tense of Rowling's own line speaks only of what comes before this last word.

Novelist Jorge Luis Borges said of one of his epilogues, "I hope that these hasty notes. . . . do not exhaust the meanings of this book; may its visions continue to unfold in the receptive imaginations of those who now close it." Rowling might concur. She has set the trajectory of the lives of her beloved characters, but she does not conclude their stories. Despite Kakutani's assertion that the epilogue "clearly lays out people's fates," this "scenic," not "summative" chapter does not take our characters to their deaths. Cadden in fact complains that the epilogue denies readers "the move into legend and myth and keeps us firmly planted in the novel tradition. . . . ironically Rowling takes what was closed and, instead of leaving it alone or providing the completion of a summative epilogue, seems to give too little by giving too much" (354). Harry's is not the immutable story of a mythological hero because life goes on, and real relationships continue.

Rowling's epilogue remains open at the close because it leaves room for imaginative interaction; and she knew full well that the fandom would bring their imaginations to bear on the years both before and after the epilogue. The epigraphs offer their thematic guidance, pointing towards the possibility of eternal communion and in their very existence modeling literary community across time and genre, but set separately on a page before the story begins, their positioning says: choose not to read them if you like. True communion is a space of give and take. This is the authentic dilemma for an author who takes human community seriously. We can never completely control, but neither do we relinquish our responsibility to speak our truth. Resistant and rebellious readers have space in which to change destinies and alter universes. In the end, Rowling's authorial audience is capacious because it is built of individuals she calls into relationship in her fourth gift to the reader: her dedication.

The reader—"You, if you have stuck with Harry until the very end"—is one of the seven dedicatees named even before the epigraphs. In the six previous books, the dedicatees were all family members and friends of the "actual" author, Joanne Rowling. Especially poignant, and resonant of the communion possible beyond life, is Rowling's inclusion of her mother in the dedication for both the first book and the last, despite the fact that her mother had died by the time that *Harry Potter and the Philosopher's Stone* was published. By this seventh novel, "the very end," Rowling acknowledges the relationship she feels not only with her family members living and deceased, but also with an authorial audience of one: "You," the loyal reader.

In my field of study, medieval literature, authors as well known as Chaucer or as anonymous as a cloistered nun routinely end their works with direct address to their readers as individuals: "Please pray for me," they ask. Scribes who copy a manuscript may do the same. The medieval ethics of reading presume a human person who has written or copied a work that will also be received by a human person. The receiver may be one who lives many years after the writer's death; but writer and receiver both believe that they have something of profound value to offer: the writer's work may help the reader achieve sanctification, the reader's prayers may save the writer's soul. James Phelan argues in the concluding chapter of *Somebody Telling Somebody Else* that readers willing to experience the narratives created by "somebody" to communicate truth and beauty and seeking to assess "the teller's mind, emotion, values, and sense of quality" are engaged in a process that is similarly profound (259). Phelan identifies the goal of this project, which he calls rhetorical poetics, to be the turn from reading to "enriched living"; he writes that "the purpose of rhetorical poetics is to contribute to human flourishing" (259). My sense is that Rowling would agree with this ambition, recognizing the true possibilities and consequences of the compact a writer makes with readers. While some critique Rowling's ethics of authorship, leery of the ways that concern for her readers may compromise her artistry, I would say rather that in the "glass" or mirror of the author-reader encounters the paratexts invite, we glimpse a reflection of the eternal community evoked by the epigraphs and the epilogue and thematically central to the novel itself: human "friendship and society," which persist beyond the borders of place, time, and even death.

Notes

This chapter grew out of a paper delivered at the Chestnut Hill College 2017 Harry Potter Conference. Special thanks are due to my children, Jack, Isobel, and Catherine, whose love for the *Harry Potter* books led me to a midnight purchase party *for Harry Potter and the Deathly Hallows* in 2007; that night, as they slept, I turned first to the epilogue, needing to know how the hearts of my young readers would fare when they reached the end. I experienced the epilogue as a gift to worried parents, for which I remain grateful to J. K. Rowling.

1. For most of the chapter, I will also speak with less precision about the author than a thoroughgoing structuralist analysis might warrant; most references to "Rowling" or the "author" of the text here would more properly, but distractingly, be the "implied author" as theorized, for instance by Wayne Booth—that is, the author we know from her rhetorical choices in her published "texts," including the novels, tweets, and on Pottermore. Towards the end, I do discuss to some degree the motives of the "actual author—that is, the person Joanne Rowling who might be knowable beyond her publications.

2. And which Rowling herself shares: compare Grove's introduction to *Literary Allusion in Harry Potter* where she quotes Rowling's description in an interview of her relationship with her readers: "My readers have to work with me to create the experience. They have to bring their imaginations to the story . . . together, as author and reader, we have both created the story" (xi).

3. Genette writes without reference to hypertexts; theorizing this spatial distinction between peritext and epitext is certainly a project subject to challenge and revision in the digital environment; see Birke and Christ who explore this landscape.

4. Genette's title in French *Seuils*, more literally translated as "Thresholds," is also more suggestive of the materiality of the text.

5. The scar of Orestes belongs not to Aeschylus's version, but is found in Euripides; nevertheless, as Groves and Granger argue, allusions to the Orsetes story draw on a web of intertexts.

6. 1 Corinthians 13:12: For now we see through a glass, darkly; but then face to face: now I know in part; but then shall I know even as also I am known.

7. Howard (Barthes 5) translates "le corselet d'un insecte" as "an insect's thorax," although corselet works in English as well.

8. See for instance Baroque era examples easily found in Google images of the dome fresco in the cathedral in Parma, Italy; the ceiling fresco of the baptistery in Padua Cathedral; the apse fresco in the Basilica di Santi Quattro Coronati in Rome. More recent examples include the Lady Chapel ceiling mural at the Basilica of the Sacred Heart at the University of Notre Dame in Indiana, and the dome fresco of the Hodges Chapel at the Beeson Divinity School at Samford University in Birmingham, Alabama.

Works Cited

Aeschylus. *Oresteia*. Trans. Robert Fagles. Introductory Essay, Notes, and Glossary by Robert Fagles and W. B. Stanford, Penguin, 1977.

Barthes, Roland. 'La Rochefoucauld: "Reflections or Sentences and Maxims"' in *New Critical Essays*, trans. R. Howard. Northwestern University Press, 2009. 3–22.

Birke, Dorothee and Birte Christ. "Paratext and Digitized Narrative: Mapping the Field." *Narrative* 21, no. 1, Jan. 2013, pp. 65–87. EBSCO*host*, chc.idm.oclc.org/login?url=http://search.ebscohost.com/login.aspx?direct=true&db=a9h&AN=84334424&site=eds-live. Accessed 3 Apr 2018.

Booth, Wayne C. *The Rhetoric of Fiction* (2nd ed.). Chicago: University of Chicago Press, 1983. p. 431.

Booth, Wayne C. "Who Is Responsible in Ethical Criticism?" in *Ethics, Literature, Theory: An Introductory Reader*, edited and introduction by Stephen K. George and Wayne C. (foreword). Booth, Rowman & Littlefield, 2005, pp. 79–98.

Booth, Wayne C. "Why Ethical Criticism Can Never Be Simple" in *Ethics, Literature, Theory: An Introductory Reader*, edited and introduction by Stephen K. George and Wayne C. (foreword). Booth, Rowman & Littlefield, 2005, pp. 23–35.

Cadden, Mike. "All Is Well: The Epilogue in Children's Fantasy Fiction." *Narrative*, vol. 20, no. 3 (October 2012), pp. 343–56. DOI: 10.1353/nar.2012.0018 Accessed 10 Dec. 2017.

Eco, Umberto. *On Literature*. Houghton Mifflin Harcourt, 2005.

Fagles, Robert, and W. B. Stanford. "A Reading of 'The Oresteia': The Serpent and the Eagle" in Aeschylus, *The Oresteia*. Trans. Robert Fagles. Introductory Essay, Notes, and Glossary by Robert Fagles and W. B. Stanford, Penguin, 1977. 13–97.

Fetterley, Judith. *The Resisting Reader: A Feminist Approach to American Fiction*. Indiana University Press, 1978.

Gennette, Gerard. *Paratexts: Thresholds of Interpretation*. Translated by Jane E. Lewin. Cambridge University Press, 1997.

Goodman, Leslie. "Rebellious Identification, or, How I Learned to Stop Worrying and Love Arabella." *Narrative*, vol. 18, no. 2 (May 2010): 163–78. http://www.jstor.org/stable/40856406 Accessed 27 Dec. 2017.

Granger, John. "The Aeschylus Epigraph in 'Deathly Hallows'" *Hogwarts Professor*, 20 Oct. 2008. http://www.hogwartsprofessor.com/the-aeschylus-epigraph-in-deathly-hallows/ Accessed 5 Dec 2017.

Granger, John. "'Deathly Hallows' and Penn's 'Fruits of Solitude'" *Hogwarts Professor*, 13 Oct. 2008. http://www.hogwartsprofessor.com/deathly-hallows-and-penns-fruits-of-solitude/ Accessed 5 Dec 2017.

Groves, Beatrice. *Literary Allusion in Harry Potter*. New York, 2017.

Johnson, Elizabeth. "Circle of Friends: A Closer Look at the Communion of Saints." *U.S. Catholic*, vol. 64, no. 11, Nov. 1999, pp. 12–18. EBSCO*host*, chc.idm.oclc.org/login?url=http://search.ebscohost.com/login.aspx?direct=true&db=a9h&AN=2460948&site=eds-live.

Johnston, Susan. "Harry Potter, Eucatastrophe, and Christian Hope." *Logos: A Journal of Catholic Thought & Culture*, vol. 14, no. 1, Winter 2011, pp. 66–90. EBSCO*host*, chc.idm.oclc.org/login?url=http://search.ebscohost.com/login.aspx?direct=true&db=a9h&AN=57631361&site=eds-live. Accessed 8 Dec. 2017.

Kakutani, Michiko. "An Epic Showdown as Harry Potter Is Initiated into Adulthood." *The New York Times*. 17 July 2007. https://www.nytimes.com/2007/07/19/books/19potter.html Accessed 3 Dec 2017.

Marshall, C.W. *Aeschylus: The Libation Bearers*. Edited by Thomas Harrison, Bloomsbury Academic, 2017. Companions to Greek and Roman Tragedy.

Penn, William. *Fruits of Solitude*. Vol. I. The Harvard Classics. P.F. Collier & Son, 1909.

Phelan, James. *Somebody Telling Somebody Else: A Rhetorical Poetics of Narrative*. Ohio State University Press, 2017.

Rowling, J. K. Interview with Shawn Adler, MTV News, 17 Oct. 2007. http://www.mtv.com/news/1572107/harry-potter-author-jk-rowling-opens-up-about-books-christian-imagery/.

Spencer, Richard. *Harry Potter and the Classical World: Greek and Roman Allusions in J. K. Rowling's Modern Epic*, McFarland, 2015.

6

COMMUNITIES OF INTERPRETATION IN JANE AUSTEN AND *HARRY POTTER*

Beatrice Groves

Proust, in his intimate portrait of the reading writer, writes of reading as a "fertile miracle of a communication affected in solitude. It enables us to receive "the communication of another's thought while still being on our own ... to be open to inspiration, with our minds still at work hard and fruit-fully on themselves" (208). Writers are readers too, and this chapter argues for the communication of J. K. Rowling's work with that of Jane Austen, her "favourite writer of all time" (*The Sunday Herald*). Additionally, it argues that the way characters interact with each other in Austen inflects the modes of communication in *Harry Potter*.

In *The Chamber of Secrets*, Ron warns that "some old witch in Bath had a book that you could *never stop reading!*" (231). Austen is trademarked as "Bath's most famous resident," and it seems plausible that this is why this literally un-put-downable book hails from Bath. Bharat Tandon has written of how Austen's prose, its riddles, its withholdings, and its surprises holds "within the texture of her narrative, invitations for disparate and successive readers to exercise their 'temper of mind'" (35). As previous commentators have explored, Rowling's debt to many aspects of Austen– her narrative voice, the gothic parody of *Northanger Abbey*, the sexual tension of *Pride and Prejudice*, the riddles of *Emma*—show how the 'temper' of Rowling's mind has responded to her own reading of Austen (Westman, Granger 23–40; Groves 98–120). Alberto Manguel calls the process of allusion the way "one book calls to another unexpectedly, creating alliances across different cultures and centuries" (14). Accordingly, books at Hogwarts are unusually conversational: some in the Restricted Section scream when opened illicitly, Ron and Harry's homework diaries are chirpily motivational, *Magick Moste Evile* wails when it is snapped shut, and Riddle's diary writes back to those who write in it. These are books that genuinely do "call out" to their readers and to each other: when Harry enters the Hogwarts library at night, he hears the books whispering to each other. This is a clue, perhaps, to the many ways that Rowling's writing communicates her reading.

Rowling's novels are in conversation with those of her most beloved author. This chapter argues that the communities of interpretation within Austen, from the small-town gossips of *Pride and Prejudice* to the networks of book readers within *Mansfield Park* and *Persuasion*, shape similar communities within *Harry Potter*. In Austen, as in Rowling, reading expresses "intellectual and moral development" (Westman 154) while gossip, which acts to subordinate individual insight to more tribal concerns, is viewed with distrust. The surveillance implicit within gossip, which tends to quash dissenting voices, stands in opposition to the way reading opens up new perspectives. While reading and gossip both involve the dissemination of knowledge and the negotiation of social identity, and both hold out the potential for the alignment of public and private spheres, they stand at opposite moral poles in both Austen (Michaelson) and *Harry Potter*. Communities of interpretation within *Harry Potter*, responding to Rowling's reading of Austen, are morally anchored by their engagement with the written word.

Gossip in *Pride and Prejudice* and *Goblet of Fire*

The Yule Ball in *Goblet of Fire* is a clear echo in *Harry Potter* of the balls that regularly punctuate Austen's narrative, acting as barometers for the feelings of the protagonists. The emotions that run riot at the Yule Ball, like those in *Pride and Prejudice*, *Emma*, and *Mansfield Park*, make it clear where Ron and Hermione's feelings for each other will eventually lead. (In a nice touch, when the Yule Ball is echoed in the final novel by the dance at Bill and Fleur's wedding, it is Ron who will be Hermione's dancing partner, while Krum is left watching from the sidelines.) These Austenian-style balls in *Harry Potter* are also occasions for gossip. Harry's peace is deeply wounded by the gossip he overhears about Dumbledore at the wedding dance in *Deathly Hallows*, echoing the over-hearings of Austen's balls. Elizabeth Bennet is clearly more affected that she acknowledges by overhearing that, for the judgmental Darcy, she is "tolerable, but not handsome enough to tempt me." The Yule Ball is likewise a focus for gossip and the rumors "flying everywhere" (391), including the idea that Dumbledore has ordered stupendous quantities of mulled mead, a rumor that recalls the claim that Mr. Bingley will bring vast numbers of ladies and gentlemen to the ball in *Pride and Prejudice* (and which, likewise, proves false).

Pride and Prejudice opens with one of the most quoted first lines of any novel but, as often happens when art becomes ossified by fame, important nuances have been lost in its translation into proverb. In this case, however, this is a peculiarly fitting fate as it is a line about the false conclusions reached by group-think. An underlying argument of *Pride and Prejudice* is that a "truth universally acknowledged" is meaningless until parsed by individuals. Austen's novel repeatedly stresses the importance of judging for oneself, as when Elizabeth, "since her being at Lambton, had heard that Miss Darcy was exceedingly proud; but the observation of a very few minutes convinced her that she was only exceedingly shy" (212). The opening ball, with its emphasis on overhearing, misinterpretation, and the shifting sands of popular opinion, sets the tone for the novel's interrogation of the universally acknowledged "truth" of its opening line. Secondhand ideas will be repeatedly proven false, from the unimportant (Mr. Bingley has only two sisters) to the crucial (Jane is in love with him). This opening ball indicates how very easily Meryton will be manipulated when Mr. Wickham arrives to spread deliberate falsehood: Mr. Darcy has not treated Wickham shamefully, and "every body"—who luxuriate in self-satisfaction at "how much they had always disliked Mr. Darcy before they had known anything of the matter"—is quite mistaken to think so (117).

The pleasures and perils of gossip are a *leit motif* in *Goblet of Fire* just as in *Pride and Prejudice*. This novel, likewise, opens with a universally acknowledged truth, the Little Hangletons all agreed that the old house was "creepy," and with a clear caution about such collective opinions: "The story had been picked over so many times, and had been embroidered in so many places, that nobody was quite sure what the truth was anymore" (1). The gossips who frequent the Hanged Man, Rowling's village inn as full of misinformation as Austen's inn at Lambton, accept the universal truth that outcasts must have done something to deserve it. They quickly find Frank Bryce guilty of the Riddle murders. Little Hangleton's character assassination of Bryce echoes Meryton's of Darcy. The Cook's assertion that "if I've offered him a cuppa once, I've offered it a hundred times" (3) recalls Mrs. Bennet's "Mrs. Long told me last night that he sat close to her for half-an-hour without once opening his lips." Both exaggerations underline the extent to which small communities judge those who do not play by their rules. The confirmation bias of appearance is accepted in both novels as if it were independent testimony—"I always thought that he had a nasty look" in *Goblet* (3) and "besides, there was truth in [Mr. Wickham's] looks" in *Pride and Prejudice* (73). In particular, confirmation for an adult crime is irrationally sought in the belief that the accused was an unpleasant child. Dot recalls that Frank Bryce had a "horrible temper . . . when he was a kid" (3); and Mrs. Gardiner (an otherwise irreproachable character), seeking confirmation for Mr. Wickham's claims against Darcy, recollects that she had formerly heard him *"spoken of as a very proud, ill-natured boy"* (121; italics mine). This is the final sentence of the chapter, and white space might give readers pause, prompting them to realize that Mrs. Gardiner is remembering Lambton gossip, not her own experience. (Indeed, when readers encounter someone who actually *knew* Darcy as a child, they will access a very different account.)

It is noticeable that Austen's use of the Anglo-Saxon place-name "-ton" (meaning "enclosed village") for the two centers of gossip in *Pride and Prejudice* (Meryton and Lambton) is echoed in Rowling's Little Hangleton. Gossip flourishes in small, tight-knit communities, and the ill-formed rumors at the beginning of both novels lay the groundwork for a character who will enter the community and attempt to wreck the networks of trust within it. In the case of *Goblet*, this is Rita Skeeter. Rita is a gossip-monger. As Mr. Weasley points out, she generates "news" by self-reporting her own rumors. She enters the series strategically at this stage because in *Goblet*, as Rowling has noted, "Harry's horizons are literally and metaphorically widening" ("Entertainment"). The novel's newly international focus links with the way that Harry has to contend with fame in a newly problematic way as he ages. The notice strangers take of him up to this point is relatively benign. All eyes are habitually drawn to him, as they are to Darcy, but from this point in the series, from Mr. Diggory's unthinking antagonism at the start of the novel, to the literally poisonous hate mail inflicted on Hermione by Harry's admirers, fame's darker side will be revealed.

Pride and Prejudice never explicitly rejects its opening sentence, but its universally acknowledged idea is only realized in the plot through the true feelings of individuals. In *Goblet*, likewise, Ron, Mrs. Weasley and the whole of the student body have to learn to test the seductive plausibility of general opinion (as voiced by Rita Skeeter) against their personal knowledge of Harry and Hermione. Rowling uses metaphor and simile, for example, the acid green of Rita's quill, or the way in which rumors fly "from student to student like highly contagious germs," to underline the corrosive and harmful effects of gossip (236). Austen's narrative, however, triumphs over gossip in an even more subtle and satisfying manner. While half-truths, overhearing and secondhand opinions have separated Darcy and Elizabeth, Austen's *coup-de-grace* is that it is the gossip network that separated them will unwittingly unite them. Readers can't trace exactly how the rumor mill has hit on the accurate idea that Darcy wants to marry Elizabeth, but Lady Catherine's response to these rumors enables the protagonists to discover the truth of their own hearts and each other. Lady Catherine threatens Elizabeth with the shaming gossip that will attend her union, and when she reports back Elizabeth's magnificent disdain of these threats to her nephew, Darcy understands that Elizabeth's feelings have truly changed towards him.

Reading at Hogwarts and Mansfield Park

Lady Catherine is far from being the worst aunt in Jane Austen, a dubious distinction that belongs to *Mansfield Park*'s Mrs. Norris, the source, of course, of the name of one Hogwarts' most unpleasant inhabitants, the cat who always accompanies Hogwarts caretaker Argus Filch (Groves 108–10). Aunt Norris's moral bankruptcy is perfectly encapsulated by her decision not to give a book to her god-daughter:

> There had been at one moment a slight murmur in the drawing-room at Mansfield Park, about sending her a Prayer-book; but no second sound had been heard of such a purpose. Mrs. Norris, however, had gone home and

taken down two old Prayer-books of her husband with that idea, but upon examination, the ardour of generosity went off. One was found to have too small a print for a child's eyes, and the other to be too cumbersome for her to carry about. (380)

In both Austen and Rowling, books and reading have a strong moral valency (Westman 154; Martin). Many of Austen's heroines are passionate bibliophiles. Hermione's predecessors include Catherine Moreland, Anne Elliot, and Marianne Dashwood, but books hold their greatest moral importance, perhaps, for Fanny Price of *Mansfield Park*. She has collected them "from the first hour of her commanding a shilling," and her childhood spent reading with her cousin Edmund nurtures her love for him (173). Reading is also something Fanny longs to share in her renewed relationship with her sister in the course of the novel. When she is exiled from Mansfield to a house that (like Privet Drive) is as empty of books as of parental affection, Fanny joins a library, longing to give Susan "a share in her own first pleasures" (391).

In *Mansfield Park*, as in *Harry Potter*, the protagonist's loved places (Mansfield Park, the Burrow, Diagon Alley, Hogwarts) are full of the books that are noticeably absent in the novels' psychologically unsafe spaces (Portsmouth, Privet Drive). In both Austen novels and *Harry Potter*, there is strongly moral understanding of reading. Dudley, Harry's fairy-tale-style ugly brother, for example, "never read anything" (*SS* 80). In *Mansfield Park*, each character's morality is even more precisely marked by his or her attitude toward books. Lady Bertram falls asleep while they are read to her; Mr. Rushworth knows nothing of them; and Mr. Crawford, the moral dilettante, displays intuitive skill in reading *Henry VIII*, but this turns out to be the first time he has touched Shakespeare since he was fifteen (as if to indicate that he *could* be virtuous, but he will not put in the effort). Tom, meanwhile, thinks nothing of moving the bookcase in Sir Thomas's room to stage *Lover's Vows*, a subtle marker of the difference between the father and the son's moral attitudes.

Harry and Fanny, as Karin E. Westman has noted, both "experience a Cinderella-like exchange of one home for another" (152), and their new adoptive home becomes, emotionally speaking, their true home. Fanny is sensitive about her slip when she refers to Mansfield Park as "home" when she is in Portsmouth (though her parents, characteristically, do not even notice). "Portsmouth was Portsmouth; Mansfield was home" for her (421). Harry, likewise, finds his home at Hogwarts, not in the house where he grew up.

Harry is "home at last" (*PA* 95) when he returns to Hogwarts. And, later, he arrives home again: "he *was* home. Hogwarts was the first and best home he has known" (*DH* 697). Rowling extends the psychological safety of Hogwarts to readers in her famous promise that "Hogwarts will always be there to welcome you home" ("Statement"). Both Harry and Fanny's new homes house superb libraries, and sharing books is, above all else, morally coded by both Austen and Rowling. Hagrid, one of Harry's most beloved friends, first takes him into a bookshop, "stacked to the ceiling with books as large as paving stones bound in leather; books the size of postage stamps in covers of silk; books full of peculiar symbols and a few books with nothing in them at all" (*SS* 80). It is a subtle sign of the Dursley's cruelty that they have not even allowed Harry to join a library. Edmund similarly shows Fanny around the library of her new home, and this transition to Mansfield Park, like Harry's entry to the Wizarding World is a doorway into the commonwealth of reading. Harry's subsequent naming of his owl, Hedwig, after "a name he had found in *A History of Magic*" (*SS* 88) marks how books become a fundamental part of Harry's engagement with his new life.

Books within Books: *Persuasion* and *Order of the Phoenix*

Hermione is, of course, *Harry Potter*'s great bibliophile, but it is noticeable the extent to which she shares her reading with her friends, constantly updating them with facts from *Hogwarts: A History*, the marginalia of *Beedle*, or the footnotes of *Secrets of the Darkest Art*. The loving relationships in *Harry Potter* often include reading. Books are regularly given as gifts among Harry's group of friends; Ron's family (unlike Harry's or Voldemort's) read him bedtime stories when he was a child; and Harry, Ron, and Hermione set out on a great fact-finding "library quest" together in most of the novels.

Sharing books is likewise characteristic of the admirable characters in *Persuasion*. Anne eagerly discusses them with Captains Benwick and Harville, while Lady Russell lends her books to Elizabeth, who, characteristically, sneers at her for it. "You may as well take back that tiresome book she would lend me, and pretend I have read it through," she tells Anne (221). Anne, a poetic reader of great sensitivity, is marooned in a home in which only one book interests the rest of her family. *Persuasion* opens, as it habitual to Austen, with a family history, but in this novel, uniquely, it happens through the medium of a book:

> Sir Walter Elliot, of Kellynch-hall, in Somersetshire, was a man who, for his
> own amusement, never took up any book but the Baronetage ... this was the
> page at which the favorite volume always opened:
>
> ELLIOT OF KELLYNCH-HALL.
>
> Walter Elliot, born March 1, 1760, married, July 15, 1784, Elizabeth, daughter
> of James Stevenson, Esq. of South Park, in the county of Gloucester; by which
> lady (who died 1800) he has issue Elizabeth, born June 1, 1785; Anne, born
> August 9, 1787; a still-born son, Nov. 5, 1789; Mary, born Nov. 20, 1791. (35)

Like Anne, Sirius Black has been raised in home in which only one book,
another book of genealogy, takes pride of place. Mrs. Black, like Sir Walter,
does not read to learn about other perspectives, but only to cement her
sense of her own importance; and Sirius, like Anne, silently underlines his
difference from the rest of his family through his ownership of books. Both
families are aristocratic and consider their family the pinnacle of their own
notions of nobility. Elizabeth's "strong family pride could see only in *him* [Mr.
Elliot], a proper match for Sir Walter Elliot's eldest daughter" (40), while the
Black family is "convinced that to be a Black made you practically royal" (*OP*
111). The cold-hearted heads of the Black and the Elliot families hold their
family pride dear, and both believe that it is the favored sibling (Elizabeth,
Regulus) who alone will bring honor to the family name. *Nature's Nobility:
A Wizarding Genealogy* appears to be the only book owned by Mrs. Black,
and it seems likely that, like Sir Walter's *Baronetage*, it would have habitually
fallen open at her own name.

   Austen's fictional *Baronetage* is closely modeled on real volumes, and
her Elliot entry is a composite creation, formed from the clipped entries of
Debrett's Peerage (1806) and the more discursive *English Baronetage* (1741).
The entry for "Eliot" in *Debrett's*, for example, has some striking parallels
with Sir Walter's favorite entry:

> Richard Eliot, esq. died in 1748; married, in March, 1726, Harriet, daughter of
> James Craggs, esq. secretary of state to George I. by whom (who died in 1769)
> he had issue E[d]ward Eliot, the first lord Eliot, who was created a baron Jan.
> 30, 178—Richard, who died young—John, died unmarried—Anne, married
> captain Bonfoy, of the royal navy, by whom she was left a widow. (1.332)

As with *Persuasion*'s fictional entry, this record ends with a blank after "*Heir Apparent*," ready for the owner's annotation. It is striking that the real Anne Eliot married a naval captain (whose name is a charming and hopeful inversion of "Malfoy") and tempting to wonder if this entry in *Debrett's* lies behind the sobering intimations of Anne's future widowhood, the "dread of a future war" with which *Persuasion* closes.

Sir Walter's *Baronetage* also shares stylistic similarities with the more discursive *English Baronetage*. Both Baronetages run through the historical achievements of each family and conclude "with the arms and motto" (36) and principal seat of the family. The arms and motto of the Black family adorn the china in Grimmauld Place and are embossed on its silver goblets and a large golden ring, but in an eloquent silence that matches that of *Persuasion*, the reader is not told what they are. Rowling, however, added them extratextually to her 2006 hand-drawn family tree of "The Noble and Most Ancient House of Black." Rowling's fictional nobility, like Austen's, engages with and critiques real aristocratic traditions, and the Black family motto, *Toujours pur* (always pure), is closely modeled on real mottos: *Toujours propice* (always propitious) and *Toujours prest* (always ready) as well as the simple, Snape-like *Toujours* (always) (*Debrett's* 1.lxxiii).

The 2006 Black family tree contains clues, and one of them lies in its engagement with "canting" heraldry. This is a tradition, particularly beloved of sixteenth-century aristocrats, in which arms punned on the family name (such as Sir Francis Bacon's heraldic badge of a pig). In the tradition of canting heraldry, the Black arms have a sable (black) field, and its supporters are dogs, pointing to the family name Sirius. However, more subtly, the arms bear the charge of two stars. The fact there are *two* stars on the escutcheon suggests that Sirius may not be the only Black who has the potential to shine. Alongside Sirius, the brightest star in the sky, his brother Regulus Arcturus, named after less well-known but nonetheless bright star, may yet shine free of his Black origins. His name, perhaps, also brings us back to Austen for in a peaceful moment of star gazing with Fanny, Edmund observes that "there's Arcturus looking very bright" (139).

The moral value that Rowling and Austen both place on books is linked to their medium, but, more fundamentally, it responds to the deeply rooted importance of the "Book" in Christian culture. *Persuasion*'s moral censure of Sir Walter's myopic reading is underlined by the irony of what this book *should* be. It would have been common, of course, for a nineteenth-century

household to own and read only one book, a book in which, like the Baronetage, the family births, marriages, and deaths would have been inscribed
by the head of the family, a book in which the reader could hope to find
consolation in a distressed hour, as Sir Walter does, a book known (just as
the Baronetage is) as "the book of books" (35, 38). The way Sir Walter has
substituted the *Baronetage* for the *Bible* sharpens Austen's satire; and perhaps
there is the faintest echo of this condemnation in the single, heavy volume
which takes pride of place in Grimmauld.

Austen, Rowling, and Their Readers

Emma is Rowling's favorite novel, and a joke from it appears to have been
lurking in her mind as she mused over her new *nom-de-plume*: "When I was
a child, I really wanted to be called 'Ella Galbraith' . . . I actually considered
calling myself L.A. Galbraith for the Strike series" (Galbraith). The punning
idea of substituting the letters "L A" for "Ella" may well have been suggested
by Mr. Weston's almost identical pun in *Emma*: "What two letters of the
alphabet are there, that express perfection?. . . . M. and A.—Em-ma.—Do
you understand?" (255–56). As I noted in *Literary Allusion in Harry Potter*,
the many riddles of *Emma* have left their trace on *Harry Potter*—Mr. Elton's
charade is echoed in the Sphinx's riddle, and the anonymous gift of the piano
forte by the gift of the Firebolt. But there is another reason that Austen is a
peculiarly fitting source for Rowling's putative alias, for the confidence of
Austen's authorial voice appears to have inspired Rowling.

The most celebrated of Austen's authorial interventions is her defense of
her chosen medium: "'Oh! It is only a novel!' . . . in short, only some work in
which the greatest powers of the mind are displayed, in which the most thor-
ough knowledge of human nature, the happiest delineation of its varieties, the
liveliest effusions of wit and humour are conveyed to the world in the best
chosen language" (*Northanger Abbey* 34). Rowling, likewise, inserts a defense
and a high claim for the moral value of her chosen medium in the final *Harry
Potter* novel. Dumbledore asserts, "That which Voldemort does not value, he
takes no trouble to comprehend. Of house-elves and children's tales, of love,
loyalty, and innocence, Voldemort knows and understands nothing. *Nothing.*
That they all have a power beyond his own, a power beyond the reach of any
magic, is a truth he has never grasped" (*DH* 709–10).

Contiguous with Austen and Rowling's strong authorial presence is the similarity in their response to a readership hungry for more detail about their novels. Austen would, if asked, tell us many little particulars about the subsequent career of some of her people. In this traditional way we learned that Miss Steele never succeeded in catching the Doctor; that Kitty Bennet was satisfactorily married to a clergyman near Pemberley . . . and that the letters placed by Frank Churchill before Jane Fairfax, which she swept away unread, contained the word "pardon." (Austen-Leigh 376).

Rowling, similarly, has revealed many extratextual details, and these include both insights about the "subsequent career" of her characters— Teddy was raised by Andromeda Tonks or Luna went on to marry Rolf Scamander—and explanations of things that are not explicit in the text, such as the smell Hermione almost lets slip when she is describing Amortentia ("Bloomsbury"). Both authors attempt to extend authorial control of meaning beyond the text. Once Rowling went so far in an interview as to suggest that her interpretation is the only correct one: "Did he actually laugh? Yes, I would say he did. Well, he did, because I've created him" ("Leaky").

Rowling has imagined her own authorship in an Austenian mold ("BBC") and is interested in Austen's life as well as her novels (she owns Austen's letters and at least one biography). As critics have noted, Austen's own tongue-in-cheek verdict on *Pride and Prejudice*, as "rather too light & bright & sparkling," seems recalled in the opening description of Dumbledore's eyes as "light, bright and sparkling" (Faye 203; Westman 145). And it is intriguing that *Harry Potter's* first Austen allusion should be not to the novels but to Austen's own voice.

Austen's phrase wittily makes light of her own achievement, and Rowling's allusion transmits some of the brio of the original. The phrase is Austen's knowing undersell of arguably English literature's most enjoyable novel, and it is also a knowing undersell of Dumbledore's eyes. Eyes are windows into the soul in the *Harry Potter* series, and this apparently incidental description of Dumbledore's eyes begins one of the circles of the series. When Dumbledore's gaze returns in *The Deathly Hallows* after his death (in the mirror fragment, in the Pensieve, and at King's Cross), it is with words that echo this off-handed opening description of them as "light, bright and sparkling." Harry notes that "the *bright* blue eyes of Albus Dumbledore would never pierce him again"; that "the mirror fragment fell *sparkling* to the floor, and he saw a gleam of *brightest* blue"; that "his tone was *light*, but his blue eyes pierced Snape"; and that "tears still *sparkled* in the brilliantly blue eyes" (*DH* 29, 466, 683, 713). *Harry Potter*'s first allusion to Austen underlines both the importance of Dumbledore's eyes and of Austen's influence on the series. Eyes as symbols of truth-telling, as markers of spiritual vision, link *Harry Potter* with many of the novels' literary forebears, from Dante and Spenser to alchemical writings and Elizabeth Goudge, and in all these works the reader learns the truth from their gaze (Granger 257–86; Groves xvii).

Rowling's love of Austen taught her to value a number of aspects of Austen's world-building that make both Austen's and Rowling's novels attractive to their readership, such as the primacy of emotional truth, using the hero as a focalizing point for the narrative, the emphasis on dialogue and narrative slow-release which rewards readers for paying attention to detail. Austen and Rowling share in uniting a strong moral core to their writing with a witty lightness of touch in its presentation, with using dialogue to move the plot forward without weighing it down. Rowling's novels, like Austen's, are novels of education in which the protagonist learns truths about themselves, as well as about the world around them.

They also share, as this essay has argued, communities of interpretation. The small-town gossips of *Pride and Prejudice* and the networks of book readers in *Mansfield Park* and *Persuasion* shape the relationships in *Harry Potter*. In Austen, as in Rowling, gossip, which acts to subordinate individual insight to more tribal concerns, is often viewed with distrust, while reading expresses "intellectual and moral development" (Westman 154). The surveillance implicit within gossip, which tends to quash dissenting voices and embrace false rumors, stands in opposition to the way reading opens up new perspectives. While gossip and reading both involve the dissemination of knowledge and the negotiation of social identity, and both hold out the potential for the alignment of public and private spheres, they stand at opposite moral poles in both Austen (Michaelson) and *Harry Potter*. The communities of interpretation within *Harry Potter*, responding to Rowling's reading of Austen, are morally anchored by their engagement with the written word.

Works Cited

Austen, Jane. *Emma*. Ed. R. Blythe. Harmondsworth: Penguin, 1966 [1816].
Austen, Jane. *Mansfield Park*. Ed. Tony Tanner. Harmondsworth: Penguin, 1986 [1814].
Austen, Jane. *Northanger Abbey*. Ed. Marilyn Butler. Harmondsworth: Penguin, 1995 [1818].

Austen, Jane. *Persuasion*. Ed. D. W. Harding. Harmondsworth: Penguin, 1965 [1818].

Austen, Jane. *Pride and Prejudice*. Ed. V. Jones. Harmondsworth: Penguin, 1995 [1813].

Austen-Leigh, J. E. "A Memoir of Jane Austen" in Jane Austen, *Persuasion*, edited by D. W. Harding. Harmondsworth: Penguin, 1965 [1818].

Debrett's Peerage of England, Scotland and Ireland [. . .]. 2 vols. London, 1806.

The English Baronetage [. . .]. 5 vols. London, 1741.

Faye, D. Le. Ed. *Jane Austen's Letters*. 3rd edition. Oxford: Oxford University Press, 1995.

Finch, Casey, and Bowen, Peter. "'The Tittle-Tattle of Highbury: Gossip and Free Indirect Style in *Emma*." *Representations* 31, 1990, 1–18.

Galbraith, Robert [aka J. K. Rowling]. FAQ answers. http://robert-galbraith.com/about/.

Granger, John. *Harry Potter's Bookshelf: The Great Books Behind the Hogwarts Adventures*. New York: Berkley, 2009.

Groves, Beatrice. *Literary Allusion in Harry Potter*. London: Routledge, 2017.

Manguel, Alberto. *The Library at Night*. Toronto: A. A. Knopf, 2006.

Martin, David. "The Role of Books in the Hogwarts Saga." http://www.hogwartsprofessor.com/guest-post-david-martin-reveals-the-role-of-books-in-the-hogwarts-saga/.

Michaelson, Patricia Howell. *Speaking Volumes: Women, Reading and Speech in the Age of Austen*. Stanford: Stanford University Press, 2002.

Proust, Marcel. *Against Sainte-Beuve and other Essays*. Trans. John Sturrock. Harmondsworth: Penguin, 1994 [1954].

Rowling, J. K. Interview, *Book Links*, July 1999. http://www.accio-quote.org/articles/1999/0799-booklinks-omalley.html.

Rowling, J. K. Interview, *The Sunday Herald*, 21 May 2000. http://www.accio-quote.org/articles/2000/autobiography.html.

Rowling, J. K. Interview, *Entertainment Weekly*, 7 Sept 2000. http://www.accio-quote.org/articles/2000/0900-ew-jensen.htm.

Rowling, J. K. Interview, *BBC Newsnight*, 19 June 2003. http://www.accio-quote.org/articles/2003/0619-bbcnews-paxman.htm.

Rowling, J. K. Interview, Leaky Cauldron, 16 July 2005 (part 2). http://www.the-leaky-cauldron.org/features/interviews/jkr2.

Rowling, J. K. Bloomsbury Live Chat, July 30, 2007. http://www.accio-quote.org/articles/2007/0730-bloomsbury-chat.html.

Rowling, J. K. Statement at premier of *Deathly Hallows* film, 7 July 2011. https://www.youtube.com/watch?v=CYVJjpk2fso.

Rowling, J. K. "The Noble and Most Ancient House of Black" (2006). https://imgur.com/GbPzUmg.

Tandon, Bharat. *Jane Austen and the Morality of Conversation*. London: Anthem, 2003.

Westman, Karin E. "Perspective, Memory, and Moral Authority: The Legacy of Jane Austen in J. K. Rowling's *Harry Potter*." *Children's Literature*, vol. 35, 2007, 145–65.

7

THE RUSSIAN FORMALIST HEART OF THE *HARRY POTTER* SERIES

John Granger

The Nobel Prize in Literature has a storied history as the most important recognition an author can receive, but it has taken quite a few hits of late with respect to its respectability. First there was the controversy when Bob Dylan was awarded the 2016 prize; many traditionalists felt the vagabond songster, however obscure in his lyrics, was insufficiently literary or serious for this honor. Then the committee that chooses the recipient each year was hit in April 2018 with its own #MeToo moment.[1] Consequently, there wasn't a 2018 prize, and the Academy offered up two prizes in 2019 to make up for lost time.

What to do, though, with the lost year? The thinking behind the New Academy Prize in Literature was both to fill the breach and to offer an implicit criticism of the elitism of all things Nobel. How about offering an *alternative* Nobel Prize for literature without the progressive agenda and old-school prejudices of the Academy? The decisions would ultimately be made by a panel, the process included a plebiscite of sorts online—we got a vote!—and the panel included the relatively humble presence of librarians instead of literati.

I bring all this up because J. K. Rowling was nominated for the 2018 New Academy Prize along with forty other authors; news coverage of the New Academy Prize inevitably mentioned her first among nominees, perhaps because of how recognizable her name is, perhaps to highlight that the New Academy Prize is not your grandfather's Nobel in Literature.[2] Which is to say, "J. K. Rowling, super-popular but no serious writer, would never have made the finalists list for the *real* Nobel Prize in Literature." Rowling didn't make the finalists list for the alternative prize (though "genre" fantasy writer Neil Gaiman did).[3] But why the whiff of patronizing dismissal in the fact that she was even nominated?

The simple fact is, though no living author's work has ever been the subject of as much critique as have Rowling's *Harry Potter* novels, this tsunami of attention has done very little to raise her reputation as a writer. Besides the rush of new work in the field—I think of Shira Wolosky's *Riddles of Harry Potter*, Beatrice Groves's *Literary Allusion in Harry Potter*, and Patrick McCauley's *Into the Pensieve*—few of the quality anthologized essays or book-length treatments that take Harry and his creator seriously as literature have penetrated the public or media mind.

The neat solution to the problem of Rowling not being taken seriously as an intentional writer is to take the most rigorous school of literary criticism and apply its tools to a very close reading of Rowling's work. The school I'm thinking of is usually called "Russian formalism," and there are good reasons for thinking this relatively obscure branch of critical history is apt and important for establishing Rowling's bona fides as even a Nobel-worthy author.

For one thing, formalism is solely about literary artistry and effect. As Rene Welleck wrote in 1954:

> Russian Formalism keeps the work of art itself in the center of attention: it sharply emphasizes the difference between literature and life, it rejects the usual biographical, psychological, and sociological explanations of literature. It develops highly ingenious methods for analyzing works of literature and for tracing the history of literature in its own terms. (qtd in Erlich 9)

The formalist school demands that the author's ability to transcend autobiographical projection and cultural influences and to write a work *about* such things be taken seriously and that the work be examined on its own terms, as if it had no author or historical context. A little overboard? Maybe. But this perspective simultaneously corrects for the excesses of prevalent critical schools today while offering an interpretation that is so pervasively literary that its judgment might correct the Cinderella story and kid lit writer albatrosses Rowling has not been able to shake.

Perhaps equally important, Rowling may be a formalist author, albeit neither Russian nor a devotee of the critics most associated with this movement, Viktor Shklovsky, Roman Jakobson, and Mikhail Bakhtin. Two of her favorite authors and most notable influences, Vladimir Nabokov and C. S. Lewis, were academic formalists at prestigious universities whose novels reflect their beliefs about what literature is and how it works.[4] Nabokov expert Michael Maar has written that Nabokov would have loved *Harry Potter*,[5] and I suspect he is right, for all the reasons he gives *and* because Rowling embeds in every book texts that the characters struggle to read and understand, mirroring reflections of our efforts to figure out her text and understand it. Think of Harry's first Chocolate Frog card, Tom Riddle's Diary, the Prophecy, *The Life and Lies of Albus Dumbledore*, and *Tales of Beedle the Bard*, not to mention every trip into the Pensieve. And consider Rowling's other writings—the online postings of Barry Fairbrother in *Casual Vacancy*, or, my favorite, *Bombyx Mori* in *The Silkworm*, the novel with the same name as the novel we're reading that isn't by the male author who is supposed to have written it but the bitter, overlooked woman not taken seriously as a writer (can you say Galbraith-Rowling?).

Rowling is, like Lewis and Nabokov, a parodist, a lover of literary allusion and polyvalent names, and a writer writing about writing and reading in each and every book and screenplay she writes. The tools of the formalist school, consequently, are important keys for unlocking her work and revealing her literary merits. To begin, two important Russian formalist words for Potter pundits to add their magical vocabulary are *syuzhet* and *fabula*, the complementary antagonists of all story telling. *Syuzhet* is the story-as-told and *fabula* the story-in-actual-chronological-sequence that the reader creates out of the story-as-told or as the characters in their universe experience them chronologically. The *syuzhet* is the story-teller's art and the *fabula* either the order of events re-created by the author or the interpretation a reader makes to understand the story events in a natural timeline. *Syuzhet* is the object of critical study, the deliberate storytelling and use of literary devices that make a story more than a police report. It is the author's intentional craft; to the formalist, nothing else about a work matters, to include the existence of the author or any predicates of the work's composition.

Because a Nobel Prize winner should be, above all, a literary craftsman of great accomplishment, the point of a formalist look at Rowling's work is to establish that she is more than a children's storyteller, a whiz-bang fabulist;

she writes consummately planned novels in which the actual story events are brilliantly represented, obscured, and revealed by various structures, symbol sets, and sequencing for the most engaging and transformative reader experience. I depart from a formalist reading for a moment to share the author's opinion of her own artistry. She has said repeatedly and consistently through more than twenty years of interviews that "meticulous" planning is the core of her work as a writer.[6] In an interview in 2018 she answered a question about whether she experiences changes in her original direction consequent to "discovery" while writing. Her response? "I don't . . . I don't change my mind . . . I do very, very detailed plans."[7] She confessed in a 2014 interview that she chose to write crime fiction "because I love crime fiction, I've always loved it, I read a lot of it. And I think that the *Harry Potter* books are really whodunnits in disguise."[8]

But you can forget what she *says*. Everything Rowling *writes* is about obscuring *fabula* via *syuzhet*. What is involved in writing great detective fiction? Read any guide to this genre and they all say the same thing. Write the *fabula* or police-report version of the story as clearly as you can, the murder as committed and concealed, and then create the story as told, the *syuzhet*, usually from the discovery of the body forward, as the point by point, clues, logic, and events leading to revelation of the writer's starting point, *fabula*, at the finish. And the closer to the finish that this revelation comes, the better. There is no genre more dependent on the *syuzhet-fabula* distinction, in other words, than Rowling's favorite, and it informs everything she writes.

It goes further than genre selection, however. Rowling is special, if not unique, in the depth of her concerns about planning and making her *syuzhet* retelling of the basic *fabula* a cathartic experience of discovery for the reader. It goes so far that she embeds in her stories reflections of the writer's efforts at this, the reader's struggle to unwind the narrative to get to the facts, and, in one extraordinary case, one writer-character's actual discussion of the distinction. Every *Harry Potter* novel, for instance, is about the Terrible Trio's up-and-down journey to figuring out that school year's core mystery. As often as not, it turns on a core text that they have to understand, a detail of which escapes them (the Chocolate Frog Card in *SS*, *Tales of Beedle the Bard* in *DH*), the narrative trickery they overlook (the Diary in *SS*, the text in *HBP*), or the meaning they either deny, misinterpret, or don't want to face, most notably the Prophecy, the ur-text of Harry's life and battle with the Dark Lord. *Casual Vacancy* similarly turns on the texts of the departed

Barry Fairbrother and what each character makes of his messages. *Cuckoo's Calling* revolves around the search for Lula's will, you might say, and all of *Silkworm* is the search for the meaning of Owen Quine's *Bombyx Mori* in its rewritten form.

Why does Hermione go to the lengths of freeing Rita Skeeter to write up her *Tattler* interview of Harry Potter in *Goblet of Fire*? Because the Ministry's *syuzhet* via the *Daily Prophet* about the Dark Lord's re-appearance and Harry being a loose wing-nut had so obscured the *fabula* that she had to take some kind of direct action to create an accurate counternarrative to begin to wake up the inattentive readers of the Wizarding World's news. Rowling's unobscured disdain for the news media is based on her writer's awareness that *syuzhet* must eventually reveal *fabula* rather than forever remaining biased spin. In *The Silkworm*, a character overtly takes on the *syuzhet-fabula* distinction. The hapless author-blogger Kathryn Kent, a writer I have speculated is a stand-in for Rowling,[9] posts on her weblog in *Silkworm* the only note of a writer-about-writing in the Rowling catalogue. Kent makes the plot-for-*fabula* miscue I mentioned earlier:

> Great talk with TFW about Plot and Narrative tonight which are of course not the same thing. For those wondering: Plot is what happens, Narrative is how much you show your readers and how you show it to them.
>
> An example from my second novel "Melina's Sacrifice."
>
> *As they made their way towards the Forest of Harderell Lendor raised his handsome profile to see how near they were to it. His well-maintained body, honed by horseback riding and archery skills—.* (66)

Garbled as Kent's definitions may be, this is definitely the formalist distinction between *fabula*-story and *syuzhet*-plot or narrative, highlighting both the facts that the reader has to get straight postnarrative as well as the artistry that makes the story literary—by defamiliarizing or just refreshing the reader's perspective.

Defamiliarization or *ostranenie* is the goal of literature according to the formalists. Viktor Shklovsky, a formalist from the post-Russian Revolution decades in the mid-twentieth century, introduced a literary technique he dubbed "the Knight's Move." Unlike the straightforward movement of the rook or bishop, the knight changes direction, turning ninety degrees to left or right from its original path on the chessboard. Shklovsky argues that the writers' "knight's move" is their break with convention and reader expectation, a break that "defamiliarizes" a reader's experience of the narrative sufficiently to create an awareness of the work's "literariness." The point of this surprise or shock, according to formalist theory, is to "'make strange' the world of every day perception and [thereby renew] the reader's lost capacity for fresh sensation" (Abrams 107).

A little critical equivalent of a poet's sudden shift in rhyme scheme, a screenwriter's breaking the fourth wall, or a novelist's unexpected departure from or blending of genre conventions is a knight's move of comparing and contrasting the work of writers who appear to have little in common—say, Nabokov and Rowling. The surprise implicit in comparing literary apples and elevators, the seemingly unrelated, has the effect, in theory at least, of all but forcing attentive readers into fresh appreciation of both of the authors in view as well as into increased awareness of their former understanding and its tired limitations.

The problem in the human condition as the formalists see it, the problem that art and literature address, is the distance from reality in human cognition consequent to mental habit, the ruts in our thinking created by repeated experience that keep us from encountering the world as it is, freshly in each moment. The author's job, as Coleridge puts it in his *Biographia Literaria*, is to remove the "film of familiarity" that cloaks and separates us from firsthand encounter with the world and relationships: "[Coleridge describes] the 'prime merit' of a literary genius to be the representation of 'familiar objects' so as to evoke 'freshness of sensation'" (Abrams 108). Our automatized thinking is best broken by imaginative defamiliarization.

Rowling's choice of the fantasy genre, to "make strange" through an enchanted world inside our own Muggle existence, reenchants a secularized, atheist existence. Her "Knight's Moves" are the genre mélange and departures from formula but especially the "Big Twist" at the end of every *Potter* and *Strike* novel where we learn that we "didn't see what we thought we saw!" The joy of discovery continues along these lines in rereadings, where we find the "Easter eggs" or hidden references and allusions to future events and realities that we missed on our first (or fifth) readings.

The primary means to *ostranenie* celebrated by the formalists was *literaturnost* or "literariness." Roman Jakobson wrote in *Modern Russian Poetry* (1921) that "the object of literary science is not literature, but *literariness*, that is, what makes a given work a literary work." Chris Baldick explains:

> The Formalists set out to define the observable "devices" by which literary texts—especially poems—foreground their own language, in meter, rhyme, and other patterns of sound and repetition. Literariness was understood in terms of defamiliarization, as a series of deviations from "ordinary" language. It thus appears as a relation between different uses of language, in which the contrasted uses are liable to shift according to changed contexts. (123)

The obviously poetic or extramundane quality of literary language "foregrounds" the literary. M. H. Abrams defines "foregrounding" as "bring[ing] something into prominence, to make it dominant in perception." He explains: "The literariness of a work, as Jan Mukarovsky, a member of the Prague Circle, described it in the 1920s, consists 'in the maximum of foregrounding of the utterance,' that is the foregrounding of the act of expression, the act of speech itself." The "primary aim of literature in thus foregrounding its linguistic medium," he goes on, is to achieve Shklovsky's estrangement or defamiliarization; "that is, by disrupting the modes of ordinary linguistic discourse, literature 'makes strange' the world of everyday perception and renews the reader's lost capacity for fresh sensation" (107–8, emphasis in original). This focus on literariness, "on the formal patterns and technical devices of literature to the exclusion of its subject matter and social values," is why the formalists were attacked by their critical opponents (107).

Literariness is a function, according to Nabokov, of "structure and style." In his *Lectures on Literature*, he described his course "Masters of European Fiction," for example, as "among other things, a kind of detective investigation of the mystery of literary structures" (xxx). He notes as he begins his discussion of Dickens's *Bleak House* that form equates to subject matter in the best writing:

> What do we mean when we speak of the form of a story? . . . In a word, we mean the planned pattern of a work of art. This is structure.
>
> Another aspect of form is style, which means how does the structure work; it means the manner of the author, his mannerisms, various special tricks; and if his style is vivid what kind of imagery, of description, does he use, how does he proceed; and if he uses comparisons, how does he employ and vary the rhetorical devices of metaphor and simile and their combinations. The effect of style is the key to literature, a magic key to Dickens, Gogol, Flaubert, Tolstoy, to all great masters.

*Form (structure and style) = Subject Matter: the why and the how = the
what.* (113)

His central dogma, recalls a student, was that "style and structure are the
essence of a book; great ideas are hogwash" (xxiii). Our principal pleasure
in reading the best fiction, Nabokov declared, is the fruit of our ability in
rereading to "keenly enjoy—passionately enjoy, enjoy with tears and shiv-
ers—the inner weave of a given masterpiece" (4).

To the formalists, the structure of greatest interest for any work's "inner
weave" was in its parallelism or internal referencing and echoing. Jakobson
cites the poet Gerard Manley Hopkins on this point: "The structure of poetry
is that of continuous parallelism, ranging from the technical so-called parallelism of Hebrew poetry and the antiphones of Church music up to the intri-
cacy of Greek or Italian or English verse" (102). Shklovsky links parallelism
to the artist's defamiliarizing mission. It is "a device of special importance,"
the purpose of which, "like the general purpose of imagery, is to transfer the
usual perception of an object into the sphere of new perception" (61).

Nabokov scholars note the mirroring and ring structures or "turtle-back"
parallelism in his novels. Jacqueline Hamrit, for example, describes *Lolita's* two
parts, each having three groups of three ten-chapter bundles that reflect one
another in turtleback fashion, so that we see "repetition, duplication, inversion,
and reversion" side by side. The essential components of a literary ring are a
latch, a story turn, and chapters in parallel before and after the turn (Douglas
1–2). We might guess from Rowling's surname that she writes in circles, and
even a look at the surface plot points in her seven *Harry Potter* novels reveals
a circular pattern and story formula, if not an "inner weave." Harry's story
begins each year on Privet Drive,[10] he escapes the Dursleys, travels on the
Hogwarts Express from King's Cross Station, explores a mystery in the castle
with friends Ron and Hermione, he makes a "saving people" choice that will
almost certainly mean his sacrificial death, the murderous black-hats defeat
him seemingly, but he rises from his faux- or near-death in the presence of
a symbol of Christ, escapes to fight another day, meets with Headmaster
Dumbledore to debrief and to learn all that he misunderstood in the past
year, and he returns to King's Cross Station for another summer with the
Dursleys on Privet Drive.[11] [See also Mars and Konchar Farr in this volume.]

This annual circular journey, curiously, brings him to an alocal, magical
place, something like what Eliade calls a "mythic center," at which Harry

confronts that year's villain, survives death, and miraculously, after learning his assumptions had been wrong, escapes. The Mirror of Erised circular chamber, the Chamber of Secrets, the Shrieking Shack, the Maze center and Little Hangleton graveyard, the Department of Mysteries, the Lake of the Inferi, and the otherworldly King's Cross in *Deathly Hallows* all act as points of origin that define the year's circle. This is a winning story formula, obviously, that successfully engages readers, and Rowling observes her formula element checklist in each book with sufficient creativity and humor that it does not seem mechanical or invite the reader to lament, "Here we go again . . ." It is not, however, the kind of *syuzhet* and narrative artistry that might interest the cultural gatekeepers who nominate writers for the Nobel Prize or even the *ad hoc* alternative.

A formalist reading of Rowling's work, however, involves a look for structures beneath the circular plot points, a parallelist scaffolding that this reading reveals. Rowling is a ring writer, the "inner weave" of whose stories is a remarkably complex tapestry of echoing correspondences, latch, turn, and chiastic parallels. It is the structural *syuzhet* and literary magic just out of sight, the story form of her *Harry Potter* novels (and Cormoran Strike mysteries, *Casual Vacancy*, and *Fantastic Beast* screenplays). Even a brief survey of the seven novels is beyond the scope of this essay.[12] Here, though, I offer a ring chart of *Sorcerer's Stone*, Rowling's shortest novel, and a brief discussion of its latch, turn, and parallels.

Latch: Harry survives meeting the Dark Lord as baby at the book's beginning and again in the finale as an eleven-year-old. He has parallel experiences, too, with a serpent at the zoo's reptile house trying to get out, then, at the end in front of the Mirror of Erised, with the Heir of Slytherin trying to get in.

Turn: "The Midnight Duel." Harry is out and under his Invisibility Cloak at midnight and survives a face-to face meeting with Fluffy the three-headed dog. Harry survives the Dark Lord, a visit with a snake, a run-in with Fluffy (and in the next chapter, with a Troll) as well as Quirrelldemort before the Mirror of Erised, giving the reader miraculous survival chapters in the beginning, middle, and end.

Chapter Correspondences: See "Rubeus Hagrid" above. Harry meets him in the House on the Rock and learns his wizard identity before he travels into Diagon Alley's hidden world; in the second half, Harry travels with Hagrid into the dark world of the Forbidden Forest, protects his protector by shipping off Norbert, and learns the identity of the mysterious stone's owner.

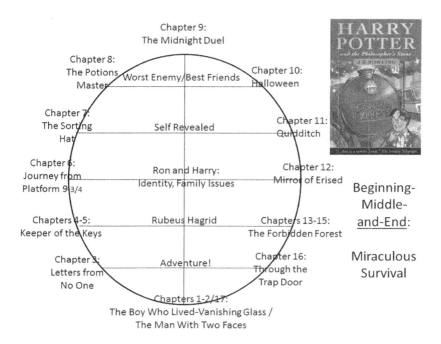

Chapter 9:
The Midnight Duel

Chapter 8:
The Potions
Master

Worst Enemy/Best Friends

Chapter 10:
Halloween

Chapter 7:
The Sorting
Hat

Self Revealed

Chapter 11:
Quidditch

Chapter 6:
Journey from
Platform 9 3/4

Ron and Harry:
Identity, Family Issues

Chapter 12:
Mirror of Erised

Chapters 4-5:
Keeper of the Keys

Rubeus Hagrid

Chapters 13-15:
The Forbidden Forest

Chapter 3:
Letters from
No One

Adventure!

Chapter 16:
Through the
Trap Door

Chapters 1-2/17:
The Boy Who Lived-Vanishing Glass /
The Man With Two Faces

Beginning-
Middle-
and-End:

Miraculous
Survival

Each of the novels follows a similar pattern, with increasing complexity, dexterity, and sophistication in every book. As surprising as this hidden artistry may be to even the most serious of Potter fans, it is only the beginning of Rowling's structural *syuzhet*. The seven-book series is also a ring cycle. For example, the story latch is *Sorcerer's Stone*, and *Deathly Hallows*, the finale, makes more than thirty references to it (see Granger, *Hallows* 265–67). The turn is *The Goblet of Fire*, whose three TriWizard Tournament trials correspond to the three adventures of *Sorcerer's Stone* and *Deathly Hallows*, and whose gauntlet running in the maze has the seven elements found in the obstacles between Harry and the Mirror of Erised in *Sorcerer's Stone* plus those he faces in the *Deathly Hallows'* Battle of Hogwarts. Finally, parallels between books 2 and 6 include the life of Lord Voldemort backstories and Horcrux revelations, match with similar parallels between books 3 and 5 and their Sirius Black stories, giving us a classic turtleback.[13]

Russian formalism is something of an acid test for the seriousness of any writer's work. It assumes that poem, play, or novel is an artifact of an author's deliberate artistry or *syuzhet*, the *literaturnost* or evident literariness of which will "foreground" the imaginative experience of reading and interpretation of story in order to "defamiliarize" our automatized thinking. "Structure and style," especially parallelist exercises in the organization of the text, are especially important signatures of a writer who knows what he or she is about. Rowling has been dismissed by cultural gate-keepers, according to James Thomas, because of the "three deathly hallows of her work," namely, that that they are "too current, too juvenile, and too popular" in the eyes of canon-setters and prize committees. But she passes the acid test of a formalist critique with flying colors.

As much as her model in Nabokov, Rowling's novels reflect her planning and concerns with their "inner weave" that transforms our vision by the various "knight's moves" of her story-crafting magic and careful parallelism. Tolkien, Tolstoy, Twain, and Joyce, not to mention Nabokov, never won a Nobel Prize in Literature, and I suspect Rowling's "deathly hallows" will mean she will not either. On the literary merits as set by the Russian formalist school of literary criticism, though, she deserves consideration as a Nabokov of novelists, a Nobel-ist for everybody.

Notes

1. "Nobel Prize in Literature" and "New Academy Prize" from *Wikipedia*, accessed 7.13.2021. https://en.wikipedia.org/wiki/Nobel_Prize_in_Literature#Controversies_about _Swedish_Academy_board_members.

2. Marshall, Alex. "An Alternative to the Nobel Prize in Literature, Judged by You" *New York Times*, July 13, 2018. https://www.nytimes.com/2018/07/13/books/alternative-nobel-prize -literature-new-academy-prize.html.

3. Liptak, Andrew. "Genre fiction is recognized with this year's alternative Nobel prize for literature" *The Verge*, September 1, 2018. https://www.theverge.com/2018/9/1/17809744/maryse -conde-haruki-murakami-kim-thuy-neil-gaiman-the-new-prize-literature-alternate-nobel -award

4. Cf. Granger, author blogs—*Hogwarts Professor: Thoughts for Serious Readers*. "Harry Potter and Lolita: J. K. Rowling's 'Relationship' with Vladimir Nabokov (Names, Politics, Alchemy, and Parody)," February 15, 2017. http://www.hogwartsprofessor.com/harry-potter -and-lolita-j-k-rowlings-relationship-with-vladimir-nabokov; "Harry Potter and Lolita: Rowling's Rings and Vladimir Nabokov's Story Mirrors (The Alchemy of Narrative Structure)," February 18, 2017. http://www.hogwartsprofessor.com/rings-mirrors-and-the -alchemical-transcendence-of-ego-reflection-in-the-structure-of-lolita-and-harry-potter/; "Seven Reasons Rowling Deserves Nobel Prize (2) CSL's Poeima: Genre and Influence." September 12, 2018. http://www.hogwartsprofessor.com/7-reasons-rowling-deserves-nobel -prize-2-csls-poeima-genre-and-influence/; and "Guest Post: Why Nabokov Would Have Liked Harry Potter (Michael Maar)." February 16, 2017.

5. http://www.hogwartsprofessor.com/guest-post-why-nabokov-would-have-liked-harry -potter-michael-maar/.

6. Cf. Granger *Unlocking Harry Potter*, 2007, pp 2–4; "I do a plan. I plan, I really plan quite meticulously." http://www.accio-quote.org/articles/2005/0705-edinburgh-ITV cubreporters.htm.

I got asked the other day, "Given the huge success of your books in America, are you going to be introducing American characters?" And I thought, "You're an idiot. I am not about to throw away 10 years' meticulous planning in the hope that I will buck up to a few more readers." http://www.accio-quote.org/articles/2000/0800-ew-jensen.html.

7. Cf. Granger, author blog—*Hogwarts Professor: Thoughts for Serious Readers*.: "*Lethal White*: Beatrice Groves on 'Galbraith Meets Graham Norton." October 9, 2018. http://www .hogwartsprofessor.com/lethal-white-beatrice-groves-on-galbraith-meets-graham-norton/.

8. "Val McDermid interviews JK Rowling (Robert Galbraith) at Harrogate International Festival 2014" on YouTube. December 1, 2014. https://www.youtube.com/watch?v=Tbv JbbgFhrQ.

9. Cf. Granger, author blogs—*Hogwarts Professor: Thoughts for Serious Readers*. "Silkworm 1: Kathryn Kent's Plot/Narrative Distinction." June 24, 2014. http://www.hogwarts professor.com/silkworm-1-kathryn-kents-plotnarrative-distinction/.

10. Exceptions are the opening chapters of *Goblet, Prince,* and *Hallows,* which then default to Harry at the Dursleys'.

11. He does not meet with Dumbledore or take the train at the end of *Half-Blood Prince,* but he meets with the headmaster and goes to King's Cross twice at the end of *Hallows.*

12. Detailed charts of the *Harry Potter* novels and the correspondences in the series as a seven-part ring are available in Granger, *Harry Potter as Ring Composition and Ring Cycle,* Unlocking Press, 2010.

13. Cf. Granger, 2010 (above n.24). The series ring structure is more involved than this simplified chart shows because of the significant correspondences between books 1 and 5 and books 3 and 7. (*Ring Composition,* 58–66, 105–24).

Works Cited

Abrams M. H. *A Glossary of Literary Terms,* 7th Edition. Boston: Heinle, 1999.

Baldick, Chris. *Concise Oxford Dictionary of Literary Terms.* Oxford UK: Oxford University Press, 1992.

Douglas, Mary. *Thinking in Circles: An Essay on Ring Composition.* New Haven CT: Yale University Press, 2007.

Erlich, Victor. *Russian Formalism: History-Doctrine,* third edition. New Haven CT: Yale University Press, 1981.

Granger, John. *Deathly Hallows Lectures.* Unlocking Press, 2008.

Granger, John. *Harry Potter as Ring Composition and Ring Cycle.* Unlocking Press, 2010.

Granger, John. *Unlocking Harry Potter: Five Keys for the Serious Reader.* Unlocking Press, 2007.

Hamrit, Jacquelin. "Structure in Lolita," *Zembla* online journal, Penn State University Press. www.libraries.psu.edu/nabokov/hamlol.html.

Jakobson, Roman and Krystyna Pomorska. *Dialogues.* Cambridge UK: Cambridge University Press, 1983.

Shklovsky, Viktor. "The Structure of Fiction" in *Theory of Prose.* Normal, IL: Dalkey Archive, 1991.

HALLOWS

8

READING *HARRY* WITH THE RISK OF TRUST AND A HOPEFUL SEARCH FOR MEANING

Patrick McCauley

I.

The phenomenon of the *Harry Potter* series is forcing us to reconsider the role literature and narrative are supposed to play in the general culture. Consider the following line from Rilke: "So we are grasped by what we cannot grasp" (Rilke, Bly). Within Rilke's beautiful line we hear a call to the question of meaning. For so many, the study of literature is also an exploration into the depths of human significance and purpose. Literature is about the aching beauty latent in language, and yet it also seeks the ground of meaning within the human condition.

There are some who see literature as a dance between the author and the audience or reader. Where the philosopher can address the reader in a concrete manner, the author of novels is often left to hope that that the reader will catch on to inference. The literary writer must trust his or her reader to independently reach into the artistry of the text in pursuit of receivable meaning. The meaning of a work of literature does not usually rest on the surface, so the author has to hope the reader is willing to descend beneath this surface, to participate or partner in the transmission of meaning. For example, an author may create a literary image with words, but it is the reader who is left to co-create the actual visual image within his or her own individual productive imagination. It is, to some degree, the reader's own image of Hogwarts that graces her reading of the story.

This kind of author/audience interaction resonates with the structure of a religious symbol. An image or artifact becomes a religious symbol in the moment that the ineffable transcendent breaks into mundane existence. An object becomes a sacred symbol when, through it, that which is beyond understanding breaks through paradoxically into human perception. However, the ineffable transcendent does not break through and appear to an entire crowd. The experience of the transcendent is a private, personal experience. One person can have a moving religious experience during a particular service even while the person sitting right next to her may feel nothing at all. The religious experience is the paradoxical interaction between the infinite and the finite. The object through which the religious experience happens can be shared, but the experience of the transcendent cannot. The object of the religious experience can be an object in the material world, but the transcendent that appears through it can never be. Such a thing can only appear as a subjective experience, as an earth-shaking yet individual glimpse.

While some may believe that any object can become the site through which an individual glimpses the divine, a walk through any church or museum will provide us with myriad examples of specific objects designed purposefully to perform this role. From the stained-glass windows in local Catholic church to the magnificent artistic achievements of the Middle Ages on display at the Philadelphia Museum of Art, we are rarely at a loss for sacred objects intentionally created by one person for the sake of another person's religious awakening. Even if some of us are not moved by the religious content of these aesthetic objects, it is not hard to appreciate the profound seriousness and dedication with which they were originally created and received.

If religion can be understood as the interpretation of meaning and purpose, what does it mean that traditional forms of religion are experiencing ever-increasing suspicion and disregard? If organized religious spaces like churches and synagogues are being relinquished a little more by each ensuing generation of the industrialized world, then where are these young people to turn for their glimpse of the transcendent and modicum of guidance? So many of our grandparents and great-grand parents would have thought nothing of turning to a rabbi, imam, or priest during times of crisis or indecision. These moments of crisis and indecision have not gotten any less frequent or pressing; even if the trust in churches has receded, the need for what they once provided has not. People of our era need inspiration, advice, and encouragement every bit as much as their great-grandparents did. Where are young people supposed to turn for trusted guidance or a glimpse of the eternal?

Friedrich Schleiermacher suggested that all humans are destined to come to an understanding of our part or role within the greater whole. We are destined to ask the question of how we fit as part of our culture and as part of the universe. He said that we are also destined to answer this question. According to Schleiermacher, we are finite parts of an infinite context and simply do not have the option of ignoring the question of our individual relevance to the big picture. For him, this was the most fundamental religious question, one inevitably posed to every human being regardless of our opinions about organized religion. The existential question of our part within the greater whole is a characteristic of the human condition, not a matter of individual discretion. We can decide not to go to church, but that will not relieve us of our deep individual need to know our appropriate place in a wide universe and in post-modern culture (Schleiermacher 18–28).

Paul Tillich, like Schleiermacher, found that human meaning is a matter of interpretation and that the interpretation of individual human meaning was inherently religious. For him, it had nothing to do with whether or not a person attended church. Each of us measures the significance of each element of our lives against that element that, to each of us individually, matters most according to Tillich. In other words, whatever we care about the most, whatever we care about unconditionally, that, in itself, measures the meaning of everything else in our lives. To Tillich, this pattern by which we interpret meaning is essential and unavoidable for each of us. We are all destined to measure meaning in reference to our own individually chosen highest priority. Whatever we care about most becomes the filter through which we see everything, *everything* else (Tillich).

So, for Schleiermacher and Tillich, religious questions are part of all of our lives regardless of our participation in or resistance to weekly religious service or practice. Religion is simply not reducible to supernatural claims, cultural traditions, or holy buildings. Every one of us is always already immersed in the personal and sacred pursuit of personal relevance whether we like it or not. However, this forces us to ask just how we see ourselves as part of the whole. What is it that we care about more than anything else? Failure to directly address these questions can so easily leave us feeling lost, our choices arbitrary. It can leave us in profound despair. The need to figure out a life of significance and character is just as important as it ever has been.

In his book *Religion for Atheists*, Alain de Botton discusses "the art of living . . . [and our] demands for relevance." De Botton suggests that art "is a medium to remind us about what matters. It exists to guide us to what we should worship and revile if we wish to be sane, good people in possession of well-ordered souls. It is a mechanism whereby our memories are forcibly jogged about what we have to love and to be grateful for, as well as what we should draw away from and be afraid of . . . we meet with a work of art that grabs us through our senses and won't let us go until we have properly remembered" (Botton 113, 215, 217). In a similar manner, David Klemm argues, "Modern thought has concentrated on the tasks of gathering reliable data and constructing adequate theories. The activities of perception and formal thinking have received special attention. But the activity of understanding, which is not reducible to either perceiving or formal thinking, has been left out of consideration. Critical consciousness thus makes the sacred power of the symbol vanish . . . The result of critical reflection is the desacralization of the world" (Klemm 12).

Tillich asserts that the symbols of the past that can grow worn with over-use must be overthrown. Sacred symbols must be able to take us by surprise, catch us off guard and unawares. It is the unpredicted, the unexpected, the unprecedented that has the best chance of quaking our accepted and stultify-ing certainties and our habitual cultural presumptions. We must be grasped by something we cannot grasp. We must find ourselves set off against the backdrop of the boundless cosmos instead of that of the food court.

There is something happening at the site where the author, reader, and text dance together. In my own life, literature was a place where I learned to take life seriously. It was where I began to take myself seriously. In a world of shopping malls and pep rallies, great works of literature not only granted me permission to see the world as an arena of crucially important ordeals and impending epic quests, but they also hinted that I myself might have a responsibility to rise to my own place within one of these marvelous quixotic adventures.

There have been moments over the last few decades during which it appeared that that meaning and purpose in our culture might just get reduced to bald consumerism, living and working for the sake of buying in an endless unexplained competition, real people aspiring to ever higher virtuosities of obsession, avarice, and conspicuous display. Young people can easily get lost in such a morass and then despair of a life any more grandiose than arbitrary mediocrity and embarrassing cliché. Within this labyrinth, complete with minotaurs, literature can lend itself as a mirror and a lamp (Abrams; Auerbach). In its role as mirror it can offer honest assessment of the human condition and of our current cultural state. In its role as lamp, it can serve a guiding light, an inspiration and a call to perhaps unexpected potential or as a lighthouse warning against unexpected perils.

So, as the art of the Middle Ages may be receding in its ability to grasp people with the ungraspable, popular literature may be emerging as another form of art intentionally created by one person for the awakening of another. Undeniably excellent writing is showing up in literature for young adults and in cable television dramas of expanding scale and ambition. In an unprecedented way, legions of people are forgoing the easy unchallenging pabulum of traditional entertainments and turning instead to the kind of writing that demands their determined attention and active participation. Literature is a dance between the author and the audience. What does it mean that the audience is growing? What does it mean that throngs of young people stood in line for midnight releases of print novels? What does it mean that throngs of adults stood right behind them? What does it mean that bookstore chains have had to create entirely new sections of their stores given over to a young adult genre that owes so much to the work of J. K. Rowling? What does it mean that a series of popular children's novels has inspired academic conferences and this essay collection? It may very well be that something important is happening in this kind of literature. It may very well be the case that literature's star as a vehicle for the transmission of purpose, insight, direction, and personal seriousness is rising.

II.

This leads us to a discussion of the interpretation of literature. As far as I can tell, there are, within the tradition of Academia, at least two fairly distinct branches or schools of interpretation. There is the older and, for many, less familiar form called "hermeneutics" that is often found in departments of religious studies. It concerns itself with meaning, and references to this approach have been made in the first section of this chapter. However, by far the most famous and well-recognized school of textual interpretation is the one commonly found in departments of English and comparative literature. It concerns itself with textual challenges and is generally called *critique*. While the study and interpretation of literature in the Western world had existed for centuries in reference to classic Latin and Greek texts, the development of departments of English literature, particularly in the English-speaking world, arrives toward the latter half of the nineteenth century; these departments have not been around that long. However, for many of us, English departments have seemed ubiquitous and permanent fixtures of education.

For those of us who found ourselves fascinated and entranced with narrative, the English department was the place to be. There, the reading of mesmerizing tales leaped from the solitary activity of the individual alone in the patrolled quiet of a library to the shared experience of a class digging together into the potential meanings of a novel or poem. It is one thing to be in love with a book in the isolation of one's own reading. It is quite another thing to be in love with that book together with others in communal interpretive event. For many that I speak to, a book gained an entirely new vibrancy and life when, after passages of the work were read aloud within a class setting, we were invited into an open discussion and constructive debate on the meaning and significance of the aesthetic material. Even though I could love a book that I had experienced privately, this shared interpretive environment of the high school or college English class was a space I so deeply cherished that it quickly became clear that permanent residence there was my only option. In many instances I just could not wait to get into class and find out what the others were thinking and feeling about a particular fictional work. My own interpretive reception of the work, which included the shared experience of classroom interpretation and discussion, would often have profound and permanent effects on both my base and my peripheral character and identity.

This began to change in graduate school. There both authorial intention and individual elements of character came under sustained scrutiny. Many of my students love to discuss the *Harry Potter* series in a class context, and they do for many of the same reasons I could not wait to get back to my classes on Tolkien or Dostoevsky. They are fascinated and driven to enter into a serious and committed discussion of the ethics, justice, and identity issues arising out of their reading and discussion of the series. However, it is quite common to find graduate classes in English departments exposing just such an experience to severe critical inspection.

There can be little doubt that the *Harry Potter* series is often seen and received as a bildungsroman, a novel of development and a work of fiction intended for young people as they go through the process of developing their own principles and character. There can be little doubt that J. K. Rowling is making certain points about justice and morality within the series. Italian psychologist Loris Vezalli has pursued groundbreaking research that shows that in reading the series, many young people develop a measurably increased ability to empathize with people who are different from themselves. We can hardly imagine that Rowling did not intend such a thing. However, this is just the sort of assertion that recent poststructuralist critique has called into question.

Do we all share the apparent morality that is expressed in the *Harry Potter* novels? Is morality something that we engage in only as we suspend disbelief and aesthetically enter into a fictional world? Is there such a thing as morality, conscience, empathy in the real world? Perhaps Rowling has the legitimate prerogative to establish the moral principles of her fictional world, but who should be left in charge of establishing moral principles in ours? Should anyone? Is the intention to pursue normative ethical principles merely a nostalgic reflection of abandoned patriarchal and colonial power structures?

Do any of us enjoy being told what to do or what to believe? Many if not most of us here in this twenty-first century resist any high and mighty attempt to impose authoritative beliefs. Many would find my question about Rowling's intentions quaint and deeply uninformed if not downright disturbing. Many late twentieth- and early twenty-first-century literary critics have been dedicated to a serious discussion of the nature of culture and language and its often derogatory and undermining effect on the development of authentic human individuality and character. This massive wave of scholars and academics has been driven to discover and reveal often hidden and caustic traces of dominating power structures within the traditional literary canon.

Many of these scholars find themselves in the tradition of Foucault and Adorno, Nietzsche and Marx. However, the tradition can almost certainly be traced back to Plato's Allegory of the Cave from book 7 in the *Republic*. There, Plato expresses the idea that "we accept the reality of the world with which we are presented" (Weir, Peter). We have no choice but to absorb the language and culture that surrounds us, and both the general and specific judgment criteria by which cultural value and hierarchy are determined and enforced. Perhaps the significant aspect of this process of acculturation is that we have the tendency to impose often destructive and eviscerating stereotypes on ourselves and everyone else at a subconscious level. For many of us, poststructuralist literary criticism, what is sometimes called "critique" came to expose often hidden forms of authoritative power lurking between the lines of canonical texts. Critique warns us that when we accept the reality of the world with which we are presented, we may also absorb astoundingly dangerous assumptions that only benefit those more powerful. During the summer of 1990, I watched my three female cousins consume Disney's *The Little Mermaid* four or five times a day every day. We must ask how much of this movie and its call for girls to abandon their own voice did my cousins absorb and bring to fruition as adults. Who could but applaud as critique and its legion of adherents came to cast an exposing light on these hidden power structures within often beloved texts and stories? As Plato suggested, it does no good to mistake shadows or prejudices for truth.

But what happens when critique takes over literary interpretation? What happens when the message of warning becomes the only message? It is so important to help people discover that shadows are only shadows and not the truth. However, once we begin to throw off the assumptions and power structures of the dominant hegemony, what then are we to do? In the last few years, Rita Felski of the University of Virginia and Cecilia Konchar Farr of St. Catherine University, among others, have engaged in a serious appraisal of the state of literary criticism and interpretation as it exists currently in academia. Felski, relying in part on the work of Paul Ricoeur, calls out current literary critique as a "hermeneutic of suspicion." She claims that this dominant form of interpretation "forecloses many potential readings." Konchar Farr notes that while there are many who are willing to assert that Joyce's *Ulysses* may very well be the best novel every written, she finds that few of these same people have actually read it. She suggests we should also pay attention to what avid readers are reading and why books matter to them. Felski calls for a turn toward hermeneutics and its focus on the interpretation of human meaning. She sees this as a hopeful path forward.

My criticism of the Disney plot mentioned above mirrors a much more grandiose and sweeping interrogation of Constantinian or authoritative forms of governmental or tyrannical cooption of religious texts. Claims of religious authority have been encountering a sustained onslaught of criticism ever since the invention of the printing press gave individual readers the opportunity to consider religious texts independent of immediate church mediation. There is every reason to regard claims of authority with suspicion, and yet, critique itself postures as an authority as well. Felski warns us that "to be critical is to be at odds with or opposed to reigning structures of thought and language. Yet, for younger scholars at least, critique is the main paradigm in which they have been trained; while buffing and polishing its role as agent provocateur to the intellectual mainstream, it is the mainstream" (125). And further, "For many scholars in the humanities, it [critique] is not one good thing but the only imaginable thing" (15).

There will never come a time, as far as I can tell, when there will not be a need for a critical interrogation of claims of intellectual, moral, or religious authority. Claims of revelation have so often in human history been used to manipulate and coerce that we ought never backslide into an easy reliance on accepted authoritative principles. However, this critical tool should be recognized as a tool and not misinterpreted as a destination. For so many of us in the humanities, critique itself has become authoritative. We have adopted a "skepticism as dogma . . . a rhetoric of againstness . . . many of us have come to believe that only by acting like detectives—interrogating and cross-examining the texts of culture—can we avoid being mistaken for criminals. We have a fear of 'being had'" (16, 24, 93, 95). However, the time is come to move beyond hermeneutics of skepticism, cross-examination, and against-ness. If claims of authority are a thesis claim, and poststructuralist critique is an anti-thesis claim, then we may, with Paul Ricoeur, begin to imagine a synthesis that both includes and transcends these two previous positions. At base, we must come to recognize that the insistence to resist normative principles is itself a normative principle.

Felski observes that "critique is a dominant approach, but it is far from being the only one" (1). Helen Small asserts that "the work of the humanities is frequently descriptive, or appreciative, or imaginative, or provocative, or speculative, more than it is critical" (Felski 10). Felski goes on to say:

This seems exactly right; everyday practices of teaching and writing and thinking span disparate activities and fluctuations of affect and tone. The point is obvious to anyone who has spent half an hour in the undergraduate classroom, where moods shift and slide as students and teacher commune around a chosen text: critical caveats are interspersed with flashes of affinity or sympathy; bursts of romantic hope coexist with the deciphering of ideological subtexts. And yet our language for describing and justifying these various activities remains remarkably underdeveloped. (11, 12)

Perhaps we can say with Bruno Latour that "at a certain point, critique does not get us any further" (16). It "seems increasingly evident that literary scholars are confusing a part of thought with the whole of thought, and that in doing so we are scanting a range of intellectual and expressive possibilities" (40–41):

> Ricoeur reminds us of histories and theories of interpretation that receive scant attention in contemporary Anglo-American literary studies. (How often does even Gadamer or Ricoeur appear in a theory survey?) Thanks to a lingering aura of Teutonic fustiness, not to mention its long-standing links with biblical interpretation, hermeneutics was never able to muster the high-wattage excitement that radiated from post structuralism; hermeneutics came to stand for a discredited form of "depth" interpretation—the hapless and hopeless pursuit of an ultimate meaning. Interpreting, Ricoeur reminds us, can be a matter of dispossession rather than possession, of exposing ourselves to a text as well as imposing ourselves on. (40)

The works of Hegel, Nietzsche, Freud, and Marx along with the landslide of literary critique that has followed in their wake have led us to a suspicion that even we ourselves cannot look with clarity into our own souls. It is not just works of fiction and works of art that have come under a critique of suspicion, but our own sense of authentic individuality has come under deep distrust as well. Paul Ricoeur observed that "Hegel believed he had superseded all recourse to conscience . . . The cruel twentieth century has taught us that it is not so" (92, 345). What does Ricoeur mean by the cruel twentieth century, and what does he claim that it has taught us? He seems to be suggesting that there are acts so unjust, so immoral, so tragic that none can honestly feign indifference. At the center of the discussion of normative principles and the authority to claim such things is the distinction between objective and subjective truth. Most criticism of normative principles springs from the inference that these are universal claims to be accepted or imposed with universal force on unconsulted subjects. However, Ricoeur seems to be referring instead to the existential and phenomenological experience of responsibility on the individual level. It is no good claiming that there are no normative principles if I find myself legitimately criticized by one that I carry and deliberately condone with my own thoughtful subjective interiority. If I find myself within the grips of stultifying moral self-condemnation due a decision I, myself, freely and deliberately entered into, your claim that moral principles are merely a relative product of linguistic cultural power interrelations becomes an argument that can find no purchase on my private consent. It may very well be that moral principles are a product of culture and thus something of the arbitrary or worse, but I myself, at the phenomenological level, will never be able to experience responsibility as such. Morality may in fact be all in my head, but why on earth should that mean that it is not real?

Karen Wendling and I teach a year-long honors seminar called "The Emergence of the Hero in the Epic Voyage." On the surface it is a class on science, philosophy, and religion, but at a deeper level it is designed to invite undergraduates into a serious and self-motivated investigation into their own character, their own principles and priorities. After a year of Plato and Galileo, Kant and Heisenberg, the course culminates with the *Harry Potter* series. The best writing of the year arises from the *Harry Potter* assignment. In these essays, our students have revealed to us that they see themselves reflected in the characters and questions of Rowling's series and that this is one of the main reasons they love it. They identify with, for example, Harry's rash use of the untried *Sectumsempra* spell that leaves Draco Malfoy on the brink of bleeding to death and far beyond any attempt at rescue Harry's meager skills could offer. They can relate to the idea that the progress toward adult responsibility can so often be marked by unanticipated self-condemnation that can result from impulsively tempting the odds.

Rowling does not talk down to her youthful readers, nor does she minimize or blunt the profound gravity of these experiences. She trusts her young readers to rise to the seriousness of the material, and they love her for it. She trusts that they can handle stark presentations of betrayal, grief and culpability. Many readers return the favor by infusing these stories with relevance in regard to their own real lives and decisions. They lean into these novels, trusting them to be a source of insight and advice. Karen and I find that our students who have repeatedly read the series have come to grant these tales and their characters permission to shape and effect their own personal deliberations, assumptions, and ambitions.

We find that this is particularly true in regard to the relationship between Harry and Hermione in the last book of the series, *Harry Potter and the Deathly Hallows*. Rowling takes advantage of earlier parts of the series to establish Hermione's interest in Ron and Harry's for Cho or Ginny. Rowling carefully crafts these romantic vectors so as to set the context for their final partnership. In *The Deathly Hallows*, she leaves Harry and Hermione alone, abandoned by Ron to face withering odds. As link upon link of the chain forged to resist Tom Riddle breaks, it is that last link between Harry and Hermione that does not fail. Neither alone could have risen to the challenges and fears of *The Deathly Hallows*. It is the shoulder-to-shoulder committed camaraderie of Harry and Hermione, their resolute mutual reliance that survives, stands, and opposes the solitary force of Tom Riddle.

The literary presentation of this relationship is one of J. K. Rowling's most significant and remarkable achievements. I am sure you can quickly name any number of Hollywood endings in which, after a long and arduous adventure, the male and female leads perform a passionate embrace before both a sunset and the ending credits. The cultural pull of this cliché is almost impossible to resist. You may find it much more difficult to name a fictional male/female adventure partnership that does not culminate in this way. However, this is just what we find in *The Deathly Hallows*. Karen and I have come to recognize that many of our students, particularly our female students, find great personal significance in this aspect of the *Harry Potter* series.

As we have said, young people often turn to narrative images for glimpses and visions of their own legitimate individual fruition. For so many individual readers, this image must exist, even if in mere fiction, if they are ever to imagine themselves into it. As events drive toward the climax of the *Harry Potter* series, everything comes to depend on the bond between Harry and Hermione. The series serves to emphasize the irreplaceable importance of this bond and commitment. And yet Rowling's skill and artistry is such that few even notice how rare such a central portrayal of partnership is in popular culture. It will now always be easier to imagine such a thing in one's own real life. Legions of little girls and little boys have now, with Rowling's series, grown up with the image of a profound and resolute male/female partnership that is not defined by romantic roles or culminations. Can we imagine what it may mean for them, what it may mean for us? What will it mean that almost an entire generation can envision life shaping male/female friendships that exist beyond the bounds of romantic/sexual presupposition? The students of our class are not waiting to find out. They are already applying these principles to their lives. Our undergraduates cannot afford the spirit of suspicion at the center of poststructuralist critique. They report to us that they need and cherish these moments of insight in inspiration that guide their real-world self-determination.

J. K. Rowling indicates something of her own feelings by means of leaving a nearly direct quote of Nietzsche within the climax of her first *Harry Potter* novel. Her Professor Quirrell asserts, "A foolish young man I was then, full of ridiculous ideas about good and evil. Lord Voldemort showed me how wrong I was. There is no good and evil, there is only power, and those too weak to seek it. . . ." Did she really place one of the founding concepts of poststructuralism in the voice of villain Tom Riddle?

This returns us to the precious and fertile undergraduate classroom experience in which an interpretive discussion of novels, plays, and poetry was shared in good faith and with the intention to discover relevant subjective meaning. Konchar Farr calls us to remember "what makes novels work for readers: main characters they can imagine themselves into, recognizable depictions of their lives and fantasies, reaffirmation of key cultural values, and, dammit, good solid entertaining stories that make you want to run to the bookstore to buy another one" (88). Konchar Farr addressed this idea at the Sixth Annual Harry Potter Conference at Chestnut Hill College. A quick survey of the previous programs (available online at the conference website) will attest that this conference is and has been a location for the serious discussion of books that really speak to people. As Konchar Farr remarks "that to judge novels astutely and well critics need to be in conversation not just with other critics, but also with . . . its passionate advocates, the many avid admirers and consumers of novels . . . [This] calls for standards of merit different from those we use for other works of art or literature" (26–27).

The passionate advocates of the *Harry Potter* series are offering us insight that we cannot afford to miss. I think it is important for those of us who spend our time in classrooms reading books with students to come, in humility, to recognize that any form or model of interpretation can prove too small to encompass the unbounded human desire or need to find meaning in narrative. There may actually be legitimate reasons for relinquishing traditional forms of organized religion and literary interpretation. Yet the individual existentially yearning for a life of pertinence will force us to acknowledge two things. First, we must face the fact that neither science nor poststructuralist critique has any ability to respond with edifying insight or advice in response to that yearning. Second, we must not miss the fact that there has emerged an overwhelming and voracious audience for new form of bildungsroman. The traditional hermeneutics of suspicion that swallowed so many English departments whole may have to make room for a modern demythologizing form of hermeneutics, itself grounded on many of the same principles as that of critique.

People who are looking to narrative for a personal glimpse of perspective have no choice but to encounter texts with a personal hope for trust. These readers must take the risk of trust. They must risk a hope that they find something there that resonates productively, something that inspires a hope for their personal authenticity and trajectory. These people simply cannot afford to immerse themselves exclusively in a vortex of cascading suspicion and incredulity. Many of our students are taking that risk and granting that trust. This transition is already underway and it is time for those of us trained in interpretation to take notice.

Works Cited

Abrams, M. H. *The Mirror and the Lamp: Romantic Theory and the Critical Tradition.* Oxford University Press, 1971.

Auerbach, Erich, and Willard R. Trask. *Mimesis: The Representation of Reality in Western Literature.* Princeton University Press, 2013.

Botton, Alain De. *Religion for Atheists: A Non-Believer's Guide to the Uses of Religion.* Penguin, 2013.

Felski, Rita. *The Limits of Critique.* University of Chicago Press, 2015.

Klemm, David E. *Hermeneutical Inquiry.* Scholars Press, 1986.

Konchar Farr, Cecilia. *The Ulysses Delusion: Rethinking Standards of Literary Merit.* Palgrave Macmillan, 2016.

Plato, and Desmond Lee. *Plato: Republic.* Penguin, 2003.

Ricoeur, Paul, and Kathleen Blamey. *Oneself as Another.* University of Chicago Press, 2008.

Rilke, Reiner Maria. "A Walk." Translated by Robert Bly, *Https://Allpoetry.com/A-Walk*, 3 Mar. 2018, allpoetry.com/A-Walk.

Rowling, J. K. *Harry Potter and the Deathly Hallows.* S.l.: ARTHUR A LEVINE, 2018.

Rowling, J. K. *Harry Potter and the Sorcerer's Stone.* S.l.: ARTHUR A LEVINE, 2018.

Schleiermacher, Friedrich. *On Religion: Speeches to Its Cultured Despisers.* Translated by John Oman, Beloved Publishing, 2016.

Tillich, Paul. *Systematic Theology: Three Volumes in One.* University of Chicago Press, 1967.

Weir, Peter, director. *The Truman Show.* Universal Pictures, 1998.

9

"ALWAYS DEPENDABLY, SOLIDLY PRESENT"
The Preeminence of Minerva McGonagall

Kate Glassman

Head of Gryffindor House, deputy headmistress, two-time member of the Order of the Phoenix, and die-hard Quidditch fan, Minerva McGonagall is one of the most respected and accomplished users of magic in the *Harry Potter* series. She consistently demonstrates how essential her presence is to the narrative, to Hogwarts, and to Harry—yet she is all but absent in most literary analyses of the series, a puzzling oversight, when you consider how valued she is by Harry and by most readers. If her exemplary abilities and achievements within Hogwarts and the greater wizarding world are not enough, then surely her relationship with the series' titular character merits a deeper look. Yet their interactions receive only cursory mention in studies focused on greater wizards, those considered proper parental (meaning, of course, proper father) figures to Harry.

Orphaned as a baby and subsequently abused for most of his childhood, Harry has never in his living memory had an adult speak a kind word to him, let alone care for him. Upon (re)entering the wizarding world, he's hardly starved for choices—as the proverbial Chosen One, there are many witches and wizards eager to ingratiate themselves with the Harry Potter. Dedalus Diggle, for example, takes abundant joy in simply shaking Harry's hand.

But admiration is not love nor care. Harry finds those qualities in a select but reasonable few: Hagrid, the genial and boisterous gamekeeper for Hogwarts; Molly Weasley, his best friend's mum, who knits him sweaters and fattens him up, as good as a seventh son; Remus Lupin and Sirius Black, his late father's best friends, prized professor, and godfather, respectively; and Dumbledore, the headmaster of his school-turned-home, who knows too well the loneliness that comes with greatness. A single witch—mother of one of his best friends—is allowed into the fold of parental figures most often cited in studies of the texts. Minerva McGonagall, head of Harry's House and the adult who would logically interact with Harry the most on a day-to-day basis is largely ignored.

Several key professors are examined in Birch's "Schooling Harry Potter: Teachers and Learning, Power and Knowledge," and the essay serves as one of the longest, focused looks at McGonagall's character in the series. However, the essay's shifting target between assessing whether she is a fully rounded character versus a successful teacher (with the implication that she cannot be both), ultimately results in a muddled conclusion: "She is a complex character with unified goals and allegiances, [but] still a detailed but hackneyed image of a teacher" (Megan L. Birch 110). McGonagall's perceived strictness is inflated into her sole identifier, so much so that all other markers of her complexity as both a character and a teacher are dismissed, crushed under the weight of her disciplinary leanings. Similarly, McGonagall's mention in Heilman and Donaldson's "From Sexist to (sort-of) Feminist: Representations of Gender in the Harry Potter Series," is relegated to her sudden change in character during the Battle of Hogwarts, wherein she takes charge rather than "defer to a male superior" and, later in the essay, how these leadership actions are read as comical (Heilman 143–44). Essays that actually reference her relationship with Harry, such as Jones's "'I'm a wizard too!' Identification and Habitus," frame their interactions as merely narrative-driving and McGonagall as an enabler of Harry's rule-breaking.

Why is it difficult for readers or scholars to recognize McGonagall's pivotal role? Or, perhaps, we recognize but feel no urge to celebrate it—after all, the stern matron with a heart of gold is a well-known figure both on and off the page. McGonagall may simply be fulfilling her archetype. Yet for Harry, her role is anything but expected. Because he is the Boy Who Lived, he inspires polemical responses—from great love and admiration to hate and loathing. To have a teacher treat him as they would any other student is a singular experience and one he never fully appreciates until the second half of the series. Harry's growing admiration culminates in his fierce defense of McGonagall in Ravenclaw Tower in the final novel of the series.

Enter McGonagall

"The door swung open at once. A tall, black-haired witch in emerald-green robes stood there. She had a very stern face and Harry's first thought was that this was not someone to cross" (SS 113). While this is not the readers' first introduction to McGonagall, who appears in chapter 1 first as a tabby cat, this is McGonagall as Harry first sees her. Usually dressed in green or plaid, her hair pulled back into a tight bun, McGonagall is described variously as "austere," "tight-lipped," and "unflappable." Harry also notes in his first year that she has "the gift of keeping a class silent without effort" (SS 137). Her formidable presence is backed by prodigious skills—one of which is the first proper display of magic in the series: Transfiguration.

While Harry first sees McGonagall as a witch, she appears on the second page of the series as a small cat with strange markings, sitting on the wall just outside Privet Drive surveilling the house where Harry Potter is to spend the next ten years. Though we will eventually encounter several Animagi throughout the series (witches and wizards who can transform at will into animals), McGonagall is the first named—and the only registered—Animagus; one of only seven in the last century (PA 351). Mastering such a prodigious feat makes it no wonder that she has taught the Transfiguration courses at Hogwarts for forty-one years, as of *Deathly Hallows*. It may also provide some insight into how three of her students acquire the skill and ability necessary to secretly do the same.

Transfiguration, unlike other branches of magic, requires the discipline not only to summon magic, but also to use it to alter the physical composition of a thing, even oneself. The word itself means a complete change of form, usually into something more beautiful. We do not see transfiguration often in the novels, yet it is required for Auror training, indicating it is a primary and specialized discipline rather than a tertiary one. Rather, the series follows the common genre tendency to linger on charms and jinxes, magic that affects. Potions, which also feature prominently, are a palatable form of magic; the combination of interacting ingredients to become something new is little more than cooking. The discipline as a whole is deemed basic to magical education, but students who cannot master Potions easily procure the necessary vials of Sleekeazy, Skele-Gro, or Wolfsbane from a licensed master or shop. Those who choose to go beyond these magical basics, however, distinguish themselves as a higher caliber witch or wizard.

In the wizarding world, it is not age that indicates limitation, but rather lack of skill. The most powerful witches and wizards in the series are well past the Muggle notion of "prime"—Voldemort is 71 at the time of his death and Dumbledore is 115. Despite being in her 70s for the duration of the series, McGonagall has clearly used the time to hone her skills, demonstrating on multiple occasions both the strength and ingenuity of her spell casting. She is responsible for the giant chessboard guarding the Sorcerer's Stone, with thirty-two pieces standing taller than any of the Golden Trio, transfigured (and presumably charmed as well) to force any entrants to not only play, but win, a game of Wizard's Chess. Such a feat is not only impressive in its scale, but also its duration; ten months pass between the stone's relocation in August and the night it is nearly stolen.

Serving on the front lines of two back-to-back wars, McGonagall is also an accomplished duelist. Every major altercation that occurs on Hogwarts grounds features McGonagall at the fore (and Dumbledore absent). Unlike other adult witches—such as Tonks and Mrs. Weasley—McGonagall is consistently given space within the text to demonstrate these acquired skills and, whether prominently, as in the "sacking" of Snape, or in the background, is shown to be a key combatant in every encounter. When Draco Malfoy's machinations allow Death Eaters into the castle in *Half-Blood Prince*, it is McGonagall who rallies the students and other Order members into battle: "It's McGonagall's orders," said Ginny. "Everyone's up there, Ron and Hermione and Lupin and everyone—" (*HBP* 612). We arrive to find "Professor McGonagall, and Lupin, each . . . battling a separate Death Eater" (599). In *Deathly Hallows*, she duels Snape with such ferocity that he's forced to flee Hogwarts: "Professor McGonagall moved faster than Harry could have believed: Her wand slashed through the air and for a split second Harry thought that Snape must crumple, unconscious" (*DH* 598). That same night, she takes on Voldemort himself alongside Shacklebolt and Slughorn (*DH* 735).

It should also be noted that these battles occur after a near-fatal attack in *Order of the Phoenix*. McGonagall takes four direct Stunners to the chest in defense of Hagrid and survives, despite Madam Pomfrey's concern that "it's a wonder they didn't kill her," and returns at the end of term "leaning heavily on a walking stick..., but otherwise look[ing] quite well" (730, 852). This is a battle-hardened hero we're dealing with.

The Quidditch Fan

McGonagall, however, is more than just a dab hand at Transfiguration or a tremendous duelist and war hero. These traits might distance her from Harry and the reader, making it easy to relegate her to the background, the necessary "helper" to launch Harry on his hero's journey, if Rowling had not carefully written her out of that mold. McGonagall has interests and passions outside of her profession, and, while they may do little to further the narrative, such details are usually reserved for prominent characters; their inclusion is what turns McGonagall into a fully rounded character rather than a useful plot device. Chief among these interests is her deep and abiding investment in Quidditch.

Her interest serves the initial purpose of bringing Quidditch to Harry's attention and Harry to the Gryffindor team. With unexpected candor after Gryffindor was "flattened" by Slytherin, she confides to Harry that she "couldn't look Severus Snape in the face for weeks" (SS 152). This is only the beginning. She attends every Gryffindor game and, when not chastising Lee Jordan for his biased commentary, is ardently cheering for her House. Quidditch is consistently one of the rare settings where we see McGonagall's stern presentation slip. She places bets with the other professors on the outcome of matches, helps Harry organize tryouts, and—when swept up into the action—will do her own share of yelling "foul!" (HBP 175; PA 311). Like Harry, she lives and dies by Gryffindor's victories and was seen "sobbing harder even than Wood, wiping her eyes with an enormous Gryffindor flag" when her House defeated Slytherin for the Quidditch Cup (PA 313). On one occasion, she even abstains from giving Gryffindor homework, under the vague excuse that they've "got enough to be getting on with at the moment" (OP 400). It's so out of character for McGonagall that her statement evinces disbelief, until she drops the pretense and reveals how badly she wants Gryffindor to win. "I've become accustomed to seeing the Quidditch Cup in my study, boys, and I really don't want to have to hand it over to Professor Snape, so use the extra time to practice, won't you?" (OP 400).

Even when Umbridge is unwilling to let the Gryffindor Quidditch team re-form under her latest decree banning school group organizations, McGonagall goes to Dumbledore behind Umbridge's back and insists they be allowed to play, a fair request as all three rival Houses were given permission without incident (*OP* 414–6). McGonagall's love of Quidditch serves not only to deepen the complexity of her personality but also to engage her further with the lives and pursuits of her students. Her Quidditch fandom is in direct defiance of the dedicated-but-distant schoolmarm role that is so easily troped and to which McGonagall is too often relegated.

The Hogwarts Professor

Partially due to the requirements of the narrative itself, McGonagall and Snape are the two professors always on hand when major events occur within Hogwarts, while the other professors and heads of house are consigned to being background spectators. Snape's professorial behavior, well-established in the texts to be harsh, biased, and antagonistic to any students but his own House, is especially highlighted in his treatment of Neville Longbottom, whose boggart, tellingly and distressingly, takes the form of Professor Snape in *Prisoner of Azkaban*. In contrast, McGonagall is fair and level-headed, and trusted by the trio with their concerns and fears, but she never quite reaches the stereotypical status of favored professor.

For one thing, Harry himself never verbalizes his respect or care for McGonagall in roughly 4,000 pages, and while McGonagall acts in ways that show particular concern for Harry, it never devolves into favoritism. When Harry doesn't have a signed permission slip to go to Hogsmeade village, McGonagall does not sign it in the Dursleys' stead, though it is presumably within her power as deputy headmistress. She empathizes with his situation, "an odd expression on her face," but remains firm: "I'm sorry, Potter, but that's my final word" (*PA* 150). She never acts outside her boundaries as his professor and head of house; rather she is the model of an invested professor, working within her position to provide the best for the students under her care.

However, when she sees aptitude displayed by any student (but, for the purpose of this chapter, Harry specifically) she rewards it, within the acceptable boundaries of the system. Suggesting Harry as seeker for the House team in *Sorcerer's Stone* is rare, but not unprecedented, and his candidacy is only brought to Captain Oliver Wood's attention after he demonstrates his innate ability by catching Neville's Remembrall. He may be the youngest seeker appointed in a century, yet it is not against school rules for first-years to try out, as several Gryffindors make the attempt in *Order of the Phoenix* when Harry is named captain. Nor is the application of school funds to order him a broom a bending of policy; it's indicated there is money set aside for such things, as in other private schools. McGonagall does not automatically award Harry passing O.W.L.s for Transfiguration but offers him additional tutoring and practice when he expresses a desire to be an Auror. These are efforts that would presumably be made by any invested professor to ensure that students pass on their own merit.

Though she may push her students harder than other professors, she is driven by a resolute faith that those in her care are both worthy and capable of performing the best magic. It is an expectation she holds herself to, a promise of presence and dedication. Therefore, one of Dumbledore's most enduring lines, "Help will always be given at Hogwarts to those who need it," is also his most revealing in its irony. It is not in Dumbledore that help is found. He is rarely even on-site to be of reliable aid, and his help, when it comes, is fleeting or by proxy, such as when Fawkes appears to Harry in the *Chamber of Secrets*. Rather, it is McGonagall who abides. It is McGonagall the trio runs to time and time again with their suspicions and their information, as when they believe Snape is trying to steal the Sorcerer's Stone, for example. When they discover via Hermione that it is a basilisk that has been hunting students in book 2, their first instinct is to ask, "What're we going to do? [. . .] Should we go straight to McGonagall?"—the beginning of a familiar refrain throughout the series (*CS* 292). In both instances, it should be noted, Dumbledore had left the building or allowed himself to be removed from Hogwarts.

McGonagall is both the head of Gryffindor House and the deputy headmistress to Hogwarts, second only to Dumbledore in rank and power at the prestigious school of magic. While Dumbledore is undoubtedly the figurehead and public face of Hogwarts, it is McGonagall who oversees the day-to-day running of the school, the one charged with "keeping the lights on." McGonagall signs and sends the acceptance letters to every incoming student and is also the one to lead the sorting ceremony, making her the principal contact for every first-year student. In Dumbledore's absence, she assumes responsibility for heading the school, which happens on a troubling number of occasions: first, in *Chamber of Secrets* when petrifications lead the board to a vote of no confidence in Dumbledore; second, in *Order of the Phoenix*, following Dumbledore's flamboyant escape from custody via phoenix before her position is usurped by Dolores Umbridge; last, following Dumbledore's death at the end of *Half-Blood Prince*. Here, McGonagall becomes acting headmistress, a position made permanent following the Battle of Hogwarts and the series' conclusion. These instances, while central to the narrative, do not constitute the entirety of Dumbledore's frequent absences from the school. He is often called away to the Ministry, as he was when the trio ventured below the trapdoor, or off on mysterious fact-finding missions that no one, not even McGonagall is privy to. This is remarked on most often in *Order of the Phoenix* and *Half-Blood Prince* because those absences nearly always coincide with trouble at Hogwarts, such as when Katie Bell is cursed by the opal necklace outside Hogsmeade:

> "The headmaster is away until Monday, Potter," said Professor McGonagall, looking surprised.
>
> "Away?" Harry repeated angrily.
>
> "Yes, Potter, away!" (*HBP* 252–53)

It is fitting that both Dumbledore and McGonagall were Gryffindors in their time at Hogwarts: as with the lion that heralds Gryffindor House, the male is seen as dominant in the pride, while the lionesses do most of the actual work. Yet, even Dumbledore acknowledges "Hogwarts needs [her]," and nothing, not even coming to his defense, should be responsible for removing her from the school (*OP* 620).

The Caring Guardian

The novels place most, if not all, of the tension in the plot in the interactions between adults and children, more so than between magic and muggle, good and evil. It becomes concerning, then, to note that within the myriad interactions and relationships, McGonagall is the only adult in the novels to see Harry as he truly is. The well-meaning witches and wizards who seek to protect and watch out for Harry do so with complicated intent.

Hagrid, the first parental figure to appear, is literally larger than life to Harry, so outside the realm of his Muggle experience that the half-giant becomes the stand-in for everything magical and good. Hagrid is the one who not only rescues Harry from the Dursleys, but also admonishes them both verbally and magically, enacting a justice that Harry has certainly longed for. He is the one who explains to Harry who he truly is and brings him into the wizarding world for the first time via Diagon Alley. It is no wonder that their friendship continues to run deep throughout the series, as the most pivotal moment in Harry's childhood memory centers on Hagrid. Harry continues to repay that first kindness, visiting Hagrid at his home and cheering him up when he's down, as any good friend would do. Hagrid, however, takes advantage of Harry's friendship often and in ways that would be suspect between peers, but that becomes downright coercive between an adult and child.

Not only are Hagrid's requests of Harry inappropriate, but they are often both irresponsible and dangerous. As early as *Sorcerer's Stone*, Hagrid, an adult fully capable of rational action and of taking responsibility for the consequences of those actions, puts Harry and Hermione in a compromising situation. Having illegally acquired a dragon egg, and subsequently hatching a Norwegian Ridgeback in his wooden house, it is not Hagrid who acknowledges the danger, both physically and legally, of his actions, but the eleven-year-olds who seem to be his only friends. They insist he get rid of Norbert before he is found out.

It is then left to Harry and Hermione to clean up Hagrid's mistake. Hagrid asks this of them so easily, never once acknowledging (nor, apparently, even considering) how great a risk it is. Young readers of the series are happy to keep Harry at the center of the action, thrilled by the rule-breaking and mischievous use of Harry's new Invisibility Cloak to sneak Norbert up to the Astronomy Tower. As readers age, however, and return to the text, the concerning implications begin to supersede the adventure itself.

In *Half-Blood Prince* we see marginal progress; here at last Hagrid acknowledges that his request for Harry to visit is inappropriate. With Voldemort's return finally public knowledge and Aurors and Order members alike stationed on Hogwarts grounds protecting students and enforcing curfew, it is no small thing to ask Harry and his friends to leave the safety of the castle. In Hagrid's reasoning, the death of Aragog—briefly his pet and longtime danger of the Forbidden Forest—must surely justify such a risk. "I know you're not supposed to be out that late, but you can use the cloak. Wouldn't ask, but I can't face it alone," he writes (*HBP* 470). Hermione, no longer the earnest eleven-year-old eager to prove her loyalty and friendship, voices her concerns: "He's asking us to leave the castle at night and he knows security's a million times tighter and how much trouble we'd be in if we were caught" (*HBP* 470). She also notes that "it's such a pointless thing to get detention for," let alone the more dire of possible consequences (*HBP* 471).

Yet we love Hagrid, as Harry loves Hagrid. There's a distinct connection that runs between Harry and Hagrid, who, having been bullied and mistreated, even made spectacles of, both find a home and a sense of belonging at Hogwarts. Hagrid is portrayed with a heart as big as his body, and though he may be a bit of a bumbling oaf at times, he cares about Harry, so we forgive him his faults. We overlook the dragon and the acromantula; we remember the photo album that gives Harry a piece of his identity back; we can't forget that Hagrid was the one who carried Harry—out of Godric's Hollow, out of the forest. We assume, because of his genial obtuseness, that the possible risks to Harry are unintended and that Hagrid's requests, while reasonable requests of a friend, are complicated by the hierarchy of power that exists in a relationship between a child and an adult.

The same cannot be said of Dumbledore.

While Dumbledore displays a certain favoritism and clear affection towards Harry throughout the series, Harry acknowledges in *Deathly Hallows* that he hardly knew Dumbledore at all, something of great concern and shock to readers and Harry alike when several aspects of Dumbledore's past are revealed in the final novel. We, like Harry, fall under the spell of his benevolence, his twinkling eyes and kind attention bookending each of the earlier books, so that it is only when we look back that we realize that Dumbledore and Harry actually rarely interact until *Half-Blood Prince*. Their brief conversations before the Mirror of Erised and in the Hospital Wing following Quirrell's attack are charged with an intense attention to Harry and his fears, something no adult has given him in all the years he's lived with the Dursleys. Harry holds onto these moments, cherishes and amplifies them beyond what could not have been more than a half-an-hour's time spent interacting in the course of an entire school year.

Much has already been said on the subject of Dumbledore's ambiguous moral compass, of his master plan to defeat Lord Voldemort centering on the sacrifice of a young boy, so his position as an unimpeachable father figure has been somewhat diminished over the years. However, it incites an interesting question of intent when juxtaposed with Hagrid's bumbling endangerment of Harry. Unlike Hagrid, Dumbledore's abuse of his relationship with Harry runs deep, his manipulations long-seeded and far-reaching. His actions are also made under the guise of affection and care, exploiting the earnest trust and loyalty from Harry that Dumbledore has spent many years cultivating. For the purpose of this argument, the most pressing offense from Dumbledore is that he intentionally places Harry in danger. After it is suggested that Dumbledore intended for Harry to go beneath the trap door and face-off against Quirrell-Voldmort:

> Hermione exploded, "if he did—I mean to say—that's terrible—you could have been killed."
>
> "No, it isn't," said Harry thoughtfully. "He's a funny man, Dumbledore. I think he sort of wanted to give me a chance. I think he knows more or less everything that goes on here, you know. I reckon he had a pretty good idea we were going to try, and instead of stopping us, he just taught us enough to help. I don't think it was an accident he let me find out how the mirror worked. It's almost like he thought I had the right to face Voldemort if I could ..." (SS 302)

From the first novel, we see both Dumbledore's careful positioning of Harry within the plot and Harry's earnest interpretation of that behavior. This is not a tricky translation in ancient runes that Harry is given to sort out. Dumbledore gives an eleven-year-old boy "a chance" to sneak past a massive three-headed dog, narrowly avoid strangulation by Devil's Snare, beheading by a transfigured chess-piece, and poisoning by a poorly reasoned choice of potion because he "thought [Harry] had the right" to try. If Harry's assertion in this moment is correct, that Dumbledore "knows more or less everything that goes on" at Hogwarts, the headmaster's actions are at best cavalier and at worst calculated. Later evidence points towards the latter, as Dumbledore's omniscience, at least regarding the events of *Sorcerer's Stone*, is confirmed through Snape's memories: "Keep an eye on Quirrell, won't you," Dumbledore instructs him (*DH* 679).

As a guardian, Molly Weasley is far from this cavalier. She is established in the first book as a surrogate mother to Harry, knitting him his own Weasley sweater for Christmas and inviting him to the Burrow the following summer. In that regard, Molly's failings as a protector come from perhaps the best intentions, those of maternal care and love. Though it is natural to shield children from unsavory truths, her attempts to keep Harry in the dark regarding Sirius Black constitute borderline endangerment. By *Prisoner of Azkaban*, it is already clear that trouble has a way of finding Harry; withheld information and half-truths do not protect him, they put him at risk (*PA* 75). She also works intentionally and tirelessly to keep the trio separate from one another as they attempt to plan their quest for the Hallows in book 7. Her control over their movements is illusory, their eventual departure something even Arthur appears resigned to. Given a mission by Dumbledore, there is nothing that will stop Harry from seeing it through, yet she persists, gaining a fleeting victory for her peace of mind at the risk of leaving Harry, Ron, and Hermione perilously unprepared.

As the focal point of both a prophecy and a Dark Lord's vengeance, Harry's adolescence isn't comparable to Ron's or anyone else's. Some, like Sirius and at times Lupin, take Molly's position to the opposite extreme: if Harry is not a normal child, then he must be an adult. These opposing viewpoints come to a head in *Order of the Phoenix*. Sirius insists "he's not a child," and, while Molly often forgets Harry is on his way to adulthood, she is the only one bold enough to point out that "[Harry is] not James," and the "adults responsible for [him] should not forget it" (*OP* 88).

While Molly sees him as a child—as good as one of her own—Sirius often conflates his godson with the friend he lost. It's no stretch to understand why: his last night of freedom was the last time he saw James alive, his twelve years of false imprisonment spent fixating on that night and on his own innocence. Sirius later affirms that it was the only thing that kept him sane; however, a twelve-year obsession with James surely accounts for why, when he encounters Harry, the two Potters begin to bleed together for him. Harry is said repeatedly to be the spitting image of his father.

Molly's desire to protect Harry's status as a child has her criticizing not only Sirius, but Remus Lupin as well. Lupin who, for the majority of the series, is level-headed and invested in Harry's education and safety, loses that rationality in *Deathly Hallows*. He is distant from most of the action in *Half-Blood Prince*, and when he returns to the narrative with a family of his own, it is to attempt to escape his perceived "mistake." He has regressed to his Marauder years, joining Sirius in willfully ignoring the consequences of his actions. Whatever his actual intentions, Harry believes Lupin to be foolishly seeking adventure when the older man appears in Grimmauld Place offering to accompany the Golden Trio on the Horcrux hunt:

"Harry, I'm sure James would have wanted me to stick with you."

"Well," said Harry slowly, "I'm not. I'm pretty sure my father would have wanted to know why you aren't sticking with your own kid, actually." (*DH* 212)

The man who has always treated Harry with kindness and understanding, who took the time to teach a young boy how to defend himself against dementors, is all but unrecognizable. The text even goes so far as to have Remus draw his wand against Harry: "There was a loud bang and [Harry] felt himself flying backward as if punched; as he slammed into the kitchen wall and slid to the floor, he glimpsed the tail of Lupin's cloak disappearing around the door" (*DH* 214). That Harry's father was one of his best friends, that he was the only decent DADA teacher Hogwarts has had in years, that he acts as a father figure to Harry—all irrelevant. In his perceived closeness to Harry, he has lost sight of the boundaries that must exist.

Though the presence of each of these adults fluctuates depending on the book, Sirius and Lupin don't appear until *Prisoner of Azkaban*, and three of the five are dead by the end of the series, all of them have their parental roles acknowledged explicitly within the text. The manner of their care for Harry is superseded by the depth of it, allowing for the numerous indiscretions mentioned above, yet McGonagall, reserved and measured in her regard, constant in her attention and care, cannot claim that textual, parental space even though she does the most to deserve it.

Harry and McGonagall

It should come as no surprise that McGonagall's first appearance in the series should coincide with Harry's. Just as she initiates eleven-year-old Harry's first contact with the wizarding world via his Hogwarts letter, it is also McGonagall who watches over the infant Harry's delivery into the hands and of his only Muggle relatives, with full knowledge and insight of what that will mean. McGonagall spends hours observing the Dursleys, a reasonable precaution, considering it's meant to be the new home of the newly orphaned Boy Who Lived. Her protestations at Dumbledore's indifference are immediate and fierce:

"You don't mean—you can't mean the people who live here?" cried Professor McGonagall, jumping to her feet and pointing at number four. "Dumbledore—

you can't. I've been watching them all day. You couldn't find two people who
are less like us." (SS 13)

Though her loyalty to Dumbledore is (and remains) unwavering throughout the novels, McGonagall confronts him beside the hedge of Privet Drive.
Though she trusts Dumbledore and, by extension, the information he alone is
privy to, she fears for Harry, all but insisting that whatever Dumbledore's reasons, they cannot be sufficient to counteract the abuse she has already foreseen.

At Hogwarts, McGonagall consistently sees Harry as he is, a first-year
with a talent for Quidditch, a fifth-year who could be a great Auror given the
right guidance. Though Harry and Ron both harbor brief hopes that she will
favor Gryffindors as Snape favors Slytherin House, she quickly corrects their
thinking. If anything, McGonagall appears to hold Gryffindors to a higher
standard than the other Houses and is the first to mete out detentions or lost
points for rule breaking. The Norbert incident, for example, results in a loss
of fifty points each for Harry, Hermione, and Neville when they are caught
by McGonagall, who justifies the massive deduction by saying, "I've never
been more ashamed of Gryffindor students" (SS 244).

Though Harry is in fact a child, McGonagall never condescends to him.
She tells him what she can when she can, and in accordance with his experiences and maturity level, and expects him to act accordingly. She doesn't lie
about the Sorcerer's Stone when confronted, but she assures them "no one
can possibly steal it, it's too well protected" (SS 268). The following year, when
Harry returns from slaying the basilisk that has been slumbering beneath the
school for decades, "Professor Dumbledore was standing by the mantelpiece,
beaming, next to Professor McGonagall, who was taking great, steadying
gasps, clutching her chest"—reacting appropriately to the sight of a twelve-
year-old brandishing a bloody sword (CS 327). Often, as in this scene, relegated to the background, McGonagall is on hand for nearly every major
event, yet her presence becomes an unremarkable given, and her reactions
are easily overlooked. It is Dumbledore's lines we remember ("only a true
Gryffindor could have pulled that out of the hat") because Harry has long
sought that beaming, effusive praise (CS 334).

From age eleven to fourteen, Harry is thrust into danger with almost for-
mulaic consistency, and his reactive responses are typical of an adolescent.
Without the necessary knowledge, children rely on instincts and emotion to
navigate new or difficult situations. Harry, kept in the dark for so long about

his past and the wizarding world, initially has only those instincts to rely on, and, while those gut feelings quite often prove to be right, his successes have the detrimental effect of reinforcing that behavior. Dumbledore encourages Harry to rely on his instincts—Dumbledore, who stands to gain from an emotionally driven Chosen One. But McGonagall encourages, even insists upon, calm and reason. For example, when Harry and Ron encounter a sealed Platform 9¾ in *Chamber of Secrets*, they panic, steal the enchanted Ford Anglia, and take off, all in the span of ten minutes, to predictably disastrous results. Arriving at Hogwarts, the pair is confronted by McGonagall, and when she points out that they could have very easily owled Hogwarts rather than drive a flying car over Britain, "Harry gaped at her. Now she said it, that seemed the obvious thing to have done . . . "I—I didn't think—," he stammers. McGonagall, however, is unrelenting: "That," she says, "is obvious" (*CS* 80). McGonagall repeatedly challenges Harry's recklessness, demanding to know "what on earth were you thinking of?" (*SS* 177). Demanding he think, period.

Scholars argue that a shift in the series takes place between books 4 and 5; Voldemort has returned, the Second Wizarding War has begun, and the children of the first four books are becoming adults [See Konchar Farr and Mars in chapter 1 in this volume]. The relationship between Harry and McGonagall appropriately undergoes a similar shift toward maturity. In the wake of Umbridge's takeover of Hogwarts, McGonagall becomes the bastion against ministerial interference and Harry's stalwart defender. No longer the short-sighted eleven-year old, Harry can't ignore the consequences of his actions any more. There is no excuse for rash behavior because fifteen-year-old Harry knows better; McGonagall makes sure he knows better. Having a biscuit with her after a nasty exchange with Umbridge, Harry expresses his surprise at not being further punished for talking back to the headmistress. McGonagall, openly frustrated with him, responds: "Potter, use your common sense. . . . You know where she comes from, you must know to whom she is reporting," and she tempers her usual brusque manner with a caution to "be careful" (*OP* 247–49). It is left to McGonagall to show Harry how to navigate a wizarding world that is no longer as simple as it was in *Sorcerer's Stone*. It is her job to teach him when to act and when to wait, a skill that becomes invaluable in the final book. Dumbledore encourages him to try out his skills, often without the necessary knowledge, preparation, or planning. His godfather models recklessness. From whom would Harry have learned to look before leaping?

McGonagall is the first to point out that Harry's O.W.L. grade in her class is only "Acceptable" and that if he wishes to continue to her N.E.W.T. level courses, he'll need to work hard to scrape up the necessary "Exceeds Expectations" (*OP* 662–63). She won't accept him on name alone. Yet, when Umbridge intends to blacklist Harry at the Ministry simply because of who he is, McGonagall will not stand for it. Nothing can stop Umbridge from employing a theory-only based DADA, nor can McGonagall override Harry's O.W.L. results to ensure he is eligible for the Auror program. Yet, if it is his goal to become an Auror, there is something still within her power: she can teach. "I will assist you to become an Auror if it is the last thing I do! If I have to coach you nightly I will make sure you achieve the required results!" (*OP* 665). McGonagall seeks to arm Harry with skills that will not only outlast Umbridge's administration, but that will also protect him from the dangers that await him.

Harry knows what supporting him costs those around him. He, in turn, protects McGonagall. Each time he serves detention with Umbridge and the scar "I must not tell lies" is carved deeper, his friends insist he tell McGonagall, "[She'd] go nuts if she knew" (*OP* 324). Harry knows this is true, yet he refuses again and again because "how long d'you reckon it'd take Umbridge to pass another Decree saying anyone who complains about the High Inquisitor gets sacked immediately?" (*OP* 324). It is not just a selfless act, to which Harry is already prone, but an intentional one. He knows, more than Ron and Hermione, the myriad of consequences involved in each of his actions. Having learned from McGonagall that the immediate threat is not always the most perilous, Harry has determined that to risk McGonagall's removal from Hogwarts would be to risk the loss of the school's best protector.

Defending the Defender

McGonagall fulfills that role throughout the next two books, and when Harry is reunited with her, hidden at first beneath the Invisibility Cloak, it is to bear witness to her resistance. "Why would Harry Potter try to get inside Ravenclaw Tower? Potter belongs in my House!" McGonagall demands, summoned by the Carrows' reports of having "got Potter" (*DH* 592). McGonagall has never stated her fondness for Harry so explicitly, and it's unlikely that she would have ever knowingly done so in his presence, yet as soon as she says it, readers know it's true and ironclad. "Beneath the disbelief and anger, Harry heard a little strain of pride in her voice, and affection for Minerva McGonagall gushed up inside him" (*DH* 592). Confronted with the truth he's always been aware of, yet never heard, cements something foundational in Harry. McGonagall, "irascible and inflexible, perhaps" was, and had always been, from that first night on the Dursley's doorstep, "dependably, solidly present" (*OP* 730).

The Carrow siblings, open Death Eaters, are "fond of the Cruciatus Curse" when it comes to punishing students, something that Harry is horrified to learn only a few hours earlier. Yet Harry points out that McGonagall and the other professors faced a choice "between staying and teaching, or a nice few years in Azkaban—and that's if they [were] lucky" (*DH* 226). He believed they would "stay to try and protect the students," which, of course, is exactly what McGonagall did (*DH* 226). When Amycus threatens to blame one of the students for summoning Voldemort, McGonagall intercedes: "You are not going to pass off your many ineptitudes on the students of Hogwarts. I shall not permit it" (*DH* 593).

At the end of seven novels, we know Harry's character, his graces, and his flaws. We know, because we have been with him since that same beginning, that he feels deeply and acts sometimes rashly but always for the sake of the people around him. It is not surprising that he breaks cover to defend McGonagall at this moment in Ravenclaw Tower; he would have done the same to save Dumbledore a year earlier had he not been under a Body-Bind Curse. The manner of his defense, however, is essential:

And [Amycus] spat in her face.

Harry pulled the Cloak off himself, raised his wand, and said, "You shouldn't have done that."

As Amycus spun around, Harry shouted, "*Crucio!*"

The Death Eater was lifted off his feet. He writhed through the air like a drowning man, thrashing and howling in pain, and then, with a crunch and a shattering of glass, he smashed into the front of a bookcase and crumpled, insensible, to the floor.

"I see what Bellatrix meant," said Harry, the blood thundering through his brain, "you need to really mean it."

"Potter!" whispered Professor McGonagall, clutching her heart. "Potter— you're here! What—? How—?" She struggled to pull herself together. "Potter, that was foolish!"

"He spat at you," said Harry.

"Potter, I—that was very—very gallant of you—but don't you realize?"

"Yeah, I do," Harry assured her. (*DH* 593–94)

While it is demonstrated in *Goblet of Fire* that even fourteen-year-old school children are capable of mustering a passable Imperius Curse, the remaining Unforgivables take a great deal more intention. Not even in his grief and anger minutes after Sirius Black's death can Harry successfully cast the Cruciatus Curse on Sirius's murderer, Bellatrix Lestrange; not after Dumbledore is murdered does Harry have the "nerves or the ability" to curse Severus Snape, though he makes several attempts in the chase (*HBP* 602). Yet, when Carrow spits in McGonagall's face, Harry, without hesitation or difficulty, sends the Death Eater into fits of agonizing torture. When faced with Voldemort, Harry consistently and notoriously employs the Disarming Charm, refusing "to blast people out of [his] way just because they're there" as the Dark Lord would. But with every hero there is a line that should never be crossed; for Harry that line is disrespecting Minerva McGonagall (*DH* 71). This is the only time in the seven-book series when he successfully deploys this Unforgivable Curse.

There is a line for McGonagall as well, equally long in coming, yet as pivotal as the events in Ravenclaw Tower for both her character and for her relationship with Harry. When Dumbledore dies, she is visibly shaken but resolved, and shifts in only a few pages from twisting her handkerchief to taking charge of the Order and of Hogwarts (*HBP* 616). When the castle is besieged, she is steel, organizing the evacuation of the students with crisp efficiency and leading the defense of the school herself, calling even the statues to life. While she instructs the other professors to "establish basic protection around the place, then gather [their] students and meet in the Great Hall," and believes "most must be evacuated," she knows that many who are of age will want to stay and fight (*DH* 600). It is a chance she feels obligated to give them, despite the risk. Yet, there are some things not even McGonagall can bear; when Hagrid emerges from the forest in Deathly Hallows carrying a seemingly dead Harry, she is the first to react:

"NO!"

The scream was the more terrible because he had never expected or dreamed that Professor McGonagall could make such a sound. He heard another woman laughing nearby, and knew that Bellatrix gloried in McGonagall's despair. (*DH* 730)

It's a visceral cry of despair in an already tense moment of the narrative. Readers know Harry is alive and one step closer to defeating Voldemort, but still engulfed by his shocking resurrection, we forget that only Narcissa Malfoy knows the truth. To the resistance, their symbol, the Chosen One, has fallen. To McGonagall, a seventeen-year-old boy, her student and charge for the last seven years, has been murdered; she has failed to protect him. In this moment, the depth of their relationship at last laid bare in Ravenclaw Tower, is unquestionable.

Not only is McGonagall's unwavering strength a touchstone for Harry throughout the series, but that same strength is an example for readers who feels lost or thwarted in challenging times. She is an extremely capable witch whose priorities are to keep Hogwarts and her students safe. It is because of this commitment to educating children above all else that she, and she alone, sees Harry as he is, a young wizard with a terrible burden. McGonagall does not manipulate or misjudge Harry and, while she would prefer he never confront Voldemort again, she doesn't let her wishes interfere with reality; she makes certain that Harry is prepared for what is coming, including the ability to discern which battles are to be fought and which are better avoided.

Can we imagine Harry succeeding in *Deathly Hallows* if those lessons hadn't been carefully and intentionally taught? As impulsive as his actions may seem during his hunt for the Horcruxes, they are nothing compared to the actions of an eleven-year-old boy who, convinced his Potions professor was evil, jumped down a trapdoor without a second thought. McGonagall is more responsible than any other adult for Harry's transition from impetuous child to discerning adult. To underplay her role in the series does this complex character a grave disservice.

Works Cited

Birch, Megan L. "Schooling Harry Potter: Teachers and Learning, Power and Knowledge" in *Critical Perspectives on Harry Potter*, edited by Elizabeth E. Heilman. Routledge, 2009. 103–20.

Heilman, Elizabeth E., and Trevor Donaldson. "From Sexist to (sort-of) Feminist: Representations of Gender in the *Harry Potter* Series" in *Critical Perspectives on Harry Potter*, edited by Elizabeth E. Heilman. Routledge, 2009. 139–62.

Jones, Hillary A. "'I'm a wizard too!' Identification and Habitus" in *Wizards vs. Muggles: Essays on Identity and the Harry Potter Universe*, edited by Christopher E. Bell. McFarland, 2016. 89–109.

10

"LOONY, LOOPY LUPIN"
(Sexual) Nonnormativity, Transgression, and the Werewolf

Jonathan A. Rose

"I have always thought of Dumbledore as gay," states J. K. Rowling, author of the *Harry Potter* novels, in an interview in 2007 (EdwardTLC). The non-chalance of this statement contrasts sharply with the novels' silence on non-normative sexualities. Even moving away from Dumbledore, the only "con-firmed" queer character in the series, it is remarkable that the *Harry Potter* novels, with a central theme of accepting differences, are ominously silent and unable to truly embrace diversity when it comes to non(hetero)norma-tive desires and relationships. This fact provides the starting point for my analysis of how the novels negotiate nonnormativity in more general terms.

One character stands for acceptance as well as difference and is among the most important in Harry's coming of age—Remus Lupin. This chapter examines the werewolf as a site of negotiation that "[explores] processes and politics of othering, social abjection and political marginalization" (Saxena 162). It continues readings of the werewolf that concentrate on a variety of perspectives such as race (Chappell), class differences (Stypczynski), dis-abilities and illnesses (Weaver), or queerness (Bernhardt-House, Elliott). Here, I look at the underlying premise that makes these readings possible, positioning the figure of the werewolf as inherently uncategorizable, that is, queer, and examining the effects that follow. Returning to the initial starting point of this chapter, I begin by exploring werewolves as a metaphor for homosexuality and other non(hetero)normative desires to then broaden the analysis and ask what the werewolf can tell us about nonnormativity or queerness in more general terms.

Despite being a part of the novels from the beginning, the werewolf first remains a vague threat, a story with which to scare children, something that dwells in the forest at Hogwarts, out of sight, and is a topic in Defense Against the Dark Arts classes, where, among other things, it serves Gilderoy Lockhart for his outrageous stories. The arrival of Remus Lupin as a Hogwarts professor changes this *en passant* engagement with the werewolf. It is through him, and the later introduction of Fenrir Greyback, that the werewolf and his position in wizarding society are more extensively explored.[1]

Werewolves in the *Harry Potter* novels are wizards who have been turned by the bite of another werewolf. They are identical to other humans save during full moon nights, when they turn into wolves. The werewolf in the novels, unlike its portrayal in the film adaptations, is, therefore, a human who turns into an animal, a wolf almost indistinguishable from other wolves, rather than a human-wolf hybrid creature. The Hogwarts students learn that "the werewolf differs from the true wolf in several small ways" (*PA* 172), like "the snout shape, the pupils of the eyes and the tufted tail" (*OP* 643). In their transformed state, they prey predominantly on humans. Werewolves are rumored to live in the forest on the Hogwarts grounds—"there's all sorts in there—werewolves, I heard," says Draco Malfoy before his detention with Hagrid (*SS* 249). And already in their first year, even though they do not learn about werewolves until two years later, Harry and Ron "[copy] down different ways of treating werewolf bites" in one of their Defense Against the Dark Arts lessons (*SS* 220). Werewolves are rarely seen out in the open, or at least do not proclaim themselves to be werewolves when they live among wizards. They "[shun] normal society and live on the margins" (*HBP* 334) because of the ill treatment they receive in wizarding society. Werewolves face multiple discriminations; for example, they are "unable to find paid work," resulting in (not only) economic disadvantages (*PA* 356). The privileged Draco Malfoy, for example, "is focused on socio-economic class" in his reaction to Lupin, noting his shabby attire and patched robes (Stypczynski 92). Already in his school days, young Lupin "was terrified [his friends] would desert [him] the moment they found out what [he] was" (*PA* 354). Ron Weasley represents the rules and norms of the wizarding world (unfamiliar to Harry Potter and Hermione Granger, who grew up in Muggle society), so he provides a good example of how werewolves are treated by wizardkind. Ron likes Lupin as a teacher and is enthusiastic about his Defense Against the Dark Arts lessons. Finding out that Lupin is a werewolf immediately changes how he views his teacher: he "[gasps], '*Get away from me, werewolf!*'" (*PA* 345, emphasis in original) when Lupin approaches to help him and cannot believe that "Dumbledore hired [Lupin] when he knew [he was] a werewolf" (*PA* 346), proclaiming the headmaster "mad." Ron's "prejudice against werewolves is not isolated but of a piece with other cultural fears against non-wizard species" (Westman 323) and is echoed in his mother's reaction to her husband being treated in the same room as a werewolf at St. Mungo's Hospital for Magical Maladies and Injuries, when she wonders whether the werewolf is "safe in a public ward" and if it would not be better for him to "be in a private room" (*OP* 488). This illustrates that "the werewolves speak to intolerance, prejudice, and racism" (Stypczynski 91), to all kinds of stigma and discrimination, including, in the discussion below, linking the werewolf to sexual nonnormativity.

One way to ensure that the norms of a society are upheld is by silencing anything and anyone who does not adhere to those norms. This can be seen in the ways the werewolf can be talked about only as an other, as someone outside of wizarding society, as the dark threat lurking in the forest rather than the Hogwarts professor. Remus Lupin is very aware of these discourses and not only keeps his lycanthropy a secret but also makes sure that he is not perceived as dangerous in any way, that is, by making sure he is not read as aggressive. Rejection is part of his experience in society and one of his biggest fears. Thus, he aims to pass for a wizard. With the help of what Eve Kosofsky Sedgwick calls "a performance initiated . . . by the speech act of a silence," Lupin establishes his nonlycanthropy using silence to contain his lycanthropy (3). In line with Sedgwick, this silence can be linked to the status of "being in the closet," to keeping one's homosexuality a secret for fear of facing repercussions and discrimination.

However, it is not only he who is silent. Rather, silence is the primary mode of discourse surrounding werewolves. Euphemisms for his condition are used, like "furry little problem" (*HBP* 335). The teachers at Hogwarts, who know about Lupin being a werewolf when he is appointed as Defense Against the Dark Arts professor are forbidden to speak about it. Professor

Snape tries to point students toward the fact without telling them directly: he makes them research werewolves "hoping someone would realize what [Lupin's] symptoms meant" (*PA* 346). The fact that students at Hogwarts—and, along with them, readers—are unaware that Remus Lupin is a werewolf seems striking, considering his telling name, both first and last, linking him to wolves, and Rowling's practice of employing names that point to characteristics or traits of her characters. In Lupin's case, however, readers are faced with the texts' own practices of silencing. His first name is not mentioned until the very end of *Harry Potter and the Prisoner of Azkaban* after Hermione Granger discloses his status to her friends. The text thus mirrors the silencing practices occurring on the plot level, not speaking the name that would even better advertise Lupin's lycanthropy.

In addition to the werewolf being forced to remain "in the closet," the texts offer other links to homosexuality. The fact that parents would be at the very least reluctant to let Lupin teach their children if they knew he was a werewolf can be linked to the homophobic idea that homosexuals contaminate young people with their sexual preferences (*PA* 423). This idea of contamination, especially in connection with the aforementioned reading of werewolves as a metaphor for disability and illness, in turn, points to HIV/AIDS. The transmission by bite makes lycanthropy a disease of the blood like HIV/AIDS, which in Western cultures is primarily coded as affecting homosexuals. This reading is underlined by Lupin's worry when his wife becomes pregnant that he "knowingly risked passing on [his] own condition to an innocent child" (*DH* 213). The bite itself can be linked back to sexuality, especially because it replaces sexual reproduction for werewolves. Sexuality, specifically homosexuality, and HIV/AIDS are, however, not the only available readings from this perspective.

In order to understand and make sense of the level of discrimination that werewolves face, especially in light of the danger that they are said to pose to wizarding society, it is helpful to expand the symbolized meaning. Rather than being based solely on homophobia paired with the fear of contamination, we can make sense of the darkness and the unspeakable that linger around the werewolf by including other nonnormative sexual preferences and sexualized violence, namely pedophilia, sadism, and bestiality. These become most apparent in the character of Fenrir Greyback, who represents and embodies precisely those aspects of the werewolf that incite fear in others. Greyback is the werewolf who bit Lupin when he was a child. A "maniac who likes attacking kids," he has chosen the credo "Bite them young" (*HBP* 334). Greyback, furthermore, enjoys the werewolf's urges to bite and kill, even in human form, and thus fully embraces his sadistic nature. In the character Fenrir Greyback, "pederasty, 'unnatural' sexuality, and cruelty become an extension of the condition of being a werewolf," thus establishing the causal link between being a werewolf and being a sexual predator that results in Lupin being perceived as a threat for children at Hogwarts (Saxena 162). Greyback's actions confirm the werewolf stereotype against which Lupin is judged as a danger to children. Including sexualities or urges that are not only marginalized but also highly problematic due to the lack of consent speaks to the unease and fear that werewolves evoke in wizarding society, which are used to justify the irrational and intense reaction to all werewolves. The figure of the werewolf encompasses both homosexuality, particularly in connection with the notion of illness (HIV/AIDS) and contamination (especially that of children), and more problematic forms of nonnormative sexuality, manifested in the werewolf Fenrir Greyback.

Rather than proposing an alternative reading, the above functions as an addition to other readings of the werewolf as a marginalized figure, as the werewolf stands more generally for deviations from the norm or the expected. This nonnormativeness, or queerness, becomes apparent when comparing werewolves to other human shape-shifters in the *Harry Potter* novels. Shape-shifting itself is not unheard of in the wizarding world. One need only think about the impressive magical achievement that was the mastery of the Animagus transformations of Lupin's group of friends at school or of Tonks's Metamorphmagus abilities. Why then is the werewolf transformation treated so negatively when other human to animal or otherwise (e.g., Slughorn posing as an armchair in *HBP*) transformations are viewed favorably? Animagus and Metamorphmagus transformations are controlled and happen at the will of the witch or wizard, whereas the werewolf is at the mercy of his monthly transformations and has no control over them. Animagi and Metamorphmagi retain their mind and sense of self in their transformed state, which is not the case for the werewolf. Thus, "it is not shape-shifting itself that causes anxiety, but the shape-shifting of a werewolf which undoes the illusion of active control over one's own body" and mind (Saxena 160). Werewolves as both human and animal are "points of rupture in the narrative of 'human-ity,'" as Vandana Saxena notes (141). As they are indistinguishable from humans except during full-moon nights, it becomes impossible to even categorize them as either human or nonhuman, Being or Beast. As we learn in *Fantastic Beasts*, "there is an office for Werewolf Support Services at the Being Division whereas the Werewolf Registry and Werewolf Capture Unit fall under the Beast Division" (xiii). These points of rupture or transgressions, in contrast to other human shape-shifting, put to question the werewolf's very humanity, and it is precisely this questioning of the humanity of a particular group of humans that aligns my reading focused on nonnormative sexualities with other readings of the werewolf as a marginalized figure and exposes the processes of marginalization.

The werewolf is, thus, inherently a queer figure, one that is not fixed, that changes and transforms and poses a "threat to any enduring sense of identity" (Bernhardt-House 165). Phillip Bernhardt-House defines the werewolf as "a human divided against itself" (163). The dichotomy Beast-Being is at the core of the endeavors to make the inherently uncategorizable or queer werewolf intelligible. This is not only illustrated by the administrative set-up at the Ministry of Magic, but, more importantly, it is embodied by the werewolves Lupin and Greyback, who each stand for one of the categories. Not only that, though both are cast as "the permanent outcasts of the magical world" (Saxena 138), they stand for two different strategies for dealing with their inherent dividedness, showing that it is indeed our choices "that show what we truly are, far more than our abilities" (*CS* 333). Both make a conscious choice of how to deal with their lycanthropy. Lupin keeps his lycanthropy a secret and denies his wolf part in order to attain a place in wizarding society. Greyback, by contrast, does not hide his lycanthropy and, as a consequence, expels himself from wizarding society, as the "most savage werewolf alive today" (*HBP* 334). Both werewolves thus "remain on their own side of the divide" (Stypczynski 75) between Beast and Being: "Greyback embraces his bestial form and the aspect of his nature. . . . Lupin rejects the animalism implicit in the new shape" (Stypczynski 76). Thus, while the werewolf is a queer figure in its threat to distinctions between human and animal, it at the same time symbolizes this dichotomy. Lupin and Greyback's strategies of coping with being a werewolf suggest an either-or decision, as detailed above, that is mirrored in werewolf identity. While the werewolf is human and wolf, he is "unable to exist as both simultaneously," a werewolf's "identity [perduring] only in its rhythmic division, that is, its transformation at each full moon" (Ward, "Shape-shifting" 9, 8). The options available to werewolves in wizarding society, as presented in the novels, entail a choice between either human or wolf, between Being and Beast. Werewolves thus cannot embrace their hybridity but rather have to choose between one or the other part of themselves. As "a human divided against itself," the werewolf can only be one or the other, if he wants to find a place for himself in relation to wizarding society (Bernhardt-House 163). The discovery of the effects of Wolfsbane potion, which make the transformation manageable and renders the werewolf harmless, "does not reverse the marginal position of the werewolf" (Ward, "Shape-shifting" 10). As Renee Ward argues, society's way of managing the werewolf is casting him as a threat and ostracizing him, without regards for werewolves as individuals and as part of wizarding society ("Shape-shifting" 10). Lupin submits to the norms of wizarding society and cannot make sense of the wolf as part of himself, but rather, in line with illness and disability readings, as a condition that he has to endure. Greyback, by contrast, fully adopts his wolfish nature. His lycanthropy is not restricted to full-moon nights but rather has become the main component of his identity. Greyback fully embraces his otherness. However, he does so at the expense of his human part. He, too, denies a part of himself and, like Lupin, foregrounds the effects of being cast as queer or other. Neither werewolf, in dealing with the norms of wizarding society, actively transgresses boundaries but rather accepts and reinforces them by remaining within the spaces assigned to them as werewolves.

The way werewolves are used symbolically in *Harry Potter* can be explained by the werewolf schemata put forward by Shelley Chappell. Even though she reads werewolves as representing ethnic differences, her schemata can be applied in other contexts such as those I develop here. Chappell characterizes werewolves as either sympathetic or as monstrous, precisely the binary opposition that we find in Lupin and Greyback, who are used as examples in Chappell as well. Lupin represents the "sympathetic werewolf schema, in which the wolf remains essentially abhorrent but the human is treated with 'tolerance' for his/her embodied difference," whereas Greyback as a monstrous werewolf is "unified, evil in both human and wolf [form]" as he "willingly [gives] [himself] over to wickedness and evil because of [his] presumed essential animality and moral inferiority" (Chappell 24, 23). The only way to be accepted as a werewolf is to "try to eliminate the 'curse' of being different," Chappell concludes (25). Societal "orientations [thus] shape what becomes socially as well as bodily given," as Sara Ahmed posits (158); this, in turn, makes the two schemata problematic for an affirmative reading of the werewolf as "the essential negativity of the wolf in both monstrous and sympathetic werewolf schemata maintains a destructive vision of difference" (Chappell 27), in which "some bodies more than others have their involvement in the world called into crisis" (Ahmed 159). Embodiment does not happen in isolation but rather always in relation to other bodies and to ways of inhabiting the world. Such ways to inhabit a space or a body are shaped by what Ahmed refers to as "collective direction" (15): "ways in which ... communities might be 'going in a certain direction,' or facing the same way" (Ahmed 15). Lupin and Greyback's coping strategies are thus shaped by the collective direction of the wizarding world, which becomes apparent in Ron and Mrs. Weasley's reactions to werewolves, as referred to above. Both Lupin and Greyback's as well as the Weasleys' (re)actions are captured in the following quote by Ahmed: "We follow the line that is followed by others: the repetition of the act of following makes the line disappear from view as the point from which 'we' emerge" (15).[2] It takes "outsiders" like Hermione or Harry to call this "we" and its directions or norms into question, and even then Lupin's lycanthropy remains an embodied difference irreconcilable with the human and instrumentalized at best. For example, Lupin is useful to Dumbledore as a spy among the werewolves, just as Greyback is useful to Voldemort for the fear he inspires in others.

In fact, there is only one instance, in which the werewolf's dividedness is framed in a positive manner. Lupin is generally presented as struggling with his condition. When he feels safe, however, and accepted, this struggle loses its prominence, and Lupin shows a playful way of dealing with his condition, of integrating the wolf into his human life. This is exemplified by the following exchange that takes place during Lupin's school years:

"Did you like question ten, Moony?" asked Sirius as they emerged into the Entrance Hall.

"Loved it," said Lupin briskly. "Give five signs that identify the werewolf. Excellent question."

"D'you think you managed to get all the signs?" said James in tones of mock concern.

"Think I did," said Lupin seriously, as they joined the crowd thronging around the front doors eager to get out into the sunlit grounds. "One: he's sitting on my chair. Two: he's wearing my clothes. Three: his name's Remus Lupin." (OP 643)

Here, Lupin accepts himself as both human and wolf and thus incorporates the dividedness into a whole without giving any part of himself preference over the other.

All engagements of werewolves with their dual nature show there is no escaping the werewolf's inherent dividedness, and the only viable way to deal with it in the long term and in relation to wizarding society seems to be to choose one or the other part of the werewolf identity. At the heart of Lupin and Greyback's endeavors lies the need to find a space for themselves in a society that does not envision or provide such a space. What is most pronounced in the *Harry Potter* novels' engagement with the werewolf is its focus on the discrimination and marginalization that confront werewolves. Wizarding society provides no room for the queerness embodied by the werewolf but rather makes every effort to either oust the werewolf altogether or to use him as an embodiment of all things evil and dangerous. The werewolf thus becomes a means for wizarding society to uphold its own rules, which, in turn, reduces the werewolf to the functions he fulfills, rather than allowing for an assessment of individual werewolves and their abilities and behaviors. Considering the werewolf as an individual, that is, young Remus Lupin and his desire to visit Hogwarts like any other young wizard, as Dumbledore did, shows that small measures suffice in making possible such a customary school visit; all that was necessary was separating him from others during the full moon, a precaution made even easier with the help of the Wolfsbane Potion. By giving them insights into the effects of living in wizarding society as a werewolf, readers are positioned at "a margin from which to reread the dominant paradigms" (Saxena 165), a position familiar to them as, through Harry, they always read the wizarding world from the margins, discovering it and its rules and norms along with him. The monsters and others of this world, or those positioned as such, "expose the radical permeability and artificiality of all our classificatory boundaries, highlighting the arbitrariness and fragility of culture" (Gilmore qtd. in Stypczynski 13). According to the collective orientation of the wizarding world, Lupin cannot possibly be both human and monster, as "constructions of normality depend on equally rigorous constructions of abnormality and monstrosity" (Saxena 139). The figure of the werewolf thus fulfills a crucial function in upholding the order in wizarding society, at the same time as it always calls this same order into question. By their mere existence, werewolves challenge the naturalness of an order, which makes an essential distinction between humans, if not to say wizardkind, and others. The werewolf as, at least partly, undeniably human "[makes] things queer [which means] certainly to disturb the order of things" (Ahmed 161). What is more, it is the werewolf's body that is the site of disturbance. The involuntary changing of the body represents the struggle of the werewolf, both of coming to terms with himself and of finding a place in a society that does not provide such spaces as a "world . . . shaped by the directions taken by some bodies more than others" (Ahmed 159). In the *Harry Potter* novels, such directions and the bodies attached to them can be witnessed e.g. in how differently the body transformations of Animagi and Metamorphmagi on the one hand and werewolves on the other are perceived.

The figure of the werewolf is one of ambiguities, one that is both human and animal, gentle and savage, hero and villain. The numerous both-and constructions along which the werewolf can be read work as a basis for readings with diverse perspectives on marginalization. Furthermore, the focus on the body might also serve as a way to address the question of gender in relation to werewolves. While the werewolf's masculinity is foregrounded in the *Harry Potter* novels, it simultaneously contains many aspects that are easily linked to feminity, that is, the connection to the moon, the monthly transformations, which can be associated to the menstrual cycle. Similarly, the body-mind dyad is traditionally coded as masculine and feminine, respectively. Maud Ellmann too has noted this gender ambiguity inherent in the figure, calling the werewolf "a man with monthlies, a wolf woman, in effect; [bespeaking] the ineradicable ambiguities of gender" (88–89), which are negated by how gender functions as a binary in society. Putting the werewolf's body in focus furthermore aligns its reading with that of transgender bodies: queer bodies, which disturb the gendered order pervading Western culture, and ostracized bodies, which remain only partly intelligible, in so far as they, in Ahmed's terms, "face the direction that is already faced by others" (15). As detailed above, no matter how human a werewolf like Lupin is, he will always ultimately fail to be (regarded as) fully human, "their physical being . . . simultaneously human and monstrous" (Tudor 25). As Ward argues, the categories underlying wizarding society provide "far too reductive an understanding of the werewolf's nature" ("J. K. Rowling's Fenrir Greyback" 118), just like the gender categories in Western societies are unable to capture the range and diversity of gendered embodiment and identities. The werewolf represents unruly embodiment (Tudor 33) that, in the novels, undermines the mutual exclusiveness of the categories human and animal. This subversion can stand for all sorts of queerings and queryings of norms, as addressed at the beginning of this chapter, to which I add the questioning of binary gender in the figure of the werewolf. The ways in which the werewolf's gender ambiguity is sanctioned speak to Judith Butler's notion of gender performativity as "a reiteration of a norm or set of norms (12), not only by those aiming to uphold these norms but also through complicity (see, e.g., Ron's reaction and Lupin and Greyback's choices) and a (supposed) lack of alternatives for everyone involved. To rephrase Jay Prosser, "the real *of* [lycanthropy] . . . may be the ultimate failure of the [werewolf] . . . to be real, that is to be real-ly [human]" (84).

The werewolf is, thus, the figure in the *Harry Potter* novels that both showcases a kind of nonnormativity that challenges the very basic makings of wizarding society *and* the repercussions that follow this transgression. This dual function, underlying all sorts of discriminatory behaviors, explains why the werewolf provides such a fruitful foil for all manner of readings, be they related to health and ability, race, class, or sexualities and gender. What all these readings have in common is that the werewolf is positioned in a marginal place, stigmatized and a threat to society's order. The above reading is the attempt to bring together all readings of the werewolf as a marginal figure by focusing on the queer potentials inherent in the werewolf as the main reason for werewolf ostracism. All readings are informed by the werewolf body, which escapes categorization and questions notions of stable and unchanging identities and embodiments, thus queering the collective direction, to use Ahmed's term, shaping wizarding society. In addition to theorizing the underlying basis in the different readings of werewolf discrimination, reading the werewolf as a transgender figure furthermore highlights the pervasiveness of collective directions, which relegate nonnormative or nonconforming subjects to the margins as well as profoundly shape the way in which they are able to make sense of themselves.

Notes

1. The novels do not specify if there are any female werewolves. Although Fenrir Greyback "regards it as his mission in life to bite and to contaminate as many people as possible . . . to create enough werewolves to overcome the wizards" (*HBP* 313–14) and attacks Lavender Brown during the battle at Hogwarts (*DH* 519), there is not a single female werewolf mentioned in the novels. In the following, I will therefore refer to the werewolf as male. The gendered aspect of lycanthropy regardless of the individual werewolf's gender will, however, be discussed in further detail below.

2. The notion of repetition that renders the "doing" and its constituting aspects invisible can be linked to Judith Butler's concept of gender performativity, which will be addressed further below.

Works Cited

Ahmed, Sara. *Queer Phenomenology: Orientations, Objects, Others*. Duke University Press, 2006.

Bernhardt-House, Phillip A. "The Werewolf as Queer, the Queer as Werewolf, and Queer Werewolves" in *Queering the Non/Human*, edited by Noreen Giffney and Myra J. Hird, First issued in paperback, Routledge, 2016. 159–83. Queer interventions.

Butler, Judith. *Bodies That Matter: On the Discursive Limits of "Sex."* Routledge, 1993.

Chappell, Shelley. "Contemporary Werewolf Schemata: Shifting Representations of Racial and Ethnic Difference." *International Research in Children's Literature*, vol. 2, no. 1, 2009, pp. 21–35. doi:10.3366/E1755619809000465.

EdwardTLC. "J. K. Rowling at Carnegie Hall Reveals Dumbledore Is Gay; Neville Marries Hannah Abbott and Much More." The Leaky Cauldron, 20 Oct. 2007, http://www.the-leaky-cauldron.org/2007/10/20/j-k-rowling-at-carnegie-hall-reveals-dumbledore-is-gay-neville-marries-hannah-abbott-and-scores-more/.

Elliott, Jacqueline. "Becoming the Monster: Queer Monstrosity and the Reclamation of the Werewolf in Slash Fandom." *Revenant*, no. 2, 2016, pp. 91–110. www.revenantjournal.com/contents/becoming-the-monster-queer-monstrosity-and-the-reclamation-of-the-werewolf-in-slash-fandom/.

Ellmann, Maud. "The Woolf Woman." *Critical Quarterly*, vol. 35, no. 3, 1993, pp. 86–100.

Prosser, Jay. "A Palinode on Photography and the Transsexual Real." *a/b: Auto/Biography Studies*, vol. 14, no. 1, 1999, pp. 71–92.

Rowling, J. K. *Fantastic Beasts and Where to Find Them*. Obscurus Books, 2001.

Saxena, Vandana. *The Subversive Harry Potter: Adolescent Rebellion and Containment in the J. K. Rowling Novels*. McFarland, 2012.

Sedgwick, Eve Kosofsky. *Epistemology of the Closet*. Harvester Wheatsheaf, 1991.

Stypczynski, Brent A. *The Modern Literary Werewolf: A Critical Study of the Mutable Motif.* McFarland, 2013.

Tudor, Andrew. "Unruly Bodies, Unquiet Minds." *Body & Society*, vol. 1, no. 1, 1995, pp. 25–41.

Ward, Renee. "Shape-shifting, Identity, and Change in Harry Potter and the Prisoner of Azkaban." Accio 2005, 29–31 July 2005, University of Reading, Reading, UK, eprints. lincoln.ac.uk/26882/1/ACCIO%20paper%20final.pdf.

Ward, Renee. "J. K. Rowling's Fenrir Greyback: Identity, Society, and the Werewolf." In *Terminus: Collected Papers on Harry Potter, 7–11 Aug. 2008*, edited by Sharon K. Goetz, Narrate Conferences, Inc, 2010, 99–120.

Weaver, Roslyn. "Metaphors of Monstrosity: The Werewolf as Disability and Illness in Harry Potter and Jatta." *Papers: Explorations into Children's Literature*, vol. 20, no. 2, 2010, pp. 69–82.

Westman, Karin E. "Spectres of Thatcherism: Contemporary British Culture in J. K. Rowling's Harry Potter Series" in *The Ivory Tower and Harry Potter: Perspectives on a Literary Phenomenon*, edited by Lana A. Whited, 1. paperback print, University of Missouri Press, 2004. 305–28.

11

SORRY, NOT SORRY

The Limits of Empathy for Nonhuman Creatures

Keridiana Chez

Tasked with expelling gnomes from the Weasley garden in *Chamber of Secrets*, Harry Potter reaps a vital lesson on interspecies relationships in the magical world. Although his best friend insists that hurling the gnomes "doesn't *hurt* them," Harry is at first "shocked" by the violence and reluctant to participate. Initial compassion proves foolish when the first gnome, "sensing weakness, sank its razor-sharp teeth into [his] finger." Consequently, "Harry learned quickly not to feel too sorry," and he chucks the offender nearly fifty feet (*CS* 37). The portrayal of (defensive) violence teaches Harry that gnomes are undeserving of mercy; the reader, in turn, learns that the appropriate attitude is to feel sorry, but not "too sorry," for the suffering of nonhuman creatures.

Harry is often held up as a model of integrity—Professor Dumbledore's posthumous apparition declares him "a remarkable selfless person" (*DH* 573)—and readerly affection has shielded the hero from a critical look at the logic and limits of his empathy, particularly for nonhuman Others. A discussion of empathetic limits reconsiders humaneness as a performance in which contemporary self-identity is deeply invested. Judith Butler's term for our performance of gender discourses extends to the discourse of humaneness in its contemporary iteration, which might seamlessly merge with the biologist E. O. Wilson's "biophilia" hypothesis: the idea that humans feel a "natural" affinity for life that urges us to behave humanely toward animals. How might the assertion of humaneness as fundamentally "human" legitimize anthropocentric ideas and actions?

This chapter begins with two propositions. First, a text with nonhuman creatures likely sorts them into Hal Herzog's categories—loved, hated, or eaten. Regardless of how inconsistently any society manages these categorizations, little room remains for nonhuman beings outside of value systems defined by their usefulness to humans. In *Harry Potter* these categories are flexible but still unabashedly anthropocentric.[1] Second, a text that teaches empathy inevitably teaches where such empathy must end: how and how much to feel, as well as when and why and for whom, by defining appropriate (and inappropriate) objects, attitudes, and behaviors. *Harry Potter* reveals the psychic economy through which Harry's profound anthropocentrism is rendered legitimate: the hero performs empathy toward nonhuman Others but consistently prioritizes human concerns. The performance of both these responses is critical to the construction of the "humane" moral subject: the one who possesses the "humanity" to feel compassion but accepts status quo inequities. Throughout the series, promoting human interests happily coincides with the interests of nonhuman beings, such that anthropocentrism and humaneness become one and the same. *Harry Potter* sets a low bar for the hero to surpass, where even small acts on behalf of nonhumans are praised as humane and rewarded primarily for advancing human ends. The "right" amount of sorry preserves systemic species hierarchy, effectively undermining textual gestures towards expanding the moral circle to include nonhuman beings.

Fantastic Beasts provides background on interspecies relationships prior to Harry's generation. In the mid-1920s, American magicians "had a curse-to-kill policy on all magical creatures" (*FB* xv), and generally, "interest in magical beasts was considered dangerous and suspect" (*FB* xiv). Compared with this stark alternative, interspecies relations appear improved, yet one of the greatest compliments that can be paid to a nonhuman in the series is to be described as "dead useful" (*SS* 81). We can think of this as "useful dead": animal flesh is copiously consumed at Hogwarts feasts, animal products clothe and equip humans, and potions are hardly vegan. Living animals also serve as experimental subjects to test dubious student potions and to be

variously transfigured or vanished. Beasts of burden are routinely conscripted
for travel and mail in spite of the magical—not to mention mechanical and
electronic—alternatives that surely exist. And of course, animals are also
commodities, purchased companions, and entertainment.

Casual exploitation seems particularly prevalent with magical nonhumans, as with the "fancy hippogriff" calendar (*OP* 512) and the "live fairies"
(dubbed "decorative beast[s]," *FB* 16) hung on a Christmas tree (*OP* 501).
Consider the leprechauns and Veela, the Quidditch mascots in *Goblet of Fire*.
Leprechauns "never requested reclassification as 'beings'" (*FB* 48), suggesting
they are satisfied being "beasts."[2] The Veela's status is even more dubious,
given their instrumental function and stereotypical manipulation of men.
Although their anthropomorphic guise allows them to mate with humans,
Veela are also treated as animals whose hair may be harvested for wand-
making, as the bodies of dragons and phoenixes are (*GF* 308). "Veela were
women," yet "they weren't—they couldn't be—human" (*GF* 103). Caricatures
of the "temperamental" feminine, Veela easily revert to a bestial state, "their
faces . . . elongating into sharp, cruel-beaked bird heads, and long, scaly wings
. . . bursting from their shoulders" (*GF* 308, 111).

The most dramatic quest of the Triwizard Championship requires cruelty
to mother dragons, in the unenviable position of defending their precious
eggs from human teenagers. Offering nonhuman bait, Cedric Diggory transfigures a rock into a Labrador "to make the dragon go for the dog instead of
him." Victor Krum is "probably the best after" Harry because he "hit it with
some sort of spell right in the eye. Only thing is, it went trampling around
in agony and squashed half the real eggs—they took marks off for that" (*GF*
359). Not only is casual cruelty to nesting mothers essential to the challenge,
so is lethal danger to their eggs—and the point system accounts for this.
Harry's observation that the Horntail "was too protective of her eggs" invites
the question of what it means to be *too* protective of one's eggs (*GF* 355).
The discourse of motherhood is at first implicated (nesting mothers would
presumably protect their eggs) and then suspended (as if a mere animal has
no right to protect her eggs so ferociously).

The garden gnomes discussed earlier—"small and leathery looking, with
large, knobby, bald head[s] exactly like a potato" (*CS* 37)—are evicted because
they are less useful than actual potatoes. A defensive bite retroactively justifies
their arbitrary expulsion, despite their capacity for human language, reason,
and some measure of civil society. Giants and trolls are also excluded from

human society for bloodthirst and stupidity, respectively. Such deficiency allows the word "Troll" to be used as an epithet for low grades (*OP* 311) and a troll leg to be deployed as an umbrella stand (*OP* 77).³ Although trolls may also be employed as security guards (e.g., guarding a portrait, *PA* 269), they have value only as material resources or laboring bodies.

Professor Remus Lupin's Defense Against the Dark Arts class features creatures that may be annoying or dangerous to humans, but most are not in fact aligned with "Dark Arts" or the malevolent ambitions of Death Eaters. Hagrid's Blast-Ended Skrewts are ugly—"deformed, shell-less lobsters, horribly pale and slimy-looking, with legs sticking out in very odd places and no visible heads"—but their main failing is uselessness. Draco Malfoy wonders, "what do they *do*? . . . What is the *point* of them?" (*GF* 196). Hermione Granger retorts that even ugly creatures might still be worth raising if "useful" (*GF* 197), but she later admits, "The best thing to do would be to stamp on the lot of them before they start attacking us all" (*GF* 198). As Hermione is usually the more sensitive to the rights and welfare of nonhumans (e.g., the "far-fetched scheme" she launches to free house-elves, *OP* 326), her response is surprising.⁴

Yet greater usefulness does not necessarily garner nonhumans greater ethical value. The prescribed relation between humans and intelligent humanoids is embodied in the Ministry of Magic's Fountain of Magical Brethren, featuring "a noble-looking wizard" surrounded by "a beautiful witch, a centaur, a goblin, and a house-elf," the latter three "all looking adoringly up at the" humans (*OP* 127). The brethren's "near-human intelligence" (*OP* 754) is amplified by unique magical abilities—for example, elves can apparate in and out of restricted places; centaurs know cosmological secrets; and goblins possess incomparable metalworking skills. Transactions with these useful nonhumans are subject to the Department for the Regulation and Control of Magical Creatures for the benefit and veneration of human beings, the construct of adoring submission deployed by the fountain to conceal the codification of species inequality.

House-elves, the only truly submissive brethren, are happily enslaved in menial labor and take grotesque pleasure in self-erasure. ("The mark of a good house-elf," after all, is "that you don't know it's there" *GF* 182). For example, their castle labor occurs without human witness and is omitted from the authoritative Bathilda Bagshot's *Hogwarts: A History*. As Ron Weasley insists, "They *like* being enslaved!" (*GF* 224). Of course, insofar as happiness is not synonymous with justice, the house-elves' subjective experience is not enough. The fact that house-elves are tolerated because of their usefulness is emphasized at the final battle, wherein the castle's house-elves volunteer to fight on the side of good. Despite their alliance, their "tiny faces" are described as "alive with malice" (*DH* 588); they remain, for the most part, mistrusted and discounted.

Unlike house-elves, centaurs "are a race apart and proud to be so" (*OP* 756). Although "part-human" (*OP* 600), "the centaurs' habits are not human-like" for they "live in the wild, refuse clothing, prefer to live apart from wizards and Muggles alike and yet have intelligence equal to theirs" (*FB* xix). Nasty characters like Dolores Umbridge call them "Filthy half-breeds! . . . Beasts! Uncontrolled animals!" (*OP* 755).[5] Even nice ones like Hermione dismissively refer to them as "horses" (*OP* 599). While centaurs generally maintain the dignity and independence so lacking in house-elves, declaring that they "are not the servants or playthings of humans" (*OP* 602), the most sympathetic centaur is Firenze, who risks his life and his position in his herd by allowing Harry to ride him like a "common mule" (*SS* 257). To resist human dominion is, as with the biting gnome, to forego human sympathy and protection; assenting to be used as a beast bestows Firenze with unique appeal.

Similarly, goblin resistance to exploitation renders them less deserving of empathy. Harry's encounters with goblinkind reflect the ambivalence with which intelligent, feeling, language-capable nonhumans are regarded. Goblins are a necessary evil, to be transacted with and controlled, but granted little "protection" or "respect" (*DH* 394). The text refers to the 1612 "goblin rebellion" (*PA* 77), a name reflecting magician outrage and goblin suppression.[6] To waylay future uprisings, the "Code of Wand Use" explicitly forbids any "*non-human creature*" to "*carry or use a wand*" (*GF* 132), which is designed to "deny [goblins] the possibility of extending our powers" (*DH* 395). Goblins have "stuck up for themselves" (*GF* 449), but their expectation that humans negotiate with them in terms of equality offends: inferior species ought to keep their place.

The text subtly approves of this suppression by finding every opportunity to vilify goblinkind. Refusing "duties ill-befitting the dignity of [his] race," Gornuk explains that he has left Gringotts Bank because he "recognize[s] no wizarding master" (296). Significantly, as he asserts his "dignity," he sounds "rougher and less human" (*DH* 296)—and therefore less-than-human. Although Harry later saves Griphook, performing his innate humaneness, the goblin proves unworthy: "The longer they spent together, the more Harry realized that he did not much like the goblin" (*DH* 509). Not only is Griphook revolting because he "refused to eat the same food, insisting . . . on lumps of raw meat, roots and various fungi," but he is also "unexpectedly bloodthirsty" (*DH* 509–10). Harry's behavior takes on an even more humane cast in light of goblin repulsiveness. In fact, none of the humans much like goblins, "but they did not discuss it: they needed Griphook" to help them break into Gringotts, illustrating how nonhuman usefulness necessitates begrudging interspecies transactions (*DH* 510). The brethren are thus creatures with coveted abilities who appear worthy of empathy only in asymmetrical positions of submission and adoration. In most cases, their recalcitrance is used to justify their inferior status, a power differential mandated by law and enforced by violence if necessary.

Limit-setting seems especially important in a world where magic renders species identity fluid. In Margaret Oakes's rosy reading, categorical fluidity is part of Rowling's moral lesson: since "almost any living thing or object can be considered something which must almost be treated as an equal, a partner, or an adversary," "the students . . . quickly learn that plants and animals can possess an anthropomorphic sensibility that is absent in their Muggle world counterparts" (126). But this presumes that "sensibility" must be measured in relation to humans—and that fuzzy boundaries breed empathy rather than status panic and backlash. In the series, blurred boundaries do not typically increase "respect" or empathy for those transformed (Oakes 126). Consider Transfiguration, through which humans, animals, and things easily become one or the other or perhaps some status in between. Students turn hedgehogs into pincushions, reducing a sentient creature to an object. Unsuccessful students produce such confusing hybrids as a pincushion that "still curls up in fright if anyone approaches it with a pin!" (*GF* 233). Animagi are magicians capable of changing into animals, and it seems that this is not merely cosmetic—but they still count as human.[7] If things such as goblets are turned into living animals, to what extent do they count as animal? If someone sets fire to Professor Slughorn when he is in the form of a sofa, is murder committed or mere destruction of property?

Category blurring may be as likely to reduce the circle of empathy as to expand it. In fact, magical hybrids elicit humor, not care or respect: a Hogwarts Transfiguration exam entails turning a teapot into a tortoise, but one student finds that theirs "still had a spout for a tail, what a nightmare" and another produces a tortoise that "breathe[s] steam" (*PA* 317). Practicing Cross-Species Switches, they try to turn guinea fowls into guinea pigs, but Harry produces a "rubber haddock" whose head comically "drooped and fell . . . to the floor," severed by Ron's tin parrot (*GF* 385–6). In Charms class, Ron produces a teacup that "grew four very thin spindly legs that hoisted the cup off the desk[,] trembled for a few seconds, then folded, causing the cup to crack into two" (*OP* 679). The damage or hurt to these hybrid beings elicits no response beyond drollery; their status is fundamentally unchanged. Perhaps precisely because of this endless potential for fluidity and hybridity, wizarding anthropocentricity seems ever more pressing. When the false Mad-Eye Moody transfigures Draco into a ferret to administer a punishment that would have appalled readers if he were human, it underscores the significance of being recategorizable from protected human to abusable animal. When the ferret "flew ten feet into the air, fell with a smack to the floor, and then bounced upward once more," most readers chuckle instead of gasp (*GF* 205).

In *Harry Potter* nonhumans are largely treated in a manner commensurate to anthropocentric needs and whims, as they largely are in our own world, yet Harry's treatment of them is viewed as uniquely virtuous. Throughout the series, to underscore Harry's status as "a perennial liberator of all manner of creatures" (Dendle 168), an arbitrary selection of nonhumans are the objects of his benevolence. In *Sorcerer's Stone*, Harry liberates a boa constrictor at the zoo. Harry identifies with its captivity, but when he makes the terrarium glass disappear, he is prompted by anger after Dudley punches him (*SS* 28). No explicit intention to liberate exists, and the result (Dudley's humiliation) benefits Harry personally. In *Prisoner of Azkaban*, Harry helps free the hippogriff, not mainly out of concern for Buckbeak's impending execution but rather so he may serve as transportation. It is also essential to the construct of the human(e) that Harry both forgets the animal *and* feels guilty for forgetting: "Harry felt a nasty pang of guilt. He had completely forgotten that Buckbeak's trial was so near . . . [and] their promise about helping [Hagrid] prepare Buckbeak's defense; the arrival of the Firebolt had driven it clear out of their minds" (*PA* 272). Meanwhile, Hagrid is grateful to Hermione for remembering but is equally happy to forgive Harry's forgetting him for something as prosaic as Quidditch.

In *Deathly Hallows*, Harry liberates the captive Gringotts dragon, again not for the animal's own sake. To Harry, the viciously abused dragon is of no particular interest because it is of no particular use—until the humans are trapped, and the nonhuman appears a useful means of escape. In a fit of "inspiration, or madness," Harry instructs his friends to board the dragon (*DH* 541). The text repeatedly asserts that Harry's humaneness is a product of his instincts, while his choices conveniently align with a discourse of heroic masculinity whereby human interests remain ascendant. In the three examples—the boa, hippogriff, and dragon—Harry liberates the nonhuman, but each humane performance is depicted as not being primarily or solely for the nonhuman's well-being. Essentially, humaneness is appropriate only when it is a moment's impulse rather than a conscious choice and when humans benefit as much as nonhumans. Although this is supposedly outdated thinking, it remains "dangerous and suspect" (*FB* xiv) to actively pursue or prioritize nonhuman welfare.[8]

Even when Harry exhibits direct interest in nonhuman well-being, these relationships remain at least partially instrumental and have little or no impact on structural inequality. Harry's relationship with Hedwig is sincerely reciprocal, but she is clearly distinguished from the general population of school owls, who are mere postal technologies. Moreover, the relationship remains asymmetrical. While Hedwig is described as Harry's "only friend" at the Dursleys' (*OP* 43), he values her primarily because she constitutes "his one great link with the magical world" (*DH* 67). Once at Hogwarts, he visits her only for mail. Hedwig symbolizes his captivity while they share this condition, except it is only Harry's captivity that is categorically wrong and offensive: no one asks if Hedwig might require or desire other companions or if Hedwig should be freed.[9]

In *Chamber of Secrets*, Harry frees Dobby after having heard the house-elf "squealing with pain all the way along the corridor." "Thinking hard," the solution "came to him" to trick Lucius Malfoy into handing Dobby a sock (*CS* 337). Here, Dobby's liberation is directly inspired by Harry's instinctive empathy, but the nonhuman's freedom remains an insufficient end in itself: Dobby's freedom humiliates Lucius as much as it benefits the elf, again linking anthropocentric objectives to the humane urge. Moreover, while grateful for Dobby's ongoing assistance, Harry evinces no interest in any other of the innumerable enslaved elves. As literary critic Peter Dendle notes, Harry is inaccurately declared the "defender of house-elves" (*DH* 734) though he has, at best, "defended a single elf" (Dendle 174). Like his godfather, Sirius Black, Harry does not generally consider house-elves as "being[s] with feelings as acute as a human's" (*OP* 832). Even with Dobby, the text repeatedly asserts Harry's limits: one Christmas, Dobby gifts Harry with a pair of hand-knit socks, and Harry is surprised that Dobby thinks they are friends who exchange gifts. Scrambling, he tosses Dobby "his oldest and foulest" socks (*GF* 408), the same used pair that symbolize how little his adoptive family cares for him (*SS* 43).

Despite the asymmetry of their relationships, Rowling emphasizes that Hedwig and Dobby choose to serve Harry out of devoted free will. Most of the references to Hedwig are either when she works (like a house-elf, she is proud, even jealous, of her duties), gives affectionate nibbles (*SS* 135, *CS* 212, *PA* 7), or is peevish (e.g., for their turbulent journey, *CS* 104; at Pidwidgeon's overenthusiasm, *GF* 35; for Harry's ingratitude, *GF* 227)—a charming trope that portrays Harry as a friend rather than a master for he bears her recurrent ill humors. Her crankiness allows Harry to demonstrate humane tolerance, concealing the fact he holds complete material power in the relation.

Hedwig's function is thus similar to Dobby's—that of a satisfied subaltern. Dobby proclaims he "is a free house-elf," which mainly frees him to "obey anyone he likes and Dobby will do whatever Harry Potter wants him to do!" (*HBP* 421). A free nonhuman can choose to be subjected, which in turn is the ultimate compliment to the human master. The subaltern's agency thus sets the stage for performances of the master's humaneness, allowing the master to feel virtuous while enjoying the benefits of anthropocentric hierarchy. Throughout, Dobby exhibits obsequious gratitude, which we interpret in the context of his species' general mistreatment. Any kind or polite gesture on Harry's part initiates a well-choreographed call-and-response, wherein Dobby grovels and Harry demurs. For example, when Harry asks if he might "help" Dobby, the elf praises Harry's "greatness" and "goodness." Rather than take credit, Harry feels "distinctly hot in the face," performing the modesty required to cast his humaneness as selfless. Fulfilling the cycle, Dobby responds with "eyes aglow" that Harry Potter "is humble and modest" (*CS* 15).

A key scene is often offered as proof of Harry's heroic empathy: when Dobby tragically dies saving them all, Harry insists on burying Dobby "properly." To Harry, this entails digging the grave manually, and "every drop of his sweat and every blister felt like a gift to the elf who had saved their lives" (*DH* 478). This scene credits Harry's act as a "gift," as he could instead resort to magical burial or leave the corpse unburied. (Witness Griphook's comment that Harry is a "very odd wizard" for choosing to dig [*DH* 486] and the alternative treatment of house-elf bodies wherein heads are mounted on the wall like trophies [*OP* 113]) Harry's performance is presented as a profound sacrifice, yet all he does is dig a (small) hole. When Griphook credits Harry for burying Dobby the hard way, Harry again rejects praise, underscoring his role as unassuming defender of nonhuman subspecies. The bar for humaneness is fairly low, yet Harry's gestures are made to seem unusually virtuous by the stipulated context of other magicians' comparatively bad behavior. This context encourages readers to notice only that he could have done less, rather than wonder why he does not do more. The text then deploys the nonhuman to label Harry's behavior special: the proudest, most suspicious goblin pronounces him the only wizard who would "not seek personal gain" (*DH* 488).

The deaths of Hedwig and Dobby also serve a critical narrative function whereby the loss of the Other is staged to further the construct of exceptional human virtue. Proverbial sacrificial lambs, beloved nonhumans are dispensed with so humans may congratulate themselves for their grief. Not only is the ability to experience the pain of love lost claimed as "part of being human" (*OP* 824)—appropriating such fine feelings for the human species—but also experiencing this grief for the loss of a (mere) nonhuman is deemed extraordinarily generous. Paradoxically, the capacity for humaneness is *part* of being human, but never actively required: humans are not in danger of losing their status for failing to rescue, protect, or care for nonhuman Others; they are merely beseeched to not actively persecute, hurt, or kill them. The point is not, then, that Harry does not care about Hedwig or Dobby, but rather that the text repeatedly sets meager limits for how much a hero need care. At the same time, Harry's aggrandized gestures for two exceptionally deserving individuals whitewashes the systemic subjection of countless others. The text repeatedly validates these limits, as Hedwig is beloved, and Dobby is free to dedicate his short life to helping Harry. Meanwhile, Harry is empowered to free Kreacher, but even as the series comes to a close, we find Harry "wondering whether Kreacher might bring him a sandwich" (*DH* 749).

There are, of course, a few tantalizing moments of parity between humans and nonhumans: after the final battle, the text presents us with an image of cross-species fraternity. In this tableau, "all were jumbled together, teachers and pupils, ghosts and parents, centaurs and house-elves, and Firenze lay recovering in a corner, and Grawp peered in through a smashed window, and people were throwing food into his laughing mouth" (*DH* 745), gesturing towards a radically pluralistic utopia where we might imagine the giant enrolling in Hogwarts and house-elves and goblins wielding wands. Yet this idyllic vision is hardly sustained by *Harry Potter* as a whole: Rowling's endorsement of humane values is ultimately undercut by assertive limit-setting and reaffirmations of anthropocentrism. While the long-running series reflects evolving views of interspecies relations, it also supports surprising conservatism. Ultimately, in the moral universe of *Harry Potter*, nonhuman humanoids are of ambiguous but clearly lesser status and nonhuman animals are mostly used as instruments or overcome as obstacles. The humane hero must never cease feeling instinctive empathy, but neither must he ever surpass its designated limits. When the text repeatedly presents Harry's humane performances choices as neatly aligned with human interests, then, it beguilingly conflates the human with the humane—and the final product is the human exceptionalist in love with his own "humanity."

Notes

1. See Chez, "The Mandrake's Lethal Cry: Homuncular Plants in J. K. Rowling's *Harry Potter and the Chamber of Secrets*," in *Plant Horror: Approaches to the Monstrous Vegetal in Fiction and Film*, ed. Dawn Keetley and Angela Tenga (Palgrave, 2016). Also bracketing creatures associated with the supernatural, which implicate different discourses.

2. *Fantastic Beasts* classifies three types of magical creatures, particularly to distinguish "beings" who are "worthy of legal rights and a voice in the governance of the magical world," contra "beasts," based on varying anthropocentric measures including intelligence (*FB* xxii, xix). Yet a nonhuman's intelligence justifies increased regulation, not rights: Law Fifteen B, for example, makes punishable "Any attack by a magical creature who is deemed to have near-human intelligence, and therefore considered responsible for its actions" (*OP* 754).

3. This exemplifies the Blacks' obsession with blood purity, but it remains that under wizarding law a troll leg umbrella stand is legal.

4. See appendix for more on the house-elves and goblins as racial/ethnic Others.

5. Centaurs chose the classification of "beast" over "being" (*FB* xxiii), again representing Others as approving their own subjection.

6. Goblins attempted to subvert the distinction of beast vs. being by teaching trolls a few words to pass anthropocentric language tests (*FB* xxi, xxii).

7. Animagi, however, register with the Improper Use of Magic Office (*GF* 487).

8. Hermione, Hagrid, and Neville are examples of excessive concern for the nonhuman, but space constraints forbid elaboration.

9. A recurrent trope is Harry's resistance to being treated like an animal. Much of Harry's early experience resembles that of "something you goggle at in a zoo" (*SS* 97). The summer he is imprisoned in his room, the Dursleys feed him via the door's cat flap, symbolizing his reduction to animal status: he "dreamed that he was on show in a zoo, with a card reading UNDERAGE WIZARD attached to his cage" (*CS* 23). Any trigger and "he was . . . back to being treated like a dog that had rolled in something smelly" (*CS* 5).

Works Cited

Butler, Judith. *Gender Trouble: Feminism and the Subversion of Identity*. New York: Routledge, 1990.

Dendle, Peter. "Monsters, Creatures, and Pets at Hogwarts: Animal Stewardship in the World of Harry Potter" in *Critical Perspectives on Harry Potter*, edited by Elizabeth E. Heilman. New York: Routledge, 2009. 163–76.

Herzog, Hal. *Some We Love, Some We Hate, Some We Eat: Why It's So Hard to Think Straight About Animals*. New York: HarperCollins, 2010.

Oakes, Margaret J. "Flying Cars, Floo Powder, and Flaming Torches: The Hi-Tech, Low-Tech World of Wizardry" in *Reading Harry Potter: Critical Essays*, edited by Giselle Liza Anatol. London: Praeger, 2003. 117–28.

Wilson, Edward O. *Biophilia*. Cambridge: Harvard University Press, 1984.

12

"ALL WAS WELL"?
The Sociopolitical Struggles of
House-Elves, Goblins, and Centaurs

Juliana Valadão Lopes

In the *Harry Potter* saga, the issue of prejudice, whether leading to discriminatory actions or not, is widely explored through different groups in the
magical world. Though many critics have discussed this issue,[1] analyzing
mainly the struggles between Muggle-borns and the followers of Voldemort, in this chapter, I approach it through the relations among house-elves,
goblins, and centaurs with wizards.[2] My aim is to prove that the inferior
position that each of these groups holds within the wizarding hierarchy is
established and perpetuated by a supremacist discourse that not only glorifies
the wizards but also develops prejudicial beliefs and discriminatory actions,
institutionalized by the Ministry of Magic. Using the Marxist/postcolonial
concepts of hegemony and subalternity, I explore how the centaurs, goblins,
and house-elves are subjugated to or revolt against the dominant political
structures. I also identify the wizards' motivations for subjugating these creatures, the mechanisms they use to do it, and whether or not they succeed.
Finally, I interrogate the role of prejudice and discrimination to perpetuate
these oppressive structures and speculate about the possibility of transformed
and more equitable magical world.[3]

Cassandra Grosh notes in her essay "Freaks and Magic: The Freakification of Magical Creatures in *Harry Potter*" that "since wizards are still considered human, they have been able to create a permanent social hierarchy, *based solely on physical characteristics*, that places them in complete control at the top" (91, my emphasis). Every nonwizard is seen, directly or indirectly, as inferior, and one of the biggest reasons for wizards to subjugate these creatures is prejudice. However, there is a crucial factor that cannot be forgotten and that is rarely explored: house-elves, goblins, and centaurs are powerful and, therefore, could represent a threat to the established order.[4] Goblins and centaurs have a better perception of the institutional power of the wizarding society than the house-elves, as well as a more developed class consciousness, and because of their political awareness, they are dominated mainly through deprivation of their sociopolitical rights. Goblins, particularly, show that wizards have concrete reasons to fear a dispute for power: their own society is evidently organized, they have some control over the economy, and, most importantly, they have fought against the wizards' domination in many rebellions throughout (fictional) history. In spite of not being as politically engaged as goblins and centaurs, though, house-elves are possibly the most powerful among the three groups, since they can harm wizards without the use of wands (*SS* 338) and can also physically control other wizards (*GF* 596). It does not seem a coincidence, thus, that they are also the most subjugated race, not only through the wizarding laws, but also through a psychological domination that makes them reproduce the same discourse that enslaves them.

In order to explore how the wizards try to control these creatures, it can be helpful to understand the concepts of hegemony and subalternity. Marxist critic Antonio Gramsci's concept of hegemony describes "any political change which does not embed itself in people's feelings and perceptions–which does not secure their consent, engage their desires and weave its way into their sense of identity" (Eagleton 46). Gayatri Spivak, one of the most prominent thinkers in postcolonial studies, explains that the term "subaltern" refers to "the bottom layers of society constituted by specific modes of exclusion from markets, political-legal representation, and the possibility of full membership in dominant social strata" (xx). It is possible to conclude, then, that those who are excluded from the hegemonic sociopolitical representation can be considered subalterns. Despite the fact that house-elves, goblins, and centaurs represent different levels of subalternity, all of them fit this concept in the context of the dominant hegemony of wizard-kind in Rowling's novels. However, the concept of subalternity applied to these three creatures needs to take into account their differences, how the hegemonic power perceives each group, and what it does, specifically, to control each of them. I consider house-elves, centaurs, and goblins subalterns not only because of the aspects highlighted by Spivak, but also because, no matter how conscious or independent some of them might seem, they are all still *unwillingly* subjugated to the political power of the wizards.

One of the characteristics of the subaltern to Spivak, found in all of the three creatures, is that they do not have the possibility of full membership in the dominant social strata. In a society that discriminates against anyone who is not a wizard or a witch, their own bodies are constant reminders of their difference. Throughout our "muggle" history, dominant cultures have often highlighted physical and cultural differences to diminish "others" and establish their own appearance and beliefs as the norm. Whether intentional or not, the dominant discourse of the wizarding society resembles Victorian England's imperialist mentality. Aware of the similitudes, Grosh even compares centaurs, house-elves, and giants to those who performed in freak shows, which became quite popular during this era. The freak shows, more than just entertainment, were a mechanism deployed to perpetuate domination over those considered inferior. Since Victorian society promoted a normative look over these biologically and culturally "exotic" bodies, one can conclude that freak shows were a tool to reinforce the high standard of Victorian manners—in other words, what it meant to be British (and imperialist).

Likewise, the domination over goblins, centaurs, and house-elves is a result of this discourse that reaffirms the alleged superiority of the wizards, whose manners and traditions are preached as "natural" and "correct" (Grosh). If, on one hand, wizards constantly see other races as menacing and dangerous, on the other, as Hermione highlights, "wizarding history often skates over what the wizards have done to other magical races" (*DH* 506). One of the biggest mechanisms that legitimize and institutionalize this discourse is the classification, established by the Ministry of Magic, of any nonhuman creature between the concepts of "being" and "beast," as Keridiana Chez discusses in the previous chapter. Explored by Newt Scamander in *Fantastic Beasts and Where to Find Them*, these definitions are clearly situated in political arguments, much more than biological ones.[5] According to Scamander:

Not until 1811 were definitions found that most of the magical community found acceptable. Grogan Stump, the newly appointed Minister for Magic, decreed that a "being" was "any creature that has sufficient intelligence to understand the laws of the magical community and to bear part of the responsibility in shaping those laws." (xii)

Beings, then, would be creatures who can live in wizarding society.[6] However, when one examines the actual political representation and action of these beings, it is evident that they have very reduced participation in "shaping the laws." It is true that there is in the Ministry of Magic a Goblin Liaison Office, a Centaur Liaison Office, and an office for house-elf relocation, all of them part of the Department for the Regulation and *Control* of Magical Creatures (my emphasis).[7] Curiously, though, all of these creatures' interests are represented by wizards (which certainly reinforces their political dependence), who will probably act in favor of the maintenance of the established order. In addition, throughout the seven books, no goblin, centaur, or house-elf goes to the Ministry of Magic. In fact, the only depiction of these creatures within the Ministry is through a statue in the entrance hall that displays them in a subjugated and idealized way, reinforcing the commonsense thought that wizards are their superiors:

Halfway down the hall was a fountain. A group of golden statues, larger than life-size, stood in the middle of a circular pool. Tallest of them all was a noble-looking wizard with his wand pointing straight up in the air. Grouped around him were a beautiful witch, a centaur, a goblin and a house-elf. The last three were all looking adoringly up at the witch and wizard. (*OP* 127)

Another mechanism for control, of particularly the house-elves, is the exclusion from markets, which Spivak identifies as characteristic of subalterns. In these novels, centaurs and house-elves do not participate as active buyers or sellers. As slaves, house-elves learn that the idea of an elf earning a salary is insulting and embarrassing. Since their lack of income makes them even more dependent on wizards, it is an undeniable mechanism of subjugation.[8] The centaurs' exclusion from the market, however, is coherent with their lifestyle. In addition to rejecting any contact with the wizarding society, they live in the forest and, therefore, do not seem to need money or manufactured goods.

It is true that, unlike the other two creatures, goblins not only participate in the market but also own and run the wizards' bank, Gringotts. Their participation in wizarding society in a supposedly prestigious position, however, does not mean that they are not subjugated in other ways. In fact, their biggest struggle is to acquire the basic right to own a wand, something that is denied to all nonhuman creatures. Alice Nuttall argues in "Wand Privilege: Perceptions of Superiority and Inferiority in Wizarding Society" that "goblins are rarely in a position to defy wizards openly; on the occasions they have done so, wizards, with their superior magical resources, have triumphed" (82). In addition to the law that forbids these creatures from owning wands, wizards also developed other mechanisms of control. To restrain nonhuman creatures' basic rights (and constrain their strengths) is to restrain their undeniable power; but the wizards are also aware that each of these creatures have weaknesses they can exploit. The centaurs, for instance, do not seem to want or need wands, but the Ministry of Magic restrains what is, to them, their most precious good: their land.

Another significant mechanism of exclusion is through control of the dissemination of knowledge. One may argue that Hogwarts embraces and accepts difference, since Professor Flitwick, head of Ravenclaw, is a descendant of goblins,[9] the centaur Firenze becomes the Divination teacher, Professor Binns is a ghost, Professor Lupin is a werewolf, and Hagrid, who is a half-giant, is the Care of Magical Creatures teacher. The fact that these professors might be the most adequate to teach there is a recognition that other races also have valuable knowledge, and it certainly helps to demystify some prejudices. However, even if these creatures (or part creatures) have permission to share their knowledge with wizards, wizards are not so fond of sharing their own education with the nonhuman. Hogwarts does not have any nonhuman students, which can be seen as an evident mechanism to constrain these creatures' access to knowledge and, consequently, a way to undermine their potential to expand their powers.

These institutional discriminatory measures, which perpetuate the oppression of the nonhuman, are maintained through the propagation and repetition of prejudicial beliefs. If wizards truly believe that goblins and centaurs are violent (therefore, it would be dangerous to give them wands) and that house-elves enjoy being enslaved, no one will take action to change the restrictions placed on them. When Hermione finds out about the degrading condition that most house-elves endure, she says: "Elf enslavement goes back centuries. I can't believe no one's done anything about it before now" (*GF* 224). As Jackie C. Horne posits in her essay "Harry and the Other: Answering the Race Question in J. K. Rowling's *Harry Potter*":

> Institutional oppression leads to personal enmity, enmity that can easily lead those who experience it to forget their knowledge of a larger institutional problem. It's easier to hate a specific individual than it is to hate a faceless institution; it is also easier to hate an entire racial group than it is to consider how racial oppression may have led that group to feel enmity toward yours. (93)

Contrary to what many readers think, it is not only Voldemort and his followers who perpetuate this kind of supremacist discourse, nor it is an issue exclusive to the Ministry of Magic. If, on one hand, discrimination against muggle-borns is overtly condemned, a discriminatory discourse against house-elves, goblins, and centaurs comes across as common sense. In fact, characters who also suffer prejudice reproduce unfounded beliefs against these creatures—such as Fred, George, and Ron Weasley (who are poor), Sirius Black (who is wrongly imprisoned), Rubeus Hagrid (who is a half-giant), and even Harry Potter himself. When Hagrid, for instance, refuses to join Hermione's Society for the Promotion of Elfish Welfare, he says that "it's in their nature ter look after humans, that's what they like, see? Yeh'd be makin' 'em unhappy ter take away their work, an' insultin' 'em if yeh tried ter pay 'em" (*GF* 265). Similarly, Fred, George, and Ron perpetuate the idea that house-elves are happy within their slavery—therefore, it should not be changed.

Not even the narrator seems to be impartial. The physical differences of the nonhuman creatures, what make them "inhuman," are constantly reinforced throughout the narrative. Features such as small stature, bat-like ears, huge eyes, big noses, long fingers, ugliness, weirdness, even emotional unbalance are remarked upon, underlining the differences that would make them inferior to the wizards. In *Monsters, Creatures, and Pets at Hogwarts*, Peter Dendle calls our attention to the way house-elves are characterized at the Battle of Hogwarts:

> Our last major scene involving elves is their siding with the wizards against the Dark Lord at the Battle of Hogwarts, but here our closing visualization of them is hardly flattering: "hacking and stabbing at the ankles and shins of

Death Eaters, their tiny faces alive with malice." Why malice? Neville, Harry, McGonagall, and many others all fight in the same battle: are they too beings of malice? (168)

Similarly, goblins' legitimate attempts to earn their rights through battles are portrayed by the narrator as "bloody and vicious" (*GF* 342), and they are often referred to as menacing, unfriendly, ugly, bloodthirsty, and malicious. Despite the goblins' history of rebellions against wizarding society, and even though they are the most politicized group among the three creatures examined here, they seem to have least effective *actions* against the wizard hegemony. All of their subversion, at least in the seven years that comprise the books, is through their discourse. Centaurs' behavior, on the other hand, seem to be much more consistent with their own beliefs since their revolt against the wizards is through the refusal to join their society. Yet, with the exception of Firenze, who does not refuse to help (or to serve) wizards, the centaurs are also described as angry, murderous, and menacing.

A close reading of the novels reveals, surprisingly, that the house-elves are most successful in their transgressive actions—in other words, they are quite subversive. Though Dobby's masters, the Malfoys, expect loyalty to their family, the elf visits Harry more than once, without their permission, to warn him about "a great danger" he would face if he went to Hogwarts in his second year. When it becomes clear that Harry would not listen his warnings, Dobby acts. Not only does he block the passage to Platform 9¾, but he also tries to injure Harry badly enough so he could be sent home. Kreacher dares to be even more openly insubordinate to Harry and Sirius. In *Harry Potter and the Half-Blood Prince*, Kreacher's Christmas gift to Harry (his master then) was a package full of maggots. Remember, too, that Sirius was killed because of a lie Kreacher told to Harry. While Kreacher's loyalty was not to Sirius, but to those he thought best represented the Black family, he was purposefully, if indirectly, responsible for the death of his own master. These actions against their own masters represent an unexpected insurrection that does not generally characterize discussions of house-elves.

Yet it is insufficient to argue, using this evidence, that elves are not subjugated to wizards. In the novels, the elves truly see themselves as inferior to wizards, unlike centaurs and goblins, who do not recognize alleged wizarding superiority. One of the centaurs says to Harry and Hermione: "We are an ancient people who will not stand wizard invasions and insults! We do not recognize your laws, we do not acknowledge your superiority" (*OP* 667). Likewise, the goblin Griphook explains to Ted Tonks that he left Gringotts because the bank was "no longer under the sole control of my race. I recognize no wizarding master" (*DH* 296). If, on one hand, it is undeniable that house-elves can be considered subalterns, it is clear, on the other, that centaurs and goblins do not see themselves as such. However, since the wizards see all of them as inferior—and, most importantly, since wizards have the power to constrain their magical powers—one can conclude that, despite their consciousness of their own situation, centaurs and goblins can also be considered subalterns. Thus, the wizards succeed in their attempt to subjugate these nonhuman races, with little prospect of change in the imagined, fictional future.

Even after the Battle of Hogwarts, for example, there seems to be little improvement in these creatures' living and working conditions, despite the fact that centaurs and house-elves fight in the Battle of Hogwarts side-by-side with the wizards. Although the last sentence of *Harry Potter and the Deathly Hallows* is "All was well," we can infer that it was well only for the wizards and witches. Despite a brief moment after the battle, when "nobody was sitting according to house anymore: all were jumbled together, teachers and pupils, ghosts and parents, centaurs and house-elves" (*DH* 745), it seems that the *status quo* is reaffirmed, and no change is ahead. In fact, with the exception of Hermione, all of the characters who are wizards fight for the *permanence* of the order. Ultimately, the basic rights of nonhuman creatures are not cited as a priority, as the wizards fight to control Voldemort, a menace who endangers the established society. Harry himself, right after the battle, even wonders "whether Kreacher might bring him a sandwich there" (*DH* 749), even though Kreacher had fought by his side against Voldemort.

It is undeniable that the *Harry Potter* books deal with tolerance for the difference (especially in the relation between Muggle-borns and pure-blood wizards), and it overtly condemns certain kinds of prejudice. It must be said, however, that the novels blithely overlook other types of prejudice. After analyzing the discourse of multiple characters and the relations among goblins, house-elves, and centaurs with wizards, it is clear that the rights of the nonhuman creatures, as well as their sociopolitical claims to such rights, are not respected in the context of these novels. In fact, as long as the wizards, who represent the hegemonic power, do not alter the prejudicial discourse and do not pressure the Ministry to allow the basic rights that these non-human races should have, no change is possible; unfortunately, the narrative does not present the reader with effective solutions to improve these creatures' lives. Not even the fact that Hermione becomes minister of magic in *Harry Potter and the Cursed Child*, nineteen years after the end of the Battle of Hogwarts, seems to change their living conditions.

This apparent hopelessness, though, might serve to enhance the verisimilitude between the issues and struggles faced by subaltern peoples in a fictional wizarding society and in our actual "muggle" one. As Jackie C. Horne argues in her essay, "it is easy to imagine collective action when the enemy is clearly defined, and is clearly evil, as are Voldemort and his power-hungry followers. It is much more difficult to imagine what collective action might look like when deployed against one's own social institutions, and especially against one's own naturalized beliefs" (98). By delineating the wizarding world's social structure with all of its flaws, *Harry Potter* exposes and denounces our own; these novels make apparent what happens to subaltern peoples when no one defies discriminatory institutions or interrupts the prejudicial discourse that causes it. In fact, to attentive readers, the discomfort caused by this lack of a solution might even work as an incitement to change their own reality.

Notes

1. See Curthoys, Ostry, and Möller.

2. It is true that other nonhuman creatures, like giants and werewolves, are also discriminated against. However, I chose to deal only with goblins, centaurs, and house-elves because I believe that they are more representative of the sociopolitical tensions of the wizarding society since their subjugation or insurrection against the dominant structure is more evident in the texts than that of the other creatures. To read more about discrimination towards werewolves, see Rose in this volume.

3. Since prejudice and discrimination are often used as interchangeable concepts, it is necessary to define each one in order to discuss the role of prejudice and discrimination in perpetuating these oppressive structures. According to the Cambridge Dictionary, prejudice is "an unfair and unreasonable opinion or feeling, especially when formed without enough thought or knowledge," while discrimination is "treating a person or particular group of people differently, especially in a worse way from the way you treat other people, because of their skin color, sex, sexuality, etc." Thus, one can infer that "prejudice" refers mainly to preconceived *opinions* and "discrimination" to *actions* that come from prejudices.

4. House-elves can apparate and execute magic without wands; goblins are very talented metalsmiths; and centaurs are pointed to as remarkably intelligent, insightful, and physically strong creatures.

5. *Fantastic Beasts and Where to Find Them*, in which the fictional magizoologist Newt Scamander explains issues related to the magical creatures that appear in the books, expands

on the *Harry Potter* novels and is the text I reference in this chapter. It is now, of course, also a film franchise.

6. Goblins and house-elves are considered beings; centaurs are beasts. According to Scamander, "the centaurs objected to some of the creatures with whom they were asked to share 'being' status, such as hags and vampires, and declared that they would manage their own affairs separately from wizards. . . . The Ministry of Magic accepted their demands reluctantly" (xiii).

7. Scamander notes, though, that "no centaur has ever used [the Ministry liaison office]" (xiii).

8. It is not by chance that the house-elf who shows more signs of independence is Dobby, the one who fights to earn a salary.

9. *Harry Potter and the Philosopher's Stone*, Ravenclaw edition, 344.

Works Cited

Curthoys, Ann. "*Harry Potter* and Historical Consciousness: Reflections on History and Fiction." *History Australia*, vol. 8, no. 1, April 2011, 7–22.

Dendle, Peter. "Monsters, Creatures, and Pets at Hogwarts" in *Critical Perspectives on Harry Potter*, edited by Elizabeth E. Heilman, 2nd ed., Routledge, 2009. 163–76.

"Discrimination." *Cambridge Dictionary Online*. www.dictionary.cambridge.org/dictionary/english/discrimination. Accessed 20 February 2018.

Eagleton, Terry. *After Theory*. Penguin Books, 2004.

Grosh, Cassandra. "Freaks and Magic: The Freakification of Magical Creatures in *Harry Potter*" in *Digital Literature Review*, vol. 3, Ball State University, 2016. 89–107.

Horne, Jackie C. "Harry and the Other: Answering the Race Question in J. K. Rowling's *Harry Potter*" in *The Lion and the Unicorn*, vol. 34, no. 1, Johns Hopkins University Press, January 2010. 76–104.

Möller, Carin. "Mudbloods, Half-Bloods and Pure-Bloods: The Issues of Racism and Race Discrimination in J. K. Rowling's *Harry Potter*." Lund University, BA thesis, 2014.

Nuttall, Alice. "Wand Privilege: Perceptions of Superiority and Inferiority in Wizarding Society" in *Magic Is Might 2012: Proceedings of the International Conference*, edited by L. Ciolfi and G. O'Brien, 2013.

Ostry, Elaine. "Accepting Mudbloods: The Ambivalent Social Vision of J. K. Rowling's FairyTales" in *Reading Harry Potter: Critical Essays*, edited by Giselle Liza Anatol. Praeger, 2003. 89–101.

"Prejudice." *Cambridge Dictionary Online*. www.dictionary.cambridge.org/dictionary/english/prejudice. Accessed 20 February 2018.

Rowling, J. K. *Fantastic Beasts and Where to Find Them*. Arthur Levine, 2001.

Rowling, J. K., Jack Thorne, John Tiffany. *Harry Potter and the Cursed Child*. Scholastic, 2016.

Spivak, Gayatri. "Foreword: Upon Reading the *Companion to Postcolonial Studies*" in *A Companion to Postcolonial Studies*, edited by Henry Schwarz and Sangeeta Ray. Blackwell 2005.

13

THE FACE OF EVIL
Physiognomy in Potter

Lauren R. Camacci

J. K. Rowling's *Harry Potter* series is highly quotable. Two of the most well-known pieces of advice come from two of the protagonist's mentors: In *Chamber of Secrets*, Albus Dumbledore asserts, "It is our choices, Harry, that show who we truly are, far more than our abilities," and in *Order of the Phoenix*, Sirius Black warns Ron that "the world isn't split into good people and Death Eaters" (*CS* 333; *OP* 302). Characters throughout the seven *Harry Potter* books emphasize the importance of making good choices, about choosing "between what is right and what is easy" (*GF* 724). Rhetorically, the plot and characterization stress the moral middle ground and that good choices can undo past evils. This wise prose, however, does not consistently match the plot and characterization throughout the series. J. K. Rowling does not do a very good job backing up her characters' words with actions.

All too often, evil in the *Harry Potter* series is visible on the face, the hallmark of physiognomy. This now-debunked pseudo-science associated with the eugenics movement of the late nineteenth and early twentieth centuries linked physical features of the face to character traits and morals. While this was largely used in American and British history to perpetuate racist socio-politics, shadows of this pseudo-science appear in the *Harry*

Potter novels to identify bad or evil characters. Although the series regularly states that choice is paramount, its insistence that one can see evil in someone's face imparts a concerning lesson to young readers who may not realize this is a literary device, thus perpetuating the "beauty bias," a modern vestige of physiognomy.

Physiognomy and Phrenology

"Physiognomy" refers to the study of the physical geography of human faces in search of morality. This now outdated term requires definition. *The Oxford English Dictionary* explains physiognomy as "the study of features of the face, or of the form of the body generally, as being supposedly indicative of character." Physiognomy was studied alongside phrenology, another pseudo-science that believed the shape and size of the head indicated intelligence. As Rhonda Boshears and Harry Whitaker explain, those who studied these phenomena believed that "each aspect of character or personality, for example, a love of children, religious faith, being secretive or talkative, or mendacious or thieving, was presumed to reside in a discrete brain location" (88). By this theory, these locations in the brain altered the shape of the head; personality traits could therefore be mapped on the head and face.

Phrenology and physiognomy were nearly ubiquitous across life in the nineteenth century, both in the United States and in England, "becoming a fixture in Victorian culture, arts, and letters as well as medicine" (Boshears and Whitaker 87). From popular magazines to literature to scientific and political writing, people applied phrenology and physiognomy as scientific fact. In the United States, for example, visual rhetorician Cara Finnegan explains:

> When *McClure's* viewers claimed to 'recognize' Lincoln [in the previously unknown daguerreotypes of the deceased president, printed in 1895], they were relying upon their social knowledge about photography and exhibiting their comfort with "scientific" discourses of character such as physiognomy and phrenology. Armed with this specific yet implicit way of talking about photographs—an image vernacular—viewers not only treated the photograph as evidence of Lincoln's moral character, they used it to elaborate an Anglo-Saxon national ideal type at a time when elites were consumed by fin-de-siècle anxieties about the fate of "American" identity. (33–34)

It was important, Finnegan explains, for white Americans to "see" goodness and morality in Lincoln's facial features so they might share "beliefs about individual and collective moral character" (51). Karen Halttunen explains why this was vital: especially in the growing American middle class of the nineteenth century, white Anglo-Saxon Protestants, in particular, wanted a scientific reason to maintain the separation between "us" and "them" (28). At that time, this mostly meant maintaining the separation of whites and nonwhites (e.g., Blacks, Irish immigrants, Italian immigrants; for more on "becoming white," see Roediger), and the dominance of the former over the latter.

As much as we like to distance ourselves from this history, the United States and Great Britain pioneered "race science" and eugenics in the nineteenth century, in which phrenology and physiognomy were a central part. Evolution theorist Charles Darwin's cousin, Francis Galton, theorized eugenics, which "advocated the regulation of marriage and family size according to hereditary endowment of the parents" (Gould 107). If we can see people's morality on their face (through physiognomy) and can measure their intelligence on their head (through phrenology), we have a scientific means by which to argue for the limitation—or even elimination—of those who are inferior. While this is most well known in Nazi Germany, where eugenics was the scientific warrant for the Final Solution, less genocidal examples took their toll on (and continue to affect) the United States and Britain. In short, the reading of morality, behavior, and intelligence through measurements of the brain and on the face *as a science* was used to justify racist socio-politics and to maintain that the different groups were—and should remain—separate.

These sciences were so ubiquitous in Victorian life that their influence spread into popular culture. Boshears and Whitaker provide a detailed account of the historical evidence that Charles Dickens subscribed to these pseudo-sciences, as did Charlotte Brontë (96–100). The characterization these famed authors use in their works reflect their subscription to these sciences, as cruel people are often possessed of physical traits that, according to physiognomy, reveal their cruelty.

Although phrenology and physiognomy had lost much of their scientific credibility by the twentieth century, vestiges of this science persisted in popular culture. Famously dark children's author Roald Dahl wrote his villain's evil onto their faces. *James and the Giant Peach*, for example, describes Aunt Sponge as "enormously fat and very short" with "small piggy eyes, a sunken mouth, and one of those white flabby faces that looked exactly as though it had been boiled" (Dahl 6). James's other aunt, Aunt Spiker, is "lean and tall and bony" and "had a screeching voice and long wet narrow lips" (Dahl 6). Aunts Sponge and Spiker treat James horribly, and Dahl wrote the characters so that their ugly outsides reflected their evil insides.

J. K. Rowling's writing shares similarities with authors and genres she admires. In the past, she has acknowledged that Dickens, the Brontë sisters, and Dahl influenced her as a person and as a writer (Higgins). As a young writer especially, Rowling drew on various genres, adopting and adapting the hallmarks of the stories and authors she admired. Describing her bad characters as ugly or as animal-like is not precisely new; Dickens, the Brontës, Dahl, and many other children's authors use these physiognomic descriptors. As Rowling's models, these authors' techniques make sense in *Harry Potter*. It is the breadth of the descriptions, the abject dehumanization, and the enormous readership of this series that make the physiognomy in *Harry Potter* distinctive. Although her series over a century removed from physiognomy and phrenology's height of popularity, shadows of these "sciences" appear in *Harry Potter*'s lessons that one indeed can judge a book by its cover.

Reading Faces in *Harry Potter*

For a series that so often discusses the importance of good choices and that things are *not* predestined, Rowling often relies on physical descriptions that associate a character's physical features with morals—to show us someone's character on their face. This is extremely common in children's literature; for example, Dahl's Spiker and Sponge are physically off-putting, while James is merely a lonely little boy, illustrated in the text to look perfectly normal. In a similar way, Rowling describes all her good characters in at least charitable terms: Sweet, bumbling Neville Longbottom is "round-faced," where mean Dudley Dursley is "fat" [for more on the moral implications of fat shaming in *Harry Potter*, see Henderson]. The bad characters and the characters of (at least initially) unknown morals receive harsher descriptions. Mad-Eye Moody, for example, is an unknown quantity throughout much of the fourth book—and indeed turns out to be a Death Eater in disguise—and his physical description helps the reader feel the same apprehension towards the teacher as the Hogwarts students feel. Moody's face "looked as though it had been carved out of weathered wood by someone who had only the vaguest idea of what human faces are supposed to look like, and was none too skilled with a chisel" (*GF* 184). We later come to learn that the real Moody is a fine, though quite gruff, man who acquired his scary face through years of service to the Ministry of Magic as an Auror. As I describe below, none of the bad or villainous characters is handsome; there is always some less-attractive aspect of their physicality, such as a constant sneer, that reflects their poor morals (e.g., Mr. and Mrs. Malfoy). Rowling strategically deploys descriptions of fairness or ugliness along moral lines, but the quantity and frequency of the negative descriptors is of primary import here.

Rowling is not kind to her baddies. Among the many physical descriptions of characters are substantial references to these characters as animals. In fact, there are over 100 instances of at least 20 different animal descriptions throughout the seven *Harry Potter* novels. These descriptions range from figurative language to cruel, sometimes dehumanizing, physiognomic descriptions, revealing in each the (im)morality of the character being described.

When animal descriptions appear in the text, sometimes they are nothing more than mere description. For example, describing Professor Slughorn's and Uncle Vernon's mustaches as "walrus-like" or saying Cormac McLaggen is "the size of a troll" is not moralizing or insulting; these are just similes (e.g., *GF* 273; *OP* 25; *HBP* 64, 90, 183, 233, 416, 491; *DH* 601). Similar descriptions, such as of "Ernie [Prang]'s owlish face," McGonagall "eyeing them like a wrathful eagle," or that Neville Longbottom "pulled the [bed]covers up to his chin, looking owlishly over them" attempt to describe something the reader cannot see (*PA* 43; *CS* 82; *OP* 219). Describing a person as "owlish" suggests that their face resembles the raptor's severe, wide-eyed expression. This is common in English: When we describe someone's nose as aquiline or face as leonine, we use these animal descriptors to suggest similarities of features and no more.

Other times, animal descriptions hint not just at physical presence but also at personality. It is not always bad, however. In *Order of the Phoenix*, for example, we are told, "Professor McGonagall's dark eyebrows had contracted so that she looked positively hawk-like" (*OP* 212–13). This description comes when Dolores Umbridge interrupts Dumbledore's start-of-term welcome to make a speech and hints at the relationship between the two women: McGonagall, a hawk, is ultimately stronger than the "toadlike" Umbridge, where toads are the sometimes-prey of raptor birds. Similarly, early in

Half-Blood Prince, "The Prime Minister's first, foolish thought was that Rufus Scrimgeour looked rather like an old lion" (16). After describing Scrimgeour as "an old lion," we read about his brave deeds, commanding personality, and rough manner; he is leonine in both body and personality. Being a hawk or a lion suggests toughness, a positive personality trait.

Other times when animal descriptions indicate personality, they are casual and cruel. While Rowling's characters insult males with words like "git" and "prat," women are insulted as "batty" or as "cows." To insult males, one insults their intelligence, but to attack a female, even if referring only to her personality, one likens her to an animal. Fleur Delacour is insulted as bovine even though she is patently not vast, smelly, or stupid. Calling her a "cow" is an insult, plain and simple. In a similar way, Malfoy insults Ron Weasley in both *Chamber of Secrets* and *Order of the Phoenix* by calling him "Weasel," a common garden pest (*CS* 80; *OP* 626).

Even more often, these descriptions are mean *and* moralizing. They are an attempt to get you to dislike the character immediately, or not to trust them, and the eviler, the worse and more consistent the descriptor. Merely mean people tend to be associated with animals that are in some ways good or gentle, despite their aggressive reputation. For example, bats have a terrible reputation and are traditionally associated with things that go bump in the night, but they are actually quite beneficial and gentle (Barnes). Throughout the series, other characters call Severus Snape "bat-like," as when *Deathly Hallows* states that Snape "flapped after the girls, looking ludicrously batlike, like his older self" (665). In nearly all these descriptions, Snape seems worse than he is, just like Snape's character is ultimately revealed to be.

Similarly, Madam Pince is associated with a beneficial yet unpleasant animal. The narrator describes her thus: "They waited, and a moment later the vulturelike countenance of Madam Pince appeared around the corner, her sunken cheeks, her skin like parchment, and her long hooked nose illuminated unflatteringly by the lamp she was carrying" (*HBP* 307). Of all their avian brethren, vultures are, perhaps, the birds with the worst reputation. Being scavengers, consuming the dead, vultures serve a very important purpose and yet are undesirable and are even considered a bad omen. Characters like Snape and Pince are unpleasant, and sometimes even cruel, and their animal association reinforces these character traits.

Rowling offers a similar description for Slytherin bully Pansy Parkinson. Pansy Parkinson is "a Slytherin girl with a face like a pug" and who has a "pug-like face" (*PA* 96; *GF* 511; *OP* 409). Dogs may be "man's best friend," but pugs are not the cutest canines out there. Pugs are, to use the common parlance, "ugly-cute," a lapdog with a squished face and an off-putting bark. What is Pansy but a mean-spirited, gossipy person who wants to be Draco Malfoy's lapdog? She routinely "shrieks" and laughs cruelly at the heroic characters. Her poor character is visible on the inside and out.

Like Pansy, Malfoy's cruelty is also associated with animal descriptions. Draco has "a pale, pointed face" that the Trio sometimes refer to in rodent terms, calling Malfoy a "rat" or a "ferret" (*SS* 77; *CS* 158; *GF* 205–7, 234, 404; Malfoy "the amazing bouncing ferret" is not merely metaphorical, as Professor Moody transfigures him temporarily into a white ferret, retaliating for Malfoy's attempted attack on Harry). In nature, rodents are associated with stink, disease, and filth. When someone calls another human a "rat," they imply plague, cowardice, or untrustworthiness. This is precisely Malfoy's character: his physical "pointed" face reveals his moral filth and cowardice (e.g., *DH* 633–34, 645).

An even better example of the rat is Peter Pettigrew, or Wormtail, one of the Potters' best friends who betrays them to Lord Voldemort. We read:

> He was a very short man, hardly taller than Harry and Hermione. His thin, colorless hair was unkempt and there was a large bald patch on top. He had the shrunken appearance of a plump man who has lost a lot of weight in a short time. His skin looked grubby, almost like Scabbers's fur and something of the rat lingered around his pointed nose and very small, watery eyes. (*PA* 366)

That he was the only of the Marauders who turned into a tiny mammal, a rodent, shows Pettigrew is "smaller" than his handsomer and more talented friends, in both stature and in character. Proving this, he ended up "ratting out" the Potters, betraying them to their deaths. Wormtail's demeanor is even rat-like: he cringes and whimpers and scurries. The facial features, the behaviors, and the poor character traits reflect one another.

Rowling uses animal descriptors to inspire dislike and distrust for characters outside Hogwarts as well. The Dursleys are not nice people, and this is visible in both behavior and appearance. Six times across five of the novels, Aunt Petunia's face and teeth are called "horsey" (*CS* 4; *PA* 17; *GF* 26; *OP* 5, 31; *HBP* 46). Harry's near-sainted mother Lily, "was a very pretty woman" with "thick, dark red hair that fell to her shoulders and startlingly green almond-shaped eyes," while Lily's sister, wicked Aunt Petunia, looks like a barnyard animal (*SS* 208; *OP* 647). The Dursley side of the family is also relegated to the barnyard: Vernon, Dudley, and Aunt Marge are also described with the word "piggy" or are called "pig" outright (e.g., *SS* 21, 59; *PA* 16, 29, 196–97; *GF* 28; *OP* 13, 37, 85; *HBP* 51; *DH* 31). For example, Harry recalls thinking "that Dudley looked like a pig in a wig" (*SS* 21). It is only when Dudley begins to be kinder to Harry in *Deathly Hallows* that he is no longer an animal, but a young man worthy of Harry's kindness in return (40–42). The Dursleys neglect and abuse Harry, and these horrible people in some ways echo Dahl's Aunt Spiker and Aunt Sponge. From the beginning of the book, the muggle family that readers get closest to are horrible people, altogether morally inferior to the heroic wizards we meet.

Indeed, none of the "bad guys" in Rowling's series is handsome in his own right or remain handsome as he delves into evil. Bellatrix Lestrange was a once-beautiful woman who lost much of her beauty when she went to Azkaban as a Death Eater. She "retained vestiges of great good looks," but she consistently "hisses," "shrieks," and "screams," instead of "says" and whose emotions are always described with lots of adverbs and extreme language, like "her breast heaving" (*DH* 704). The narrator also relates, "Azkaban had hollowed Bellatrix Lestrange's face, making it gaunt and skull-like, but it was alive with a feverish, fanatical glow," an affect that does not draw the reader to her (*OP* 783). Sirius is described in a similar way in *Prisoner of Azkaban*, as readers are not to trust him until the end of the book. In *Goblet of Fire*, we read:

> Sirius looked different from Harry's memory of him. When they had said good-bye, Sirius's face had been gaunt and sunken, surrounded by a quantity of long, black, matted hair—but the hair was short and clean now, Sirius's face fuller, and he looked younger, much more like the only photograph Harry had of him, which had been taken at the Potters' wedding. (331)

It is only as readers come to know Sirius as a hero that he stops being physically frightening. Similar to Aunt Petunia and Lily, Sirius's brother, Regulus, was a Death Eater who *eventually* did the right thing and died for it. He is described in *Deathly Hallows* as "instantly recognizable as the boy sitting in the middle of the front row: He had the same dark hair and slightly haughty look of his brother, though he was smaller, slighter, and rather less handsome than Sirius had been" (*DH* 187). Regulus is still less attractive than his obviously heroic, rebellious, Gryffindor brother, Sirius. Evil and moral inferiority manifests both in the face and as a result of evil-doing.

Dehumanizing the Enemy

The aforementioned characters are mean—horrible and treacherous even—but they are not utterly evil. What does Rowling do with those truly evil characters? Two such characters, Umbridge and Voldemort are dehumanized completely. What Dungeons and Dragons lovers would call the "chaotic evil" and "lawful evil" characters transform, sometimes literally, into animals.

We first meet Dolores Umbridge in *Order of the Phoenix,* when Harry attends his disciplinary hearing at the Ministry of Magic:

> He thought she looked just like a large, pale toad. She was rather squat with a broad, flabby face, as little neck as Uncle Vernon, and a very wide, slack mouth. Her eyes were large, round, and slightly bulging. Even the little black velvet bow perched on top of her short curly hair put him in mind of a large fly she was about to catch on a long sticky tongue. . . . The witch spoke in a fluttery, girlish, high-pitched voice that took Harry aback; he had been expecting a croak. (*OP* 146)

This face as described in the text is not humanly possible. Indeed, looking at Umbridge actor Imelda Staunton, compared to the description and artistic representation of Umbridge from the book, we see that the textual Umbridge is impossible. Twenty-five times across the last three books, the narrator uses phrases such as "toadlike" or "pouchy toad's eyes," particularly in moments when Umbridge is doing something horrible or evil, like taking pleasure in others' pain or suffering. Textually, Umbridge is much more animal than human.

Lord Voldemort, that king of suffering, is similarly dehumanized. Fourteen times across five books, the text describes Voldemort as a snake: "The thin man stepped out of the cauldron, staring at Harry . . . and Harry stared back into the face that had haunted his nightmares for three years. Whiter than a skull, with wide, livid scarlet eyes, and a nose that was flat as a snake's with slits for nostrils . . . Lord Voldemort had risen again" (*GF* 643). Once again,

Figure 13.1 (left) Mary GrandPré illustration for chapter 12 "Professor Umbridge" and (right) Imelda Staunton as Professor Umbridge

the fact that this is not a humanly possible face is driven home by comparing the book descriptions and chapter art to Ralph Fiennes's portrayal of the villain in the *Potter* films.

Nowhere is this clearer, though, than in the transformation from "handsome Tom Riddle" to snakelike Lord Voldemort:

> Harry let out a hastily stifled gasp. Voldemort had entered the room. His features were not those Harry had seen emerge from the great stone cauldron almost two years ago: They were not as snakelike, the eyes were not yet scarlet, the face not yet masklike, and yet he was no longer the handsome Tom Riddle. It was as though his features had been burned and blurred; they were waxy and oddly distorted, and the whites of the eyes now had a permanently bloody look, though the pupils were not yet the slits that Harry knew they would become. (*HBP* 441)

We literally see the effects on the physical face of the villain as he delves into evil. In fact, Dumbledore attributes Voldemort's physical form to the corruption of his soul: "Lord Voldemort has seemed to grow less human with the passing years, and the transformation he has undergone seemed to me to be only explicable if his soul was mutilated beyond the realms of what we might call 'usual evil' . . ." (*HBP* 502). Umbridge and Voldemort's animal faces reveal their lack of humanity and both their inner evil and propensity for violence.

See No Evil?

If you are introduced to someone who shakes your hand and states, "A pleasure to meet you," but with a sneer on their face, how do you interpret this
interaction? Do you listen to what was said, that making the acquaintance is a
pleasure, or are the nonverbal parts of the message more important than the
words, showing that the person is, in fact, not at all pleased? Adults react to
such situations using the schemata developed over their lifetimes to interpret
the interaction. But can those who have yet to develop these schemata draw
the same conclusions?

Contrary to her insistence that there is ample moral middle ground—that
"the world isn't split into good people and Death Eaters"—the overuse of
animal descriptors for the unlikeable, bad, or evil characters perpetuates the
Manichean world of *Harry Potter*. It collapses the moral middle ground, but
even more damningly, teaches readers that evil is visible in physical appearances. Adult readers know that this is a literary device, but would younger
readers come to the same conclusion, or would this offer a confusing lesson?

In *Sorcerer's Stone*, newly initiated wizard Harry asks Hagrid some clari-
fication questions about the wizarding world: "'And what are Slytherin and
Hufflepuff?' 'School Houses. There's four. Everyone says Hufflepuff are a lot
o' duffers, but—''I bet I'm in Hufflepuff . . .' 'Better Hufflepuff than Slytherin.
There's not a single witch or wizard who went bad who wasn't in Slytherin.
You-Know-Who was one'" (*SS* 79–80). Attempt to view this interaction from
eleven-year-old Harry's perspective. His "concierge" to this new world tells
him something, and this child has no mental script to understand Hagrid's
words as hyperbole. Harry's beliefs and behavior throughout the series are
evidence that he took Hagrid literally; his Slytherin paranoia and Quidditch
mania remain constant throughout the series.

As Hagrid is for Harry, Rowling is the reader's "magical concierge," and
like Hagrid, Rowling shapes how we understand this world. In her world,
we can physically spot the bad guys. Of course, Harry's world is fictional; it
is not our world; but to suggest that we can extrapolate lessons about brav-
ery by reading about a preteen who fights a gigantic snake-monster with a
sword and a bird means we can reasonably conclude that there are implied
real-world lessons about evil.

This perpetuates myths that we can see goodness or evil manifest in flesh.
Although physiology and phrenology have been debunked as legitimate

sciences, they have not died. The contemporary concept of the "beauty bias" suggests that good-looking people often get privileges and exceptions that average-looking and especially bad-looking people do not. Citing studies from the preceding decades, Wiley's 1995 study notes:

> Physical appearance discrimination plays a substantive and all-too-frequent role in American criminal trials. Research suggests that people viewed as facially unattractive are more likely to be perceived as criminal than are facially attractive persons. Similarly, physically unattractive people are more likely to be reported for committing a crime than are their physically attractive counterparts. (193)

A more recent study by Johnson and King "found that more attractive and baby-faced individuals are judged to be less threatening in appearance" and "more attractive defendants and defendants with stronger baby-faced features are less likely to be sentenced to prison, whereas offenders with facial tattoos are substantially more likely to be incarcerated" (538). While they found some unclear data correlating threatening appearances to higher sentences, they did find that being good-looking was a benefit, as did Wiley two decades earlier. Simply, people are more likely to think you are morally good if you look physically good, even though this is a patently false association. Notorious serial kidnapper, rapist, and killer Ted Bundy relied entirely on the beauty bias for his ruse; his female victims trusted him and went with him because he was a "handsome and charismatic" white man. The beauty bias meant that Bundy's good looks made it nearly impossible for victims or the general public to spot him for the monster he was. Bundy is just one example that, in real life, villains do not usually look literally like snakes or toads or give "piggy squeals" or any of the other animal descriptors so very often used to describe evildoers in *Harry Potter*.

J. K. Rowling uses a surprising number of animal descriptors in her text, especially to describe villains, ranging from descriptive to cruel to moralizing and all the way to dehumanizing. In doing so, Rowling has perpetuated the beauty bias by making none of her obviously heroic characters into "bad" animals and by, sometimes literally, transforming her most evil characters into animals or other visible nonhumans. These choices draw on the pseudo-sciences of phrenology and physiognomy and their contemporary cousin, the beauty bias, all of which perpetuate our differences and use "science" to maintain the boundaries between "us" and "them." Perhaps "the world isn't split into good people and Death Eaters," as Sirius tells Ron, but through Rowling's animal descriptions, it is hard to take him at his word.

Works Cited

Barnes, Tom. "Backyard Bats." *Kentucky Woodlands* Magazine, vol. 5, no. 1 (2010): 16–17. Web. 28 Oct. 2018 http://www2.ca.uky.edu/kywoodlandsmagazine/Vol5_No_1/pdf/batspg16-17.pdf.

Boshears, Rhonda, and Harry Whitaker. "Chapter 5—Phrenology and Physiognomy in Victorian Literature." *Progress in Brain Research* 205 (2013): 87–112.

Dahl, Roald. *James and the Giant Peach*. New York: Puffin Books, 2016.

Finnegan, Cara A. "Recognizing Lincoln: Image Vernaculars in Nineteenth-Century Visual Culture." *Rhetoric & Public Affairs*, vol. 8, no. 1 (2005): 31–57.

Gould, Stephen Jay. *The Mismeasure of Man*. New York: W. W. Norton & Company, 1996.

Halttunen, Karen. *Confidence Men and Painted Women: A Study of Middle-Class Culture in America, 1830–1870*. New Haven: Yale University Press, 1982.

Henderson, Tolonda. "I Don't Think You're a Waste of Space": Activity, Redemption and the Social Construction of Fatness," in *Inside the World of Harry Potter*, edited by Christopher E. Bell. Jefferson, NC: McFarland & Company, Inc., Publishers, 2018. 33–43.

Higgins, Charlotte. "From Beatrix Potter to Ulysses . . . What the Top Writers Say Every Child Should Read." *The Guardian*. 31 Jan. 2006. Web. 25 Oct. 2018. https://bit.ly/2O7cLWK.

Johnson, Brian D., and Ryan D. King. "Facial Profiling: Race, Physical Appearance, and Punishment." *Criminology*, vol. 55, no. 3 (2017): 520–47.

"Physiognomy." *The Oxford English Dictionary*.

Roediger, David. *Working Toward Whiteness: How America's Immigrants Became White*. New York: Basic Books, 2005.

Wiley, David L. "Beauty and the Beast: Physical Appearance Discrimination in American Criminal Trials." *St. Mary's Law Journal*, vol. 27, no. 1 (1995): 193.

14

SLYTHERIN SAFETY
The Rhetoric of Antiassimilation
in the Wizarding World

Nusaiba Imady

"Every drop of magical blood spilled is a loss and a waste."
—Lord Voldemort (DH 745)

In the early chapters of *Harry Potter and the Sorcerer's Stone*, we are introduced to the dichotomy of assimilation, showcased through mainstream wizarding society, and separation, as seen in pureblood culture, and how loyalty to one or the other is the touchstone of moral principle within the Wizarding World. Harry Potter, a newcomer to this world, is expected to choose between these groups, a decision that will determine how his personal morality is viewed by this new world, while also directing the narrative arc of *The Sorcerer's Stone* and the novels that follow. Harry is offered the choice to either follow in the footsteps of Dumbledore and his path of assimilation (the "good" side), or to assert the right to exist as separate and distinctive in a separatist movement, represented by Voldemort and his followers (the "evil" side).

It is important to understand these opposing views in a more nuanced way than their initial presentation to a young adult audience. A common reading creates a parallel between Nazi ideology and Slytherin separatism (see Fuerst).

Sarah Wente, in *The Making of a New World*, claims that the "fundamental connection between Harry Potter and Nazism is the blood purity racism in both worlds" (89). Wente draws a further correlation between the genocide of Jews in World War II and the ideologies and acts of Voldemort, which lead his followers to willfully torture and kill Muggles and Muggle-borns (102). However, if we dive deeper into the ideology behind separatism in the Wizarding World, we might perceive not a dominating force of power but a minority population attempting to configure how best to survive in a world determined to bring about its destruction. Specifically, we might find that Salazar Slytherin and Tom Riddle embody an ideology of tactical separatism, not of hierarchical racism, as I will demonstrate in the following discussion.

The *Harry Potter* series is written in a context wherein the experience of what it means to be a wizard has shifted dramatically within the last few centuries, based on actual historical shifts: from holding a central role within a multitude of cultures, to being the subjects of a widespread quest for extinction, to the twenty-first century where witches (and wizards) inhabit a greatly mythologized existence beyond the handful of faith-based magic users in the world. Magic is the stuff of TV and fantasy (Cawthorne 25). Examining the *Harry Potter* fantasy series within a real-life context of persecution, both rhetorical and actual, it becomes clear that identity formation among those targeted in the Wizarding World is consistently marked by trauma (see Singer). This chapter argues for the possibility of reading wizard separatism as a force for self-preservation, as opposed to a supremacist ideology as a force for oppression, in the context of the Potterverse and the histories and cultures it calls on.

Harry Potter and the Unreliable Narrator

The motivation for examining the *Harry Potter* series through this shifted perspective is to identify how the dichotomy of separatism and assimilation is negotiated within a minority culture in the novels. This constitutes a form of literary witnessing of how the power dynamic and narration shift a doctrine of self-preservation into a social evil, with clear parallels to white supremacist ideologies. As the titular Harry Potter is the protagonist, the books are constructed through his perception, guided, albeit heavy-handedly, by his mentor Albus Dumbledore. Evil as a concept has been examined in more philosophical, literary, and scientific ways than could possibly be summarized in this research; however, if we assume that the concept of evil is influenced and formed by a subjective audience, we can conclude that judging what is evil is formed and informed by our culture through collective narrative and historical experience.[1] The formation of a rhetoric of evil provides a way to construct reality: who to trust, what to trust, and how to navigate various power dynamics. Recognizing, then, that the *Harry Potter* series is generally narrated within a third-person limited viewpoint allows the confirmation of a fallible subject and unreliable narrator, which invites an excavation of views beyond those that are offered to the reader.

The necessity of understanding a narrator's perspective is articulated by Gerald Prince in "On a Postcolonial Narratology." Prince writes, "The simple characterization of the points of view selected . . . in particular narratives can help to shed light on the nature and functioning of the ideology those narratives represent and construct" (372). In essence, what we are *not* told in the *Harry Potter* novels is in some ways as important as, if not more so than, what we are told for the construction of narrative relies on eliminating other points of view, or, in this case, casting them as antagonists.

Unreliable narration in the *Harry Potter* series is established through the naivety of the titular protagonist's perceptions. Harry begins the series as an eleven-year-old and ends it at seventeen, precluding the epilogue. Though these years are formative in developing one's ultimate cognitive awareness or ethical development, few of us could say we maintain the same viewpoints that we did in young adulthood. Harry's perspective is, without much effort, discernible as at least partially limited, and Harry's mercurial nature remains our only baseline for judgment of truth in the Wizarding World. Harry jumps to dramatic conclusions about those he has decided are Other that, while in congruence with a teenager's perspective, is shaky ground on which to base the morality of an entire culture. For instance, Harry decides at intermittent times that Draco Malfoy, Severus Snape, Remus Lupin, and Sirius Black are the villains in his life, only to be proven partially wrong on each count.

Even Hermione, who becomes Harry's most reliable friend, is first described as "interfering" and a know-it-all, until after the troll incident in which she saves him (*SS* 155, 179). What is important to note here is that Hermione does not change anything about herself; she remains vocally intelligent and generally hell-bent on following the rules. However, what does change is Harry's perception of her. Readers, therefore, are led to assume that "Hermione had become a bit more relaxed about breaking rules . . . and she was much nicer for it" (SS 181). Hermione does not transfigure into a new variant of herself, only the way Harry (and following that, the way the reader) perceives her changes. How can we take Harry's perspective as infallible when one of his closest friends is assumed to be an antagonist at the start of the first novel? Harry's perspective is further compromised when, in *The Sorcerer's Stone*, he risks his life and the lives of his friends to stop Snape from stealing the stone. He refuses to believe that Snape isn't the villain, despite being told by almost every adult that Snape is a person to be trusted, and Harry continues to defy evidence that demonstrates Snape consistently protects him. Here, Harry's view of Snape doesn't change. He continues to cast Snape as the villain, even as he is proved wrong repeatedly. Harry is so convincing in his perception that is difficult for a reader to look beyond this and explore different truths. This is not to assume that Snape is not an incompetent or abusive instructor—he is not an innocent blacklisted by our narrator—however, he is also not the personification of evil that Harry is adamant he become for us.

Harry Potter and the Materiality of Oppression

Harry's perspective, however, is not shaped solely by his own opinions. He is highly influenced by those around him. Upon discovering that Hogwarts is sorted into Houses, Harry is immediately told that there wasn't "a single witch or wizard who went bad who wasn't in Slytherin" (SS 80). The factual inaccuracy of such a statement is baffling, specifically because Hagrid himself believes, at the time of this utterance, that Sirius Black, a Gryffindor, was behind the betrayal that led to Harry being orphaned. Furthermore, Hagrid is telling a child that all that is required to be bad is to be sorted into a community by an enchanted hat. It becomes impossible to divorce Slytherin House from its crest, with its image of a slithering serpent. This symbolism acts as a warning to all wizards that this House and all those who belong to it have come to tempt them to bite the apple of evil. It is easy, when analyzing the novels, to rely unquestionably on a reading that establishes "evil" as a man cloaked in black, with a disfigured face and a morbid chosen name (Voldemort literally meaning "flight from death"). However, if the narration is at least fallible, if not completely skewed to present a single perspective, is it possible to find instead a foundation for the necessity of a Slytherin-inspired separatist movement in the Wizarding World? To examine the materiality of oppression towards wizards, I will now analyze examples of Muggle antiwizard violence within the series, as well as the historical oppression of magic-users in a lived context. This line of argument is driven by the assumption that the series is set within a reality that is not far removed from its own historicity.

No example of Muggle cruelty towards wizards is clearer and more consistent than that of the Dursleys' mistreatment and exploitation of Harry. The abuse Harry suffers at the hands of the Dursleys is extreme; by the age of ten he has already been beaten, starved, and manipulated.[2] This is our first introduction to Muggles in the series, and they are a prime example of Muggles who know about wizards. Their response, tellingly, is to persecute the child associated with wizards.

It is possible to assume that the Dursleys represent a specialized case, a "not all Muggles" case if you will, and that there are many Muggles who would not act with such violence or antipathy towards wizard-kind. Hagrid admits that Harry grew up with "the biggest Muggles I have ever laid eyes on" (*SS* 59). Perhaps what makes a Muggle is not just the lack of magical capabilities, but rather the aversion they exhibit to the Wizarding World. As the Dursleys themselves admit that the reason behind their disgust for Harry is his wizard nature, even going as far as to say that the only way they agreed to care for their newly orphaned nephew is that they "swore we'd stamp it [magic] out of him" (*SS* 53), this could very well cement their status as the "biggest Muggles." Hermione's parents' reaction to her magical abilities, for instance, is kept to a throw-away comment of it being "ever such a surprise when I got my letter" (*SS* 105). The books, however, do not support a "not all Muggles" position; the Dursleys are less an exception than a rule. For instance, the Dumbledores offer a strong example of wizard oppression by Muggles. Ariana Dumbledore remains a family secret revealed only towards the end of *Deathly Hallows*, a revelation cementing the fact that Muggles who are aware of magic's existence will primarily cause violence. Ariana was six years old when "she was attacked, by three Muggle boys [who had] . . . seen her practicing magic" (*DH* 564). The trauma Ariana endures leads to an inability to control her magic, which results in the need to isolate her. Her early and violent death is caused by her now uncontrollable magic. While Ariana's father seeks revenge against the Muggle boys and is punished as a result, this does not take away from the fact that Ariana was targeted and tortured for being a witch.

Beyond the examples of Muggle violence towards wizards found within the series, there are obvious parallels, in our own context, with the persecution of those who practice witchcraft, which is clearly condemned in the religious doctrines of Christianity, Judaism, and Islam.[3] Execution was and remains a reality for people accused of witchcraft. Nigel Cawthorne states that in Europe, on "the continent and in Scotland . . . over a hundred thousand perished in the flames" (23). Even as recently as 2012, a man accused of witchcraft was executed in Najran ("Saudi Man"). While in *Prisoner of Azkaban* we learn that wizards were able to cast a cooling charm on the fire if they were condemned to burn, the multitudinous ways one can be executed for witchcraft would not allow for a constant expectation of safety. Nor would they secure the safety of wizarding children or, in the Potterverse, those without wands (*PA* 2).

The presence of these oppressive forces is proof that the ideology of pure-blooded wizards and their drive for an insular community is not necessarily a reiteration of white supremacy and Nazi ideology, nor is it resurrection of a *sangrelimpia*, as Wente, Lyubansky, and Rowling herself claim. Rather, it can to be read as a movement of self-preservation and protection. Furthermore, to conflate the separatist movement with Nazi ideology implies that an oppressed minority is somehow capable of oppressing their oppressor, which the *Encyclopedia of Race and Ethnic Studies* notes, "suggests that racism [or Wizard separatism] today can be studied by examining beliefs and without careful consideration of the vastly different historical experiences of the group involved" (373). Attempting to draw a clear parallel between an oppressed minority claiming a safe space and an oppressor furthering the reach of their oppression is, at best, misguided. At worst, it makes the claim that wizards are responsible for their own oppression because they failed to be accepted by Muggle society.

Harry Potter and the Chamber of Muggle-Borns

The Sorting Hat attempts to provide a history of the initial ideological split of the Wizarding World in the yearly welcome song, recalling "the clash of friend on friend. / And at last there came a morning / When old Slytherin departed" (*OP* 205). Salazar leaving Hogwarts, whether by force or by choice is never extrapolated upon. His leaving, however, becomes a point of proof that he abandoned the school and his students. What Salazar leaves behind, on the other hand, is an important part of the history of this split; when he departs, he makes sure to announce that he has left a "Chamber of Secrets" to protect his students. Significantly, the era in which the Hogwarts School was founded is roughly around the tenth century, a peak time for persecution of those accused of witchcraft in what became Great Britain, where the story is set. Contextually, therefore, for Salazar to be wary of Muggles and Muggle-born wizards should not only be expected, but it would be dangerous for him to consider otherwise. When he leaves Hogwarts, he leaves his students and school without the protection his presence provides. Leaving the Chamber of Secrets behind is thus a substitute protection, in lieu of his physical being.

By way of comparison, in *The Disappearing L*, Bonnie Morris describes the phenomena of lesbian activist attempting to "pass the torch" to the next generation, and finding that generation rejecting the torch. She asks, "what does it mean if that next generation is disdainful of the torch, welcomes its dousing or lacks the data or the will to learn how it was lit and carried forward in the first place?" (178). Perhaps Salazar, aghast that the rest of the Wizarding world and those he started a school with do not want the torch of self-preservation he has been offering, decides to leave the school. He is unable to pass a torch of protection to a new generation of wizards and witches. Importantly, many of those who embrace and preserve Salazar's ideology were those with a long line of wizarding existence, ancient families who would be more likely than others to be carrying the weight of ancestral pain and trauma in their collective history.

The presentation of Muggles as oppressors and wizard society as an endangered culture within its boundaries provokes the question: Is there a place for Muggle-borns in the Wizarding World? Muggle-borns come into Wizarding World having exhibited an affinity towards magic, which allows them the right to participate in wizarding society. The pushback against Muggle-born integration into wizarding society might be correlated with the gatekeeping exhibited towards transwomen in feminist separatism. Morris notes that many long-time lesbian-feminist activists have found their work, which in its early days was deemed man-hating for excluding men, is now deemed oppressive, that is, to be "cisgender lesbians becomes an oppressive act" (183). That the more "lesbians insist on an issue-driven identity of their own as women, or claim spaces of their own to address those issues, the more their essentialism is perceived as transphobia" (185). In *The Lesbian Body*, Monique Wittig attempts a drastic linguistic reformation as an attempt to remove the pain of patriarchy from her very tongue and its utterances. She begs for a way to experience an act of linguistic creation that does not bend to a structure that has done nothing but enslave and harm her gendered existence. Wittig's writing was part of a wider separatist lesbian ideology, which insists that the way to live outside of patriarchy is to completely remove oneself from the influence of men. As a movement, separatism proved unsustainable, due to various factors of schismatic nature and other political and social challenges. However, as an ideological movement, it remains relevant to many theorists, specifically in relation to transwomen, as it demands a rigid biological definition of womanhood that excludes transwomen, and, in fact, perceives them as a threat to the very definition. Germaine Greer highlights this in *The Whole Woman*, where she says that "Governments that consist of very few women have hurried to recognize as women, men who believe that they are women and have had themselves castrated to prove it, because they see women not as another sex but as a non-sex" (74).

Parallels between lesbian separatists and the pureblood movement can be found in that: (1) both stem from a need for protection against a perceived oppressor; (2) in some ways, both have had a necessary involvement with that oppressor, including genetically; (3) both are accused of being unnecessarily exclusionary. Transexclusionary rhetoric provides a way to understand the concept of Muggle-born beyond a narrative of racialization. That is, wizards born into wizarding families are socialized as wizards, while Muggle-born wizards are socialized as Muggles—strange Muggles, but Muggles nonetheless. Many trans-exclusionary radical feminists (in the current vernacular: TERFs) argue that to claim the identity of "woman" is to cut one's teeth on it. Robin Morgan, in her keynote address at the West Coast Lesbian Conference in 1973 said, "I will not call a male 'she'; thirty-two years of suffering in this androcentric society, and of surviving, have earned me the title 'woman' . . . [and] he dares to think he understands our pain? No, in our mothers' names and in our own, we must not call him sister" (Goldberg). It is important to note that many trans-exclusionary radical feminists have experienced forms of silencing and threats of violence in response to their position. For example, a recent Twitter attack suggests that we "slowly and horrendously murder TERFs in saw-like torture machines and contraptions" (Goldberg). Much like the pureblood movement, the very existence of the ideology of preservation is met with hate and violence, in an irrational attempt to appease one's oppressor by allowing them to break down safety barriers. This is not to condone exclusionary and harmful behavior exhibited by trans-exclusionary radical feminists, but rather to draw parallels between these modalities of exclusionary behavior and to suggest how the logical trajectory of both seem to align.

This position against Muggle-borns is not limited to the novels' antiassimilationist movement. Many of those in the assimilationist movement display a disdain for Muggle-borns, unless they can prove themselves a "model Muggle-born," similar to the way many self-proclaimed "non-TERF" feminists will accept only transwomen who meet their standards, if they accepted transwomen at all. Even despite a supposed antipathy towards the "Magic Is Might" mentality, the use of magic is seen by many wizards as mark of exceptionalism. Hagrid, who spends a good portion of his introduction to the Wizarding World explaining to Harry that Slytherins are evil, also does not proffer favorable opinions of Muggles nor Muggle-borns. He even goes as far as to comfort Harry by asserting, "Yer not *from* a Muggle family," as though be from such a background would be a source of shame (*SS* 79). Hagrid later backpedals this statement, declaring, "Some o' the best I ever saw were the only ones with magic in 'em in a long line o' Muggles—look at yer mum! look what she had fer a sister!" (79). Here he demonstrates the hypocrisy of vilifying Slytherin House while espousing rhetoric that casts Muggle-borns as only good when they are useful (79). Even Hermione, who is called the brightest witch of her age, is only allowed her lineage because she is able to perform with excellence. An average Muggle-born is not used as an example of why Muggle-borns deserve entry into Hogwarts or the greater Wizarding World. Rather, Muggle-borns within the assimilationist movement seem to be allowed space only when they are useful, in contrast to the separatist movement, which disallows their right of entry into the Wizarding World, useful or not; unfortunately, neither approach seems to have a good answer as to what to do, so to speak, with Muggle-borns.

Harry Potter and the Revisionist History of Postwar Rhetoric

The epilogue to the series in the final pages of *Deathly Hallows* is meant to provide a glimpse into a postwar society, where all wizard-kind live without prejudice. Harry names his second-born son Albus Severus, a move meant in part to signify solidarity with Slytherins. Harry even tells his son that he should feel honored to be placed in Slytherin House. While not untrue, it is highly suspect that in the course of less than one generation all prejudice or hate towards the pureblood separatist movement has ebbed. That is, until we are reminded that those who had the audacity to believe in a world not organized around their own oppression have, by and large, been wiped out. Draco Malfoy, one of the only pureblood movement survivors we see, is presented in the epilogue as a wisp of a man; and Ron Weasley tells his daughter to make sure to pummel Draco's son.

It is reasonable to assume that assimilation of the Wizarding World into Muggle society could not be possible. Assimilation or absorption offered to wizards could only be predicated on a denial of their core beliefs and identity, an invitation to invisibility or genocide. However, even assuming an optimistic attempt to integrate into Muggle society, the witchhunts, the hate crimes, and the religious doctrine of condemnation are so present there (in the corresponding "real world"), that any effort to create an assimilated wizard-Muggle community would, in essence, put the entire Wizarding World in danger. And the danger rises if we take into consideration the reality of violence against existent so-called minorities in that same (Muggle) society, particularly those living as women, queers, people of color, or disabled, to name but a few.

I argue, then, for the possibility of a reading of the pureblood movement in the Wizarding World as a separatist movement with the hope of self-preservation at its heart. It is possible to imagine Salazar Slytherin's entire philosophy driven by his contextual reality, a world where wizard children could be executed merely for existing—or for accidentally revealing their abilities. Reading the *Harry Potter* series as an interminority conflict of assimilation versus perseveration allows the reader to step away from a simplistic black-and-white reality of good versus evil, away from a dominant narrative controlled by Harry's standpoint. Doing so, readers can more easily recognize a complex fictional culture that, as Konchar Farr and Mars argue in chapter 1, progresses from black and white to shades of gray. Then the endangered community at the center can be seen struggling to survive in ways they assume are best, none of them completely good or bad.

Notes

1. In research on *The Construction of Social Reality*, John Searle suggests that the creation of institutional facts operates to give utterance to brute facts as well as form symbolic boundaries that are then practiced as institutional facts, and treated as brute facts, even though they are not. In such cases, it is also possible that construction of fact occurs without the conscious recognition of those who formulate the hierarchy and practice of said facts. Hence, the definitions of good and evil are formed and actualized within social institutional realities and, though treated as brute facts, are in reality only expressions of institutional norms.

2. The instances of abuse towards Harry by the Dursleys are impossible to list in their entirety, but include, among other things making a child live in a cupboard under the stairs, treating him like a pariah, showing no affection or emotional care towards him, neglecting him, withholding food from him, allowing and even encouraging the physical abuses of his cousin over him, expecting his physical labor as a given, and treating him with the utmost disrespect.

3. Recorded in Leviticus 19:26, Deuteronomy 18:9–12, Quran 2:101–2.

Works Cited

Cashmore, Ernest, editor. "Reverse Racism/Discrimination." *Encyclopedia of Race and Ethnic Studies*, Routledge, 2008. 373.

Cawthorne, Nigel. *Witch Hunt: History of a Persecution*. Chartwell, 2004.

Fuerst, Orly Eleonore. "J. K. Rowling, Voldemort and Hitler." *Aish.com*, 21 Jan. 2017. www.aish.com/ho/i/JK-Rowling-Voldemort-and-Hitler.html.

Goldberg, Michelle. "What Is a Woman?" *The New Yorker*, 19 June 2017. www.newyorker.com/magazine/2014/08/04/woman-2.

Greer, Germaine. *The Whole Woman*. Doubleday, 1999.

Konchar Farr, Cecilia, et al. *Wizard of Their Age: Critical Essays from the Harry Potter Generation*. SUNY, 2015.

Morris, Bonnie J. "Points of Erasure" in *The Disappearing L: Erasure of Lesbian Spaces and Culture*. SUNY, 2017.

Mulholland, Neil, and Mikhail Lyubansky. "Harry Potter and the Word That Shall Not Be Named." *The Psychology of Harry Potter: An Unauthorized Examination of the Boy Who Lived*, BenBella, 2007. 233–48.

Phelan, James, et al. "On a Postcolonial Narratology" in *A Companion to Narrative Theory*. Blackwell, 2008. 372–81.

"Saudi Man Executed for 'Witchcraft and Sorcery.'" *BBC News*, BBC, 19 June 2012. www.bbc.com/news/world-middle-east-18503550.

Searle, John R. *The Construction of Social Reality*. NY: Simon and Shuster, 1995.

Singer, Thomas, and Catherine Kaplinsky. "The Cultural Complex" in *Jungian Psychoanalysis: Working in the Spirit of C. G. Jung*, edited by Murray Stein, Open Court, 2010. 22–37.

Uris, Leon. *Exodus: Leon Uris*. Bantam, 2012.

Wente, Sarah. "The Making of a New World: Nazi Ideology and Its Influence on *Harry Potter*" in *A Wizard of Their Age*, edited by Cecilia Konchar Farr. SUNY, 2015. 95–123.

Wittig, Monique. *The Lesbian Body*. Translated by David Le Vay, Beacon, 1986.

15

HARRY POTTER AND THE MANAGEMENT OF TRAUMA

Tolonda Henderson

The penultimate chapter of the *Harry Potter* series is by far the most peculiar. Set in what Harry eventually identifies as a version of King's Cross station, it features surroundings that only come into existence as Harry looks at them, a whimpering piece of Voldemort's soul, and a conversation with a dead headmaster. In this essay I will argue that the chapter "King's Cross" is best understood as the crowning moment of a series-long exploration of trauma and its management. Even though she uses the word "trauma" only once in seven books, the author consistently constructs experiences that overwhelm her main character's ability to process life in real time.[1] Harry's traumatic experiences escalate from fragmented access to the trauma of his parents' deaths in *Prisoner of Azkaban* to fighting Voldemort after witnessing the death of a classmate in *Goblet of Fire* to being hit with the killing curse with no defense and no one to die for him in *Deathly Hallows*. "King's Cross" is a chapter where Harry will either be destroyed by trauma or find a way to survive. The liminal space Harry inhabits after being hit by the killing curse becomes something, and someone, he recognizes so that he can consolidate everything he knows into a coherent narrative and thereby develop the resilience necessary to finally defeat Voldemort.

Much of the existing scholarship on the relationship between trauma and the *Harry Potter* series approaches the topic from a psychological perspective, asking such questions as how the series can help people talk about intergenerational trauma (Katz) and whether Freud or Lacan best explains the impact of the murder of Lily and James Potter on Harry's identity development (Cox). Other works take a more literary approach but are concerned with the struggles Harry faces in trying to be believed about the traumatic events he has experienced and witnessed at Voldemort's rebirth (Debling) or with establishing Voldemort's relationship with Harry as one of "homoerotic child abuse" (Sanna 4). While these are interesting questions, I am more interested in how the books represent trauma to the reader and what strategies the characters use to process that trauma. In other words, this chapter examines those moments in the text where Harry remembers or experiences traumatic events.

Judith Herman differentiates between "commonplace misfortunes" and traumatic events, stating that the latter "generally involve threats to life or bodily integrity, or a close personal encounter with violence and death" (33). Harry grapples with two types of trauma: intrusive memories of the violent murder of his parents when he was a toddler and threats to bodily integrity—both his own and others'—as a teenager. In *Prisoner of Azkaban*, we watch Harry manage his exposure to traumatic memories by developing a magical defense against the effects of dementors, dark creatures who cause people to relive the worst moments of their lives. When faced with the most intense and direct attack in *Deathly Hallows*, however, Harry does not defend himself, allowing the piece of Voldemort's soul living within him to be killed. The pseudo-King's Cross he then encounters is not a magical defense against traumatic events, but rather a transitional space between life and death, much like the actual King's Cross serves as transitional space between the Muggle and Wizarding worlds throughout the novels. The elements that make "King's Cross" such a peculiar chapter are, in fact, extended episodes of a narrative technique known as peritraumatic dissociation, which the author uses to mark traumatic events going back at least as far as the death of Cedric Diggory in *Goblet of Fire*. Both the interruption of the dementors and the disruptions captured by peritraumatic distortion demonstrate that a trauma aesthetic is present in the *Harry Potter* series.

The earliest trauma that Harry experiences is the murder of his parents by Lord Voldemort. Though Harry is only fifteen months old at the time, he

retains memories of that night. At first, these memories are vague: a burst of
green light and a dream about a flying motorbike (*SS* 29, 19). More specific
memories of his parents' deaths come back to Harry in his third year when
he is in the presence of dementors. Typically found guarding the wizard
prison Azkaban, dementors "glory in decay and despair" while they "drain
peace, hope, and happiness out of the air around them" (*PA* 187). When they
are close at hand, dementors force you to relive the worst moments of your
life (*PA* 187). This closely resembles the intrusion that Herman observes as a
core feature of post-traumatic stress disorder: "Long after the danger is past,
traumatized people relive the event as though it were continually recurring
in the present. They cannot resume the normal course of their lives, for the
trauma repeatedly interrupts" (37). Most of the inmates of Azkaban "go mad
within weeks" because they are "trapped inside their own heads, incapable
of a single cheerful thought" (*PA* 188). Those in constant close proximity
to dementors lose the ability to function properly in part because any past
trauma in their lives "repeatedly interrupts."

No character in the series enjoys the company of dementors, but their presence disrupts Harry's life more than it does his companions. When a dementor
enters his compartment on the *Hogwarts Express* on his way back to school
for his third year, Ginny curls up in a corner, Neville describes the experience as "horrible," and Ron reports that he felt he would "never be cheerful
again" (*PA* 85). For his part, Harry goes rigid, falls out of his seat, and begins
to twitch as he hears screaming that no one else can hear (*PA* 83–84). Later,
Harry falls off his broom when the dementors enter the Hogwarts grounds
during a Quidditch match (*PA* 178–79). Humiliated, he asks Remus Lupin,
his Defense Against the Dark Arts teacher, why the dementors bother him
more than his peers. Lupin tells him "The dementors affect you worse than the
others because there are horrors in your past that the others don't have" (*PA*
187). What Lupin describes as "horrors" can also be called traumatic events.

In their article on the different ways in which trauma is remembered,
Dori Laub and Nanette C. Auerhahn observe that "we all hover at different
distances between knowing and not knowing about trauma" (288). Over the
course of *Prisoner of Azkaban*, Harry moves between these two poles, first
not knowing and then knowing his early trauma. At first, the experience of
encountering a dementor yields fuzzy memory of someone screaming. This
is nothing that Harry has conscious memory of, so he can't place it. The
more time he spends around dementors, however, the clearer everything

becomes, and a narrative emerges. When hundreds of dementors flood the Quidditch pitch, their combined presence means that the screams in Harry's head become specific words (PA 179). The added detail allows Harry to iden- tify the screaming woman as his mother pleading with Voldemort not to kill him. Even more detail becomes available to Harry when he is practicing the Patronus charm in Professor Lupin's office. The first time he faces the shape-shifting boggart in the form of a dementor, he hears his mother's voice once more. The second time Harry tries to produce a Patronus, he hears his father telling his mother to take him and run, something that happened before his mother pleaded with Voldemort (*PA* 240). In other words, with prolonged exposure to the boggart-dementor, Harry's memory of his parents' last moments becomes longer. Laub and Auerhahn discuss the path from not knowing to knowing one's trauma as having therapeutic benefit, but this applies to those whose knowledge of their trauma has been stymied by the trauma itself. Harry's lack of knowledge of the details of his early trauma stems largely from his age at the time of his parent's deaths, so becoming aware of these details is distressing to him.

Harry's response to the detrimental effects of dementors is typical of the resilience and stubbornness that exemplify his character throughout the series. Instead of taking steps to keep himself from encountering dementors, Harry places himself in the presence of a dementor substitute on a regular basis so he can practice the Patronus charm and learn to protect himself (and others) from the intrusion of traumatic memory. Harry's chief motiva- tion to seek anti-dementor lessons is his desire to win the Quidditch Cup. The captain of his team worries that he will have to replace Harry if Harry doesn't get a grip on his dementor problem, so learning the Patronus charm is critical to Harry's ability to continue to do the activities that bring him joy, even if he is confronted with painful memories (*PA* 234). Indeed, it is happy thoughts that anchor the spell that drives the dementors away.

Harry not only gains access to traumatic memories from his past during the course of the series, but he also lives through new traumatic events. Even before he walks into the Forbidden Forest during the Battle of Hogwarts and allows Voldemort to hit him with a killing curse, Harry watches classmates and loved ones die. At these times, the narrative frequently includes what Joshua Pederson refers to as peritraumatic dissocation: "depictions of expe- riences that are temporally, physically, or ontologically distorted" (339). For example, after Harry witnesses the murder of Cedric Diggory, the text tells us that Harry stared into his classmate's blank eyes "for a second that contained an eternity" (*GF* 638). The traumatic shock of Cedric's death causes Harry to experience epochs and eons compressed into the single second in which he has to try to "[accept] what he was seeing" (*GF* 638). The competing realities of the short time Harry looks into Cedric's eyes and realizes the reverberating magnitude of the significance of Cedric's death yield a beautiful contrast in language—"a second that contained an eternity"—that pulls the reader into the trauma. The author uses the same technique at the end of *Order of the Phoenix*: when Harry watches his godfather move through a veiled archway in the Department of Mysteries, "it seemed to take Sirius an age to fall" (*OP* 806). Harry is once again experiencing time outside of time as he attempts to process an overwhelming event.

Having established temporal distortion as a means of conveying the traumatic experience of witnessing death, the author turns to physical and ontological distortions when describing Harry's reaction to watching Snape kill Dumbledore. When hit with the Avada Kedavra curse at the end of the chapter, Dumbledore is "blasted into the air" before falling "slowly backward" over the edge of the Hogwarts' tallest tower (*HBP* 596). The next chapter begins with these words: "Harry felt as though he too were hurtling through space" (*HBP* 597). Harry's sense of physicality is warped as immobility and the sensation of movement clash inside of his body in the same way that eternity is contained in a second when Cedric Diggory is killed. The remainder of the sentence is broken up by ellipses: "It had not happened. . . . It could not have happened. . . ." (*HBP* 597). This narrative fragmentation can be understood as an ontological distortion. Harry's very being is rattled to core by an event so overwhelming he is unable to process it in real time.

This sense of unreality is echoed in *Deathly Hallows* during the Battle of Hogwarts. First, the death of Fred Weasley sends Harry reeling:

> The world had ended, so why had the battle not ceased, the castle fallen silent in horror, and every combatant laid down their arms? Harry's mind was in free fall, spinning out of control, unable to grasp the impossibility, because Fred Weasley could not be dead, the evidence of all his senses must be lying—. (*DH* 638)

As with Dumbledore, Harry both knows that Fred has been killed and rejects that fact. The push and pull of these contradictory beliefs articulate the warped sense of reality, the ontological distortion, into which Harry has been forced by the sudden death of a friend. He wants everything around him to stop in respect for the dead, he yearns for an eternity in which to process what has happened, but the press of the narrative does not allow for such luxuries. Later, the author returns to spatial distortion to describe Harry's reaction to the deaths of Lupin and Tonks. When Harry sees their bodies, "the Great Hall seemed to fly away, become smaller, shrink, as Harry reeled backward from the doorway" (*DH* 661). This recalls Harry's reaction to watching Dumbledore's death, although here it is his surroundings that seem to be moving rather than Harry himself. In both instances, the traumatic nature of encountering these deaths detaches Harry from a commonplace experience of his physical reality.

The deaths of others have tremendous impact on Harry, but the necessity (and then the reality) of his own death sits at the heart of the series' trauma narrative. Harry spends most of *Deathly Hallows* searching for Voldemort's Horcruxes, fragments of the Dark Lord's soul existing outside his body that must be destroyed before he can be killed. After identifying and destroying inanimate objects such as a cup that belonged to Hogwarts founder Helga Hufflepuff, Harry believes that only Voldemort's snake, Nagini, remains. He is shocked, therefore, to learn that when Voldemort had tried to kill him sixteen years prior to the Battle of Hogwarts, the curse had rebounded, and a fragment of Voldemort's soul had broken off and attached itself to Harry's soul. In other words, Harry himself is a Horcrux and must die at Voldemort's hand before Voldemort will be truly mortal again.

The author conveys the traumatic nature of this discovery with a string of peritraumatic distortions. Harry no longer experiences his body in the same way once he knows that he must die: "He felt more alive and more aware of his own living body than ever before" (692). In particular, Harry could feel "his heart pounding fiercely in his chest" because "it knew it had little time left [and] was determined to fulfill a lifetime's beats before the end" (691, 694). His relationship to his closest friends is also changed: "Ron and Hermione seemed a long way away, in a far-off country; he felt as though he had parted from them long ago" (693). In other words, Harry no longer experiences space or time in the same way. With these distortions, the author paints a picture of someone whose grasp on reality is coming unraveled, whose ability to process the world has been altered.

Finding out that he is a Horcrux is, therefore, a key event in Harry's trauma narrative. It does not "occur to him . . . to try to escape, to outrun Voldemort" because "Harry would not let anyone else die for him now that he had discovered that it was in his power to stop it" (*DH* 692, 693). Instead, Harry will seek Voldemort out with the intention of allowing himself to be killed. In other words, the fact that he is harboring a fragment of Voldemort's soul represents a dire threat to Harry's bodily integrity, to his life. This threat is eclipsed only by its fulfillment: the most intense representation of response to trauma in the series occurs just after Harry is struck by Voldemort's killing curse. Understanding "King's Cross" as an extended episode of peritraumatic distortion allows us to appreciate the importance of Dumbledore's presence in that space. Healing from trauma cannot happen in isolation, and Harry needs a conversation partner to work through several traumatic experiences in his life (Herman 134). The conversation with Dumbledore in "King's Cross," then, enables Harry to reenter the world of the living and grants him the focus necessary to vanquish Voldemort.

The first few paragraphs of "King's Cross" establish the experience of being hit with a killing curse as a deeply traumatic one by using all three of the types of distortions outlined by Pederson, starting with the ontological. Over the course of seven books, the author typically describes Harry in a clear and direct manner: he is somewhere, he is doing something, he is talking to someone. The opening of "King's Cross" completely ignores this pattern, informing the reader that Harry "was not perfectly sure that he was there himself" (*DH* 705). This uncertainty as to the nature, or even the fact, of his being is the most profound distortion we see in the series. The story revolves around Harry, so the possibility that he might not exist tugs at the fabric of the narrative. Having immediately established how far off the edge of the map this chapter is, the author has Harry conclude that he does in fact exist, but only after warping his sense of time: the realization that he "must be more than disembodied thought" comes to him "a long time later, or maybe no time at all" (*DH* 705). The fact that time refuses to be perceived normally is reinforced midway through the chapter: "Harry sat in thought for a long time, or perhaps seconds. It was very hard to be sure of things like time, here" (*DH* 712). Woven among the ontological and temporal distortions are those relating to Harry's physical surroundings. After "[discovering] that he had eyes," Harry sees that he is lying in "a bright mist, though it was not like mist he had ever encountered before. His surroundings were not hidden by cloudy vapor; rather the cloudy vapor had not yet formed into surroundings" (*DH* 705). Harry is unsure of what to make of these surroundings because they are unsure of what to make of themselves.

Just as Harry's sense of his own being evolves from ambiguity to a level of certainty, his sense of the physical space around him also becomes more solid. The text tells us that as Harry "turned slowly on the spot, . . . his surroundings seemed to invent themselves before his eyes" (*DH* 706). The mist resolves itself not into a generic physical space but one that is highly symbolic: King's Cross Station marks a boundary between the Muggle and magical worlds; here it marks a boundary between life and death. Time, too, begins to take shape again. Near the end of the chapter, Harry and Dumbledore "[sit] in silence for a long time;" a few paragraphs later, Harry speaks after a "short pause" (*DH* 719). Just before Harry returns to the world of the living, we learn that "Harry and Dumbledore sat without talking for the longest time yet" (*DH* 721). Each of these references to time is definitive and free from the waffling that is characteristic of the beginning of the chapter. Time, space, and being operate more predictably as Harry processes his trauma with his dead headmaster.

"King's Cross" is not the first time the novels have seen Harry and Dumbledore discuss trauma Harry has endured. At the end of *Goblet of Fire*, for example, Dumbledore insists that Harry narrate his experiences in the graveyard of Little Hangleton despite Sirius's objections and attempted interruptions because he knows that talking about it will help with the pain (*GF* 695). The conversation in the pseudo-King's Cross is different, however, because this time the impetus to talk comes from Harry. The Dumbledore he addresses here does not insist on hearing the details of Harry's trauma, but rather is conjured into the liminal space by Harry's need for advice. Just as robes appear when Harry decides he does not want to be naked (*DH* 706), a conversation partner appears when Harry cannot decide whether to comfort the whimpering but repulsive creature whose presence makes him want to be clothed in the first place (*DH* 707). Herman states that during recovery, "the survivor tells the story of the trauma" (175). This implies that there is someone to whom the story is told. For Harry, that someone is Dumbledore. The trauma of being hit with the killing curse has pushed Harry so far beyond his ordinary reality that the dead appear before him, ready for a chat.

Early in their conversation, Harry looks to his headmaster for answers only to be thwarted by Dumbledore's insistence that the answers lie within.

When Harry asks where they are, Dumbledore responds, "I was going to ask you that" (*DH* 712). Later, Harry asks Dumbledore to explain why Voldemort's curse did not kill him, and Dumbledore replies, "But you already know" (708). Harry then muddles his way through to an explanation of why the curse failed, encouraged at every step by Dumbledore. Harry survives the killing curse as a baby because his mother dies for him. Voldemort, knowing this, uses Harry's blood to regenerate himself in *Goblet of Fire*, to mitigate Harry's mother's protection. What Voldemort didn't know was that taking that protection into his own body would mean that Harry could not be killed while Voldemort still lived (*DH* 709). While this is the kind of explanation readers have come to expect of Dumbledore at the end of each book in the series, it is one that, in this book, Harry more or less supplies for himself.

Over time, Dumbledore becomes less evasive in response to Harry's inquiries, but most of what he says, from his explanation of a tricky bit of magic that Harry's wand performed to his admission of resentment towards his family, are things Harry could have deduced on his own. For example, for most of *Deathly Hallows*, Harry is tormented by the idea that Dumbledore had once been friends with Gellert Grindelwald, a dark wizard with powers and ambitions rivaled only by Voldemort's. Harry also hasn't known what to make of the accusations that Dumbledore's younger sister, Ariana, was mistreated because she didn't display magical ability. In the pseudo-King's Cross, Dumbledore explains that he developed a relationship with Grindelwald at a time when he wished he could escape from his family responsibilities and that he lived with guilt, grief, and shame after the death of his sister. In the midst of this explanation, however, is a telltale return to the earlier insistence that Harry already possesses information critical to understanding these points. Dumbledore marks a transition in his narrative with the statement "You know what happened" (*DH* 717). And Harry does, indeed, know what happened, having heard the story of Grindelwald's arrival in Godric's Hollow and the death of Ariana from Albus's younger brother, Aberforth, only hours before. This is not to say that Dumbledore's presence in "King's Cross" is unnecessary, but rather to emphasize how the dialogue is really between Harry and a version of himself he conjures in the midst of peritraumatic dissociation to help him cope.

Just before returning to the world of the living, Harry asks his headmaster a pressing and deeply philosophical question: "Is this real? Or has this been happening inside my head?" Dumbledore responds with characteristic ambiguity: "Of course it is happening inside your head, Harry, but why on earth should that mean that it is not real?" (*DH* 723). The fact that Harry's dialogue with Dumbledore is "happening inside [his] head" means Harry had all the answers when he entered the Forbidden Forest. What he hadn't had was space and time to process what he already knows and come to conclusions about it. His experience in the pseudo-King's Cross provides that opportunity while reinforcing the idea that healing from trauma does not happen automatically. "King's Cross," then, not only shows response to trauma but also a path through it: dialogue and conversation about the trauma itself.

One of the intriguing things about the *Harry Potter* series is that the author has woven "a vast number of genres," from mystery and detective stories to folk and fairy tales, into a complex "mosaic" (Alton 199, 221). I maintain that one of those genres is trauma fiction. Trauma is not only the reason the dementors affect Harry differently than they do his peers, but it is also a consistent theme as the books grow darker later in the series. The author's use of peritraumatic distortions grows from single sentences to paragraphs to an entire chapter. The "King's Cross" chapter ties up narrative loose ends and sees Harry come to terms with his trauma and gain the perspective and certainty he needs to defeat Voldemort.

Notes

I owe a debt of thanks to Professor Marshall Alcorn, chair of the English Department at George Washington University, and his honors student Julia Weiss for helping me to conceptualize and frame this essay.

1. The one occurrence of the word "trauma" is when Rita Skeeter asks Harry if the trauma of losing his parents compelled him to enter the TriWizard Tournament (*GF* 306). The fact that the author gives this word to a writer who delights in exaggeration could be the basis for an entirely new essay.

Works Cited

Alton, Anne Hiebert. "Playing the Genre Game: Generic Fusions of the Harry Potter Series" in *Critical Perspectives on Harry Potter*, 2nd ed, edited by Elizabeth E. Heilman. Routledge, 2009. 199–225.

Cox, Rachel. "Freud, Lacan, and Harry Potter: Two Readings of Trauma." Diss. University of South Dakota, 2010.

Debling, Heather. "'You Survived to Bear Witness': Trauma, Testimony, and the Burden of Witnessing in *Harry Potter and the Order of the Phoenix*." *Topic*, vol. 54, Fall 2004, 73–82.

Herman, Judith. *Trauma and Recovery: The Aftermath of Violence—From Domestic Abuse to Political Terror*. Basic Books, 1997.

Katz, Maureen. "Prisoners of Azkaban: Understanding Intergenerational Transmission of Trauma Due to War and State Terror (With Help from Harry Potter)." *Journal for the Psychoanalysis of Culture and Society*, vol. 8, no. 2, Fall 2003, 200–207.

Laub, D., and Auerhaun, N. C. "Knowing and Not Knowing Massive Psychic Trauma: Forms of Traumatic Memory." *International Journal of Psychoanalysis*, vol. 74, 1992. 287–302.

Pederson, Joshua. "Speak, Trauma: Toward a Revised Understanding of Literary Trauma Theory." *Narrative*, vol. 22, no. 3, Oct. 2014. 333–53.

Sanna, Antonio. "'I can touch him now': Harry Potter as a Gothic Narrative of Trauma and Homoerotic Sexual Abuse." *[sic]: A Journal of Literature, Culture and Literary Translation*, vol. 1, no. 5, 1–17.

A CODA
She-Who-Must-Not-Be-Named

You may or may not have noticed, but the name of the author of the *Harry Potter* series does not appear in the preceding essay. This is intentional. I am a genderqueer—which for me means nonbinary transgender—*Harry Potter* scholar, something that grew increasingly difficult to be throughout the summer of 2020. I had stopped using the author's name in conversation and presentations about Harry Potter in December of 2019 just after she came to the defense of a Maya Forstater, a woman in Britain who had gone to court arguing that she should have the right to misgender transgender people in the workplace because of freedom of speech. When the court came back and affirmed that misgendering transgender people—referring to transwomen as men or he or him, for example—constitutes hate speech and therefore is not protected speech, She-Who-Must-Not-Be-Named got onto Twitter and made it clear that she stood with Forstater. This was not the first indication we had had that the author was transphobic, but it was the clearest articulation of her beliefs about transgender people and could not be explained away as a middle-aged moment in the way that her PR firm has attempted to do when the author had earlier followed a transphobic Twitter account. I stopped saying the author's name not because I felt it would hurt her in any way but because making that stand publicly protected me, insulated me in some small fashion, from the hurt she was inflicting. I was prepared to stay in that relationship with She-Who-Must-Not-Be-Named for quite some time, but alas, she was not.

In June of 2020, J. K. Voldemort (as one of my friends has taken to calling her) responded to a tweet about people who menstruate insisting that there is a word for such people. Implied was the idea that the word for people who menstruate is "woman," a stance that invalidates nonbinary people like me and transgender men like my friends as people who also menstruate. When confronted about this bigotry, the author doubled down and posted a letter on her website outlining her position on issues of sex and gender. Reading the essay was a head trip. I don't recommend it. She has a way with words (of course, or we wouldn't know of her existence) and I felt gaslit and brainwashed at the same time after reading it. I had to reach out to friends and YouTubers to feel confident in my assessment that she was, in fact, doing everything she said she wasn't doing, namely, being transphobic.

Fortunately, I was not alone in my assessment. I actually first learned of the Twitter commentary when Daniel Radcliffe released a statement denouncing it. He said, in part, "To all the people who now feel that their experience of the books has been tarnished or diminished, I am deeply sorry for the pain these comments have caused you. I really hope that you don't entirely lose what was valuable in these stories to you." For someone of such prominence in the *Harry Potter* franchise to reach out in this way, and to do so through the Trevor Project, was a balm. Many online memes had a similar effect, especially the one of Umbridge being labeled as She-Who-Must-Not-Be-Named standing apart while McGonagall (labeled as the Harry Potter fandom) comforts and shields Professor Trelawney (labeled as transgender people). Many organizations, including MuggleNet and the Leaky Cauldron, issued statements similar to Radcliffe's: the author is wrong, and we get to keep the texts anyway.

Now, it would be easy to invoke Roland Barthes's concept of "The Death of the Author" here to completely evict She-Who-Must-Not-Be-Named from our enjoyment of the world she created. I have two difficulties with this approach. First, she won't shut up. Given her proclivity for revealing details about the wizarding world on Pottermore and Twitter, we shouldn't be surprised, but it would have been nice to have gone two weeks this summer and early fall without her name making its way into my Facebook feed. I have forgotten—or blocked out—most of the details, but I will never forget the news that her new adult murder mystery was about a man who dressed as a woman to kill women; or that a human rights organization moved to take back an award from her, but before they could do it, she announced that she was giving it back; or that she started an online shop with transphobic merchandise. These actions have wedged themselves between me and the series that gave me my start as a literary scholar, and I will probably never forgive her for that.

The other reason I have a hard time divorcing the author from the books is that there are trans-exclusionary themes baked right into the text. I say more about this in a forthcoming essay, but think for a moment about both Dumbledore and Harry calling Voldemort "Tom" or "Riddle." This action establishes our heroes as having power in their interactions with the evilest wizard in the world, but it also disrespects that wizard's right (yes, evil people have rights) to change his name and have that change honored even by his enemies. Not all transgender people change our names, and name changes don't only happen in transgender communities, but the act of changing one's name is a fundamental part of many trans people's gender affirmation journeys. The fact that this act is only given to the evilest character in the books and then is dismissed by our heroes is troubling to me.

So, what's a nonbinary *Harry Potter* scholar to do? One thing I have chosen to do—and that I feel immensely grateful for the opportunity to do—is to go through and rephrase each of sixteen times I had used the author's name when I first wrote this chapter. Again, I know that this will not harm J. K. Voldemort, but it gives me back a sense of power and agency in my scholarship. Another thing that I am seriously pondering, even though it breaks my heart, is putting down my quill and referring to my time as a *Harry Potter* scholar in the past tense. I simply do not know if I have the wherewithal to do work that feels like it is centering her. What I will not do, however, is stop being a fan of the wizarding world. She doesn't get to take that from me, too.

—TH

CONTRIBUTORS

Lauren R. Camacci earned her PhD from Penn State in 2017. She is an independent scholar who works as a content writer in Cleveland, Ohio. Dr. Camacci has four previous publications in *Harry Potter* studies and is an assistant chair of the Harry Potter Academic Conference at Chestnut Hill College.

Keridiana Chez is associate professor at Borough of Manhattan Community College, City University of New York. Her research generally focuses on nineteenth-century animal studies, such as *Victorian Dogs, Victorian Men: Affect and Animals in Nineteenth-Century Literature and Culture* (Ohio State University Press 2017); "Wanted Dead or Alive: Rabbits in Victorian Children's Literature," in Brenda Ayres's *Beasts on a Leash* (Routledge 2020); and "Man's Best and Worst Friends: The Politics of Pet Preference at the Turn of the Century," in Dominik Ohrem's *American Beasts: Perspectives on Animals, Animality, and U.S. Culture, 1776–1920* (Neofelis 2017).

Kate Glassman is a perennial academic, teacher, and multigenre writer whose work ranges from shark poetry to mass media studies across film, books, and video games. Her analysis of the boy wizard and his series also appears in *A Wizard of Their Age: Critical Essays from the Harry Potter Generation*. She is currently a middle school English teacher at Saint Paul Academy and Summit School, where, in true Slytherin fashion, she routinely and unironically dabs for the sole purpose of upsetting her students.

John Granger, who was memorably tagged "The Dean of *Harry Potter Scholars*" by *TIME* magazine's Lev Grossman, writes and speaks on the intersection of literature, philosophy, faith, and culture. The author or editor of eight books, Granger has been a keynote and featured speaker at more than twenty academic and fan conferences and spoken at twenty-five major universities and colleges, from Princeton and Pepperdine to Yale and the University of Chicago. His books include *Unlocking Harry Potter* (Zossima 2007), *How Harry Cast His Spell* (Tyndale, 2008), *The Deathly Hallows Lectures* (Zossima 2008), *Harry Potter's Bookshelf* (Penguin, 2009), and *Harry Potter as Ring Composition and Ring Cycle* (Zossima 2010). Granger was also a finalist in the 2016 Witch Weekly "Most Winning Smile," house-elf division. He lives in Oklahoma City with his wife, Mary, and the last of their seven Harry-and-Narnia-and-Redwall-loving children. Keep up with John at his weblog, HogwartsProfessor.com.

Beatrice Groves is research fellow and lecturer in Renaissance English at Trinity College, Oxford. She has published books on both *Harry Potter*— *Literary Allusion in Harry Potter* (Routledge, 2017)—and Renaissance literature—*The Destruction of Jerusalem in Early Modern English Literature* (Cambridge University Press, 2015); *Texts and Traditions: Religion in Shakespeare, 1592–1604* (Oxford University Press, 2007). She has written numerous articles on early modern literature and blogs regularly about *Harry Potter* at Leaky Cauldron, Hogwarts Professor, and at her dedicated column on mugglenet.com "Bathilda's Notebook." She is also a regular contributor to the MuggleNet podcast formerly called *Reading, Writing, Rowling* now *Potterversity*.

Tolonda Henderson is PhD student in the English Department at the University of Connecticut. Their specialization in children's and young adult literature was inspired by their work as a *Harry Potter* Scholar. Mx. Henderson has been a guest lecturer in a Harry Potter and Literary Theory class, at the DC Public Library, and at the National Symphony Orchestra.

Nusaiba Imady is doctoral student in the Asian and Middle Eastern Department at the University of Minnesota. She has her master's degree in gender studies from the University of London-School of Oriental and African Studies. Her master's focused on the creative outputs of cultures in the aftermath of surpassing disaster. Her PhD work explores madness in the Arab literary renaissance. Her other research interests include romance novels, postcolonial desire, and fandom studies.

Cecilia Konchar Farr is professor of English and dean of the College of Liberal and Creative Arts at West Liberty University in West Virginia. Her work centers on modernism, popular literature, feminist theory, reception studies, and the history of the novel. Among her publications are a study of literary merit, *The Ulysses Delusion: Rethinking Standards of Literary Merit*; an examination of Oprah's Book Club, *Reading Oprah: How Oprah's Book Club Changed the Way America Reads*; and a student-generated collection of essays about the *Harry Potter* novels, *A Wizard of Their Age: Critical Essays from the Harry Potter Generation*.

Juliana Valadão Lopes is Brazilian and has been living in Porto, Portugal, since 2016. She has a master's degree in Anglo-American studies from the Faculty of Arts from University of Porto with a dissertation entitled "'They Like Being Enslaved'? British Imperialist Rhetoric and the Wizards' Hegemonic Discourse in *Harry Potter*," in which she develops some of the themes presented in this book. Her bachelor's degree was in Portuguese and Anglo-American languages and literatures at Pontifical Catholic University of Rio de Janeiro (PUC-Rio), and she also has a taught postgraduation course in literature, art, and contemporary thought at the same university.

Amy Mars is research and instruction librarian at St. Catherine University, where she is liaison to the humanities. Amy takes an active role in advising and collaborating on digital humanities projects around campus and author of the open access, peer-reviewed article "Claiming Expertise from Betwixt and Between: Digital Humanities Librarians, Emotional Labor, and Genre Theory." She also leads the annual campus reading program, One Read for Racial Justice. Amy received her master's in library and information science from St. Catherine University.

Patrick McCauley received a PhD in philosophical theology and literature from the University of Iowa in conjunction with the University of Glasgow and its Centre for the Study of Literature, Theology and the Arts. He received a master's in English literature from Binghamton, and a bachelor of science degree in cinema production from Ithaca College. He teaches religion, literature, and philosophy at Chestnut Hill College in Philadelphia. Along with Karen Wendling, PhD he coordinates the Annual Harry Potter Academic Conference every October in Philadelphia. His *Into the Pensieve: The Philosophy and Mythology of Harry Potter* was published in 2015. He is currently working on a large project centered on the emergence of strong female protagonists in recent young adult literature tentatively called "The Diana Archetype."

Christina Phillips-Mattson received her PhD in children's and young adult literature from the Department of Comparative Literature at Harvard University in 2015. She is a writer and the host of "Exquisitely Ever After," a podcast that focuses on reading children's literature to cultivate kind, intelligent, and successful kids and that expanded into a YouTube channel and blog in 2020 (www.exquisitelyeverafter.com). Her book, *Children's Literature Grows Up: Harry Potter and the Children's Literature Revolution*, was published in 2016.

Jennifer M. Reeher is currently a PhD student in rhetoric and composition at the University of South Carolina; she earned her master's degree in literary history and a graduate certificate in women's, gender, and sexuality studies from Ohio University in 2018. Her research, both literary and rhetorical, is centered on intersectional feminist theory and the rhetoric of health and medicine, and her work focuses primarily on the intersections of medical history, social anxieties, and illness/patient narrative as a literary genre.

Jonathan A. Rose is lecturer and PhD candidate at the Professorship of English Cultural and Media Studies at the University of Passau, Germany. He holds undergraduate degrees in economics and management as well as philosophy, English, and literary studies. He graduated from the Free University Berlin with a master's degree in English studies. His research and teaching center around digital and popular fiction, new media, adaptations, and trans(gender) and fan(fiction) studies. His dissertation project looks at transgender representations and negotiations of gender in fan narratives. Among his publications are book chapters on *Harry Potter* fanfiction and on the continuing popularity of the *Harry Potter* phenomenon: "Breaking the Scales: Refusal, Excess and the Fat Male Body in *Supernatural* and *Harry*

Potter Fan Fiction," published in *Representing Kink: Fringe Sexuality and Textuality in Literature, Digital Narrative, and Popular Culture* (2019), and "Who Tells Me Where I Ought to Be?: The Sorting Community *Hogwarts Is Home* and *Pottermore*," published in *Harry Potter and Convergence Culture: Essays on Fandom and the Expanding Potterverse* (2018).

Marie Schilling Grogan is associate professor of English and director of the Honors Program at Chestnut Hill College in Philadelphia. Her academic research explores hagiography and women's spiritual writings of the Middle Ages. She is also a published poet.

Emily Strand has a master's degree in theology and has taught religion at the collegiate level for more than fifteen years. She is author of two books on Catholic sacraments (Liguori Publications) and serves her diocese as an educator for adult learners. With Kathryn McDaniel, she cohosts the academic *Harry Potter* podcast "Potterversity" and has written many essays on religion and popular fiction for John Granger's HogwartsProfessor.com website and for her own blog, LiturgyandLife.com. Her essay on the symbolic nature of Quidditch was included in 2015's *Harry Potter for Nerds II*, her essay "Harry Potter and the Sacramental Principle" was included in the Fall 2019 edition of the journal *Worship*, and her essay "Dobby the Robot: The Science Fiction in *Harry Potter*" in the October 2019 edition of the journal *Mythlore*. In her almost nonexistent spare time, she enjoys reading and writing fiction.

INDEX

Abrams, M. H., 111–12, 125

Adams, Richard, *Watership Down*, 45–46

Advanced Potion Making (Libatius Borage), 58, 64n12

"Allegory of the Cave," 127

Anatol, Giselle Liza: *Reading Harry Potter*, xxviin2; *Reading Harry Potter Again*, xxviin2

Anatomy of Literary Nonsense, An (Tigges), 48

Animagi, 50, 63n3, 137, 158, 163, 171, 176n7

Austin, J. L., *How to do Things with Words*, 55–56

Azkaban Prison, 151, 195, 214

Bakhtin, Mikhail, 108

Barthes, Roland, 84–85, 91n7; *The Death of the Author*, xxvi, 224

battles: Battle of Hogwarts, 115, 136, 142, 164n1, 183, 185, 186, 215, 216, 217; Battle of the Department of Mysteries, 17, 30; Battle of the Seven Potters, 30

beast and being, 159–60, 176n2, 176n5–6, 180, 187n6; Beast-Being, 159

beauty bias, 189, 199

Bennet, Alanna, xix. *See also* Black Hermione

Bernhardt-House, Phillip, 154, 159–60

Black, Regulus, 100, 101, 195

Black, Sirius, 16, 84, 100–101, 115, 183, 195–96, 203–4, 219; death of, 30, 152, 184, 216; and

dementors, 60–61; "good people and Death Eaters," 188, 200; as Harry's godfather, 26, 60, 173; as James Potter's friend, 25–26, 136, 146–47, 161

Black Hermione, xix

Bloom, Harold, xxviiin16, 38, 41

Borges, Jorge Luis, 88

Bryce, Frank, 96

Burrow, the, 28, 30, 50, 98, 145; table, 29

Butler, Judith, 164, 165n2, 166

Carroll, Lewis, 48–50, 54, 56–57; *Alice in Wonderland*, 48, 50, 52–53, 56, 63n1; *The Hunting of the Snark*, 50, 54; "Jabberwocky," 50, 56

Chang, Cho, xvi, 25, 88; "To JK Rowling, from Cho Chang," xviii, xxviiin12

Chappell, Shelley, 154, 160–61

Chestnut Hill College Harry Potter Conference, xxiv, xxviin3, xxviiin16, 90, 133

communities of interpretation, 93–97

coursework at Hogwarts: Care of Magical Creatures, 182; Charms, 172; Defense Against the Dark Arts, 20, 72, 147, 150, 155–56, 169, 214; Divination, 16, 182; N.E.W.T., 58, 64n12, 150; O.W.L., 59, 141, 150; Potions, 20, 22, 24, 55, 64n12, 137–38, 153; Transfiguration, 137, 139, 141, 171

Cursed Child, The (Rowling), xi, xix, 32n6, 186

Dahl, Roald, 190–91, 195
Daily Prophet, 17, 110
Dark Arts, 14, 20, 28, 72, 155, 156, 169, 214
Death Eaters, 30, 33n9, 58, 138, 151, 169, 184, 188, 198, 200
"Death of the Author, The" (Barthes), xxvi, 84–85, 91n7, 224
defamiliarization, 110–12
Delacour, Fleur, xvi, 193
Diagon Alley, 28, 30–31, 98, 114, 143; table, 29
Díaz, Junot, xix
Diggory, Cedric, xvi, 16, 168, 213, 215–16
Disappearing L, The (Morris), 207
Dobby, 15, 24, 173, 174, 175, 184, 187n8
Dumbledore, Albus, 15, 37–38, 63n2, 95, 102, 103–4, 108, 117n11, 140, 166, 188, 192, 197, 205, 225; age, 138; on choices, 188; death of, 152, 216–17; dwelling on dreams, 51; Dumbledore's Army, xviii, xxii, 17, 61; explains everything, 28, 31, 218–22; eyes, 103–4; as gay, xviii, 154; and Lupin, 72, 156, 161, 162; as mentor, 16, 24–28, 31, 52, 61, 136, 141–52, 201, 202, 218–21; and Snape, 4, 59; table, 29; on words, xxvi. See also *Life and Lies of Albus Dumbledore, The*
Dumbledore, Ariana, 205–6, 220
Dursleys, xii, 14, 24, 30, 36, 99, 113, 117n10, 140, 143, 144, 147, 173, 176n9, 194–95, 205, 211n2; Aunt Marge, 195; Dudley, xv, xvi, 28, 30, 36, 61, 98, 172, 191, 194–95; Petunia, 28, 36, 44, 194; table, 29; Vernon, 29, 195

fabula, 108–10
fandom. *See* Harry Potter fandom
Fantastic Beasts and Where to Find Them: book, 167, 176n2, 180, 186n5; films, 54
Feeling for Books, A (Radway), xiv
Felski, Rita: *Limits of Critique*, 128–29; *Uses of Literature*, xiv
Fetterley, Judith, 88
Fic: Why Fanfiction Is Taking Over the World (Jamison), xvii
First Five Pages (Lukeman), 37
Flamel, Nicolas, 63n4; and alchemy, 51
Flitwick, Filius, 182
Forbidden Forest, 64n15, 114, 143, 215, 221
Forgotten Readers (McHenry), xxviin8

Genette, Gerard: and epitexts, 79; and paratexts, xxiv, 78–79, 90
Godric's Hollow, 31, 144; table, 29
Golden Trio, 15, 22, 24, 27, 85, 138, 146
Goodman, Leslie, 88
Grace, George W., 66, 75n2
Gramsci, Antonio, and hegemony, 179
Granger, Hermione, xv, xvi, 97, 141, 169, 184, 194, 204; as Black, xviii–xix; as brightest witch, 98, 99, 110, 144, 169, 180, 209; as friend, 83, 172, 203; Harry, Ron and, 15, 22, 80, 85, 113, 146, 150; and house elves, 170, 182–83, 185–86; male/female friendship, 25, 28, 30, 32n8, 132–33, 143, 145, 148; as Muggle-born, 68, 73, 82, 156, 161, 205; "said earnestly," 35–47; with Ron, 95, 103, 217
Granger, John, 44, 80, 82–83, 91n5, 94, 104, 106–17; as "Dean of Harry Potter Pundits," xxiv, 32n6; ring chart, 114–15
Greer, Germaine, 208
Greyback, Fenrir, xxiv, 69, 155, 157–58, 163, 164n1
Grimmauld Place, 20, 25, 27, 101–2, 146; table, 29
Grindelwald, Gellert, 220
Grosh, Cassandra, 179–80
Groves, Beatrice, *Literary Allusions in Harry Potter*, 44–45, 79, 80, 91n5, 107

Hagrid, Rubeus, xv, xxviiin12, 28, 30, 114, 205; and creatures, 15, 155, 169, 172; and Dumbledore, 30; as gamekeeper, 136; as half giant, 73, 182, 183; and McGonagall, 139, 152; as mentor, 22, 24, 25, 99, 143–45, 198, 204, 209
hallows. *See* magical objects
Halttunen, Karen, 190
Harry Potter: A History of Magic (British Library exhibition), xxviiin12
Harry Potter and the Sacred Text (podcast), xxi
Harry Potter books: artistry of, 35–47, 85, 90, 107, 109, 114–15, 121, 132; as bildungsroman, 17, 23, 27, 31, 32n6, 127, 134; as children's literature, xxii, xxiii, xxviin1, xxviin2, 6, 23, 28, 33n10, 40–41, 42, 46,

48–64, 108, 125, 190–91; epigraphs, xxiii, 77–90; epilogue, xxiii, 31, 77, 78–79, 85–90, 203, 209–10; as fantasy novels, xii, xxii, 11, 15, 28, 50, 55, 86, 107, 111, 202; literary devices, 11, 53–54, 75, 85, 102–5, 108, 110, 189, 198; as literary phenomenon, xii, xxviin1, 40–42, 121; midnight book releases, xi, xiv, 90, 125; and Millennials, xi, xix; omniscience, 14, 36, 42, 44; popularity of, xxii, 3, 32n5, 39–43, 46, 106–7, 116, 125

Harry Potter central themes, 22, 24, 27–28, 61, 62, 102, 104, 126, 128, 130, 135, 146, 151, 159, 173, 188, 191, 203; choices, 18; complexity of, xxiii, 3–34, 49, 53–54, 57, 78, 115, 140; love, xxi, 19; truth, xxii, 21

Harry Potter contexts: diversity, xxi, xxviin2, 154, 163; George Floyd, xx; #MeToo, 106; HIV/AIDS, 157–58

Harry Potter fandom, xvii, xix, xxi, 89, 140, 224; fan fiction, xvii, xxviin9; Harry Potter Alliance/Fandom Forward, xxi; Leaky Cauldron, xxi, 103, 224; MuggleNet, xiii, xxi, 224; Pottermore, xi, xviii, 76n7, 79, 90n1, 224

Harry Potter films, xi, 54, 79, 197

Harry Potter linguistics and language studies, xxiii, 3, 31, 37, 39, 40–44, 48–64, 65–69, 74–76, 192, 195, 216; adverbs, xxiii, 37–38, 39, 42–43, 45, 195; character names, 52–53, 157, 210; clichés, 39, 42–43, 125, 132; creature names, 53–54; Latin, 56–58, 60, 63n7, 71, 126; prose style, 38–43, 54, 93. *See also* spells

Harry Potter literary criticism: anthropocentrism, 167, 176; assimilation, xxv, 201–11; close reading, 3–34; critical race studies, 182–83; digital humanities, 3–34; distant reading, 5–13; eco-criticism, xxiii, 166–77; feminist, xvii, xxii, xxiv, xxviin8, 135–53, 207–8, 209; genderqueer, xxvi, 223; healing, xxiii, 65–76, 218, 221; hermeneutics, xxiv, 121–34; intertextuality, xxiv, 77–78, 80, 82; and Jane Austen, 93–105; lexical density, 5–6, 10–12; medical humanities, 65–76; new criticism, xxii, 4; nonhuman other, xxv, 62, 159, 166–77;

180–86, 199; non-normativity, 154–64; postcolonial, xxii, xxv, 178–87, 201–11; psychological, xiii, 98, 107, 213; queer and gender studies, xxi, xxii, xxiv, xxvi, 154–65, 210, 223; readability, 6, 9–10, 12, 17, 32n5; reception studies, xii, xviii–xxii, 126; Russian formalism, 106–19; and ring structure, 114, 116; separatism, 201–8; structuralist narratology, xxiv, 77–92, 203; subaltern, xxv, 174, 178–80, 185–86; supremacy, 178, 183, 202, 206; table, 8, 115; TERF, xx, 209; transwomen, xx, 207–9, 223; trauma studies, 212–22; word frequency, 11–12, 32n5, 102, 112, 121, 127–30, 168, 170, 192

Harry Potter literary qualities, xiii–xviii, 28, 32, 39–46, 79, 86, 107, 111, 112–16, 121–22, 127–30; absorption, xiv–xvi, 43

Harry Potter point of view, 36, 38, 44, 45; free indirect discourse, 14; relatability, xiv–xvi; third person limited, 14, 42, 44; unreliable narrator, 202–3, 204

Hedwig, 99, 173, 174, 175

History of Magic, A, (Bathilda Bagshot), 99

Hogwarts. *See* coursework at Hogwarts

Hogwarts: A History (Bathilda Bagshot), 99

Hogwarts Express, 28, 30, 113, 214; table, 29

Hogwarts Houses: Gryffindor, 14, 24, 26, 142, 148, 196, 204; Heir of Slytherin, 15, 114; Hufflepuff, 198, 217; and Quidditch, 51, 135, 139–41; Ravenclaw, xvii, xxviin2, 52, 137, 182; and Ravenclaw Tower, 150–53; Slytherin, xxv, 24, 73, 139, 148, 193, 198, 201–10

Holden, Anthony, 40–46

Hooked (Edgerton), 37

Hopkins, Gerard Manley, 113

horcruxes. *See* magical objects

How to Do Things with Words (Austin), 55–56

Illness Narratives, The (Kleinman), 70, 75n5

intertextuality. *See* literary influences

Into the Pensieve (McCauley), 32, 107

Jakobson, Roman, 108, 111, 113

Johnston, Susan, 86

Kakutani, Michiko, 32n6, 85
King, Stephen, 45
King's Cross Station, xxv, 30, 31, 61, 103, 113–14, 117n11, 212–21; table, 29
Klemm, David, 124
Konchar Farr, Cecilia: *Reading Oprah*, xxvii; *The Ulysses Delusion*, 39, 43, 113, 128, 133, 149, 210; *A Wizard of Their Age*, xvi
Kreacher, 175, 184–85

Latour, Bruno, 130
Laub, Dori and Nanette C. Auerhahn, 214–15
Lesbian Body, The (Wittig), 208
Lestrange, Bellatrix, 55, 151–52, 195
Lezard, Nicholas, 39–43
Life and Lies of Albus Dumbledore, The (Rita Skeeter), 108
Limits of Critique (Felski), 128–29
Literary Allusions in Harry Potter (Groves), 44–45, 79, 80, 91n5, 107
literary influences: Arthurian legend, 32n6; Jane Austen, xxiv, 39, 44, 93–104; Joseph Campbell, 32; *Oresteia/The Libation Bearers*, 79–82; Vladimir Nabokov, xxiv, 108–16
Little Hangleton, 64n15, 95–96, 114, 219
Lockhart, Gilderoy, 24, 55, 67–69, 75n3, 155
Longbottom, Neville, xvi, 83, 140, 141, 148, 176, 184, 191, 192, 214
Lovegood, Luna, xvi, 26, 54, 83–84, 87, 103
Lovegood, Xenophilius, 31, 54
Lupin, Remus, 31, 62, 64n14, 138, 146–47, 169, 203; as James Potter's friend, 25, 136; as mentor, 22, 24, 67, 214–15; as werewolf, 71–76, 154–65, 182
lycanthropy, 71–72, 76n6, 156–57, 159, 160, 161, 164

magical creatures: acromantula, 53, 144; Aragog, 143; basilisks, 15, 53, 141, 148; Blast-Ended Skrewts, 169; centaurs, xxv, xxvi, 53, 169, 170, 175, 176n5, 178–86, 187n6; Crumple-Horned Snorkack, 54; dragons, 15, 54, 143, 144, 168, 172–73; erumpent, 53–54; garden gnomes, 166–70; giants, 73, 143, 168, 175, 180, 182–83, 186n2; goblins, xx, xxv, xxviii, 169–71, 175, 176n4, 178–86, 187n6; Grawp, 175; the Grim, 16; Griphook, 170–75, 185; hippogriffs, 168, 173; house-elves, xxv, 15, 102, 169–76, 178, 186n2, 187n8; leprechauns, 168; merpeople, 53; obscurus, 54; phoenixes, 142, 168; sphinx, 53, 102; unicorns, 53; vampires, xix, 187n6; Veela, 168; werewolves, xxiv, 69, 71–72, 76n6, 154–64, 182. *See also* Dobby; Greyback, Fenrir; Kreacher; Lupin, Remus
magical objects: hallows, 116, 146; horcruxes, 22, 28, 31, 58, 63n10, 115, 146, 153, 217–18; Invisibility Cloak, 114, 143, 150; Mirror of Erised, 15, 24, 50, 114, 115, 144; Pensieve, 59, 64n11, 103, 108; Sorcerer's Stone, 14, 51, 138, 141, 148, 204
Malfoy, Draco, xvi, 15, 53, 63n7, 138, 155, 169, 172, 194, 210; as Harry's nemesis, 24, 28, 55, 62, 131, 203
Malfoy, Lucius, 53, 173
Malfoy, Narcissa, 153
Marx, Karl, xxv, 127, 130, 178–79
Matthews, Carrie, xvi
McCauley, Patrick: Chestnut Hill Harry Potter Conference, v, xxiv, xxviiin16, 47, 133; *Into the Pensieve*, 32, 107
McGonagall, Minerva, xxiv, 22–23, 37, 52, 63n5, 135–53, 184, 192, 224
McManus, Kate, xvii, xxvii
Ministry of Magic, 25, 53, 159, 178, 180, 181, 182, 196
Moaning Myrtle, 28, 58
Monsters, Creatures, and Pets at Hogwarts (Dendle), 183
Moody, Mad-Eye, 25, 191
Moretti, Franco, 32n3
mortality, 13, 16, 27, 43
Mudblood, 59, 72, 73
Muggles, xi, xxiii, xxviiin1, 24, 28, 57, 61, 76n6, 111, 138, 142, 170–71, 180, 186, 202; Harry raised by, 143, 147, 156, 195; King's Cross as gateway, 30–31, 213, 219; Muggle-born, 15, 53, 59, 64, 178, 183, 185; Muggle medicine, 64–74; table, 29; violence against wizards, 205–10

Nazis and Slytherin, xxv, 73, 190, 201–2, 206
Nearly Headless Nick, 26
New York Times: Bestseller List, xi; book critics, 32, 38, 42, 85. *See also* Kakutani, Michiko
Nobel Prize in Literature, 106–8, 114, 116
Nonsense Songs and Stories (Lear), 48
Nuttall, Alice, 182

Occlumency, 20
Order of the Phoenix, 135

Park Dahlen, Sarah, xxviin2, xxviiin12
Parkinson, Pansy, 193
Penn, William, 79–84
Pettigrew, Peter, 16, 25, 60, 194
Phelan, James, 78, 90
Platform 9¾, 85, 86, 87, 149, 184
Plato, 127–28, 131
Pomfrey, Madame, xxiii, 67–70, 139
Potter, Harry: as "Dumbledore's man," 23–25; as having his mother's eyes, 24, 195; and mother's love, 24–25, 215, 220; scar, 17, 44, 80; as the Boy Who Lived, 136; as the Chosen One, 26, 153. *See also* Golden Trio
Potter, James, 4, 24, 26, 59, 146–47, 161, 213
Potter, Lily, 59, 64n13, 194, 195, 213
Privet Drive, 28, 30, 44, 98, 113, 137, 148

Quidditch, 28, 31, 67, 135, 139–40, 148, 168, 172, 198, 214, 216; table, 29
Quirrell, Quirinus, 14, 15, 51, 114, 133, 144, 145

Radcliffe, Daniel, xvii, xxi, 224
Reading, Writing, Rowling (podcast), 42
Religion for Atheists (Botton), 124
Ricoeur, Paul, 128–30
Riddles of Harry Potter (Wolosky), 107
Rostad, Rachel, "To JK Rowling, from Cho Chang", xviii–xix
Rowling, J. K.: and anti-trans statements, xx–xxi, 208–9, 223–25; as Christian/moral, 81, 86, 127–31, 171, 174, 176, 206; and gender, 154, 163; as *Harry Potter* series writer, xi, xiv, xv, xvi, xxiii, xxiv, xxvi, 28, 35–46, 82, 106–7, 125, 132–33, 139, 191;

and Jane Austen, 93–104; and language, 48–62, 83, 157, 191–200; Maya Forstater, 223; and Nabokov, 108–16; other works, 5, 32n4, 108; and race, xviii, xix, xxxviii, 73, 183; and readers, 77–79, 85–90, 131; on Twitter, xix, 79, 208, 223, 224

Saint Mungo's Hospital for Magical Maladies and Injuries, 68, 156
Scamander, Newt, 180, 186n5
Scamander, Rolf, 103
Schleiermacher, Friedrich, 123
Searle, John, 211n1
Self-Editing for Fiction Writers (Brown and King), 36–37
Shanoes, Veronica L., 14
Shklovsky, Viktor, 108, 110, 112–13
Skeeter, Rita, 25, 63n3, 96–97, 110, 221n1
Snape, Severus, 157, 193; "Always," xvi, 58, 101; and Dumbledore, 4, 59, 104, 145, 216; as the Half-Blood Prince, 22; and Harry, 14, 15, 24, 25, 152, 203–4; and James Potter, 26, 59; and Lily Potter, 59, 64n14; and Lupin, 157; and McGonagall, 138–41, 148; and Occlumency, 20, 28; and potions, 58, 76n7
spells, xxiii, 48; *Avada Kedavra*, 57–58, 61, 62, 63n9, 216; Body-Bind, 151; *Crucio*, xxiv, 61, 63n9, 151; *Episkey*, 67; *Expecto Patronum*, 60–61, 215; *Expelliarmus*, 57, 60, 61, 62; expertise with, 138, 168; *Ferula*, 67; for healing, 55–74; *Imperio*, 63n9, 152; linguistic roots of, 54–62; as nonsense language, 48–62; for protection, 77, 88; *Sectumsempra*, 55, 58, 59, 131; *Stupefy*, 61
Spivak, Gyatri, 179–81
standards of literary merit, 39, 43–44, 133
syuzhet, 108–10, 114–15

Tales of Beedle the Bard, The (Rowling), 82, 108, 109
Tandon, Bharat, 93
Tillich, Paul, 123–24
Tonks, Nymphadora, 66–67, 75n3, 138; and Lupin, 31, 64n14, 71, 72, 217; as metamorphmagus, 158

Tonks, Ted, 86, 185
Triwizard Tournament, 16, 115, 168, 221;
    table, 29

Umbridge, Dolores, 33, 140, 142, 170, 197, 224;
    abuse of Harry, 25, 149, 150; defiance of,
    61, 150; as toadlike, 192, 196
Uses of Literature (Felski), xiv

Vezalli, Loris, 127
Voldemort, Lord, 14–16, 53, 57–58, 63, 73, 99,
    115, 138, 151, 183; connection with Harry,
    17, 31, 51, 145, 214; Dark Lord, 59, 109, 110,
    114, 146, 152, 183, 217; defeat of, 20, 22,
    26–27, 37, 61, 62, 64n15, 144, 152–53, 185,
    212, 217–18, 221; He-Who-Must-Not-
    Be-Named, 14; and Hitler, xxv, 201–2;
    killings, 25, 59, 60, 194, 215; and naming,
    204, 225; and power, 102, 133, 161, 186,
    220; return of, xii–xiii, 17, 30, 149, 196–97;
    Tom Riddle, 24, 28, 108, 132, 133, 137, 202,
    225

Ward, Renee, 160
Watership Down (Adams), 45–46
Weasley, Arthur, 16, 68, 71, 96
Weasley, Bill, 69, 71
Weasley, Fred, 183, 216; and George, 30, 32n9,
    183
Weasley, Ginny, xviii, xxviiin12, 16, 24, 83, 85,
    132, 138, 214
Weasley, Molly, 25, 26, 68, 97, 136, 138, 145–46,
    161
Weasley, Percy, xvii, 17, 86
Weasley, Ron, 16, 22, 25, 67, 83, 97, 113, 161,
    169, 172, 188, 193, 200, 210; as Harry's
    friend, 24, 80, 94, 138, 146, 148, 149, 155;
    and Hermione, 95, 132; leaves the Golden
    Trio, 31, 132; as wizard-raised, 68, 73, 82,
    93, 156, 164, 169, 183. *See also* Golden Trio
Weasley family, 17, 24, 50, 99, 166; table, 29.
    See also Burrow, the
Wendling, Karen, v, xxiv, 131
Wente, Sarah, 202
Wizard of Their Age, A (Konchar Farr), xvi,
    xxviin10, xxviiin15
Wizarding World, Orlando, xiv

Wizarding world vs. Muggle world, xii, xviii,
    14, 16, 30, 82, 135, 143, 149, 198, 213. *See
    also* Diagon Alley; King's Cross Station
wizards: education, 62, 99; ghosts, 26;
    language of, 50, 54, 183; magic, 60, 61, 66,
    138; medicine, 65, 68–69; Muggle-born,
    59, 73; professions, 51, 192; purebloods, 73,
    100, 156; rules, 53, 57–58, 162, 169, 176n3,
    180, 187n6; separatism, 201–10; society,
    155–64, 178, 181–86; travel, 50; war, xiii, 17,
    20, 31. *See also* coursework at Hogwarts;
    Ministry of Magic
Wolosky, Shira, *Riddles of Harry Potter*, 107

Yule Ball, 94–95

Made in the USA
Coppell, TX
10 October 2022

84396447R00163